ECONOMICS
ON TRIAL
Lies, Myths, and Realities

ECONOMICS
ON TRIAL
Lies, Myths, and Realities

Mark Skousen

BUSINESS ONE IRWIN
Homewood, Illinois 60430

Acquisitions editor: Amy Hollands
Project editor: Susan Trentacosti
Production manager: Carma W. Fazio
Compositor: Weimer Typesetting Co., Inc.
Typeface: 11/13 Century Schoolbook
Printer: R. R. Donnelley & Sons Company

Library of Congress Cataloging-in-Publication Data

Skousen, Mark.
    Economics on trial / lies, myths, and realities / Mark Skousen.
        p.   cm.
    ISBN 1-55623-372-8
    1. Economics. I. Title.
HB171.S5637   1990   90–34339
330—dc20   CIP

Printed in the United States of America
2 3 4 5 6 7 8 9 0 DO 7 6 5 4 3 2 1 0

Dedicated to the supply of students whose demand was never satisfied in college economics.

And to my wife, Jo Ann, who took one course in economics, and that made all the difference.

ACKNOWLEDGMENTS

When I was an undergraduate majoring in economics, I searched in vain for a book that would simply but thoroughly dissect the large number of dubious theories and questionable doctrines taught in the classroom. A few books were helpful, but I was unable to find a systematic critique of mainstream economics. Now, 20 years later, I find myself writing the very book I searched for then.

No one's work is entirely his own. Over the years, I have depended on a large number of fellow economists and scholars with diverse views to help me develop my own understanding of economic science: Kenna C. Taylor, Wayne Hales, Charles P. Rock, and Harry Kypraios at Rollins College; Roger Garrison and Leland Yeager at Auburn University; Israel Kirzner at New York University; Larry T. Wimmer and Clayne Pope at Brigham Young University; Murray N. Rothbard at University of Nevada at Las Vegas; Gary North at the American Institute for Economic Research; Steve Hanke at Johns Hopkins University; Gerald P. O'Driscoll, Jr., at the Federal Reserve Bank in Dallas; Richard Ebeling at Hillsdale College; Hans F. Sennholz at Grove City College; James Buchanan, Walter Williams, and Don Lavoie at George Mason University; Milton Friedman, Martin Anderson, Alvin Rabushka, and William Bartley III at the Hoover Institution; Mark Blaug at the University of London; Peter F. Drucker at Claremont Graduate School; John Kenneth Galbraith at Harvard University; Paul A. Samuelson and Franco Modigliani at MIT; Michio Morishima and P. T. Bauer at the London School of Economics; Roger LeRoy Miller at Clemson University; F. A. Hayek at the University of Freiburg; G. C. Harcourt at Cambridge University; Eamonn Butler and Madsen Pirie at the Adam Smith Institute; and Robert Poole, Jr., at the *Reason*

Foundation. My conversations with each of these scholars have contributed to the development of this book, although I don't expect any consensus about the ideas contained herein.

In writing this work, I acknowledge the help of three individuals in particular. First, I wish to thank Kenna C. Taylor, professor of economics at Rollins College, for painstakingly reviewing this work and making a number of worthwhile suggestions. He will no doubt be disappointed that I did not incorporate all of his points, although I did rewrite several sections in response to his cogent critique. But there is a bright side to these omissions. Professor Taylor can tell his associates that he can't be held responsible for this new and irreverent challenge to mainstream economics.

Second, I appreciate attorney Gary Burnett, a longtime friend, for reading the manuscript. Gary took an introductory course in economics many years ago, but most of his background in economics comes from practical business experience. I wanted to see if he, as an intelligent layman, would be able to follow the logic of my arguments and, more important, find the information useful. He made a number of suggestions that have improved the final version.

Third, I appreciate the support of Amy Hollands, acquisitions editor, at BUSINESS ONE IRWIN, and especially her astute recognition of the importance of this much-needed work.

Finally, I thank my wife, Jo Ann, for her enthusiastic editing. She spent many hours trying to make layman's sense out of the sometimes obtuse jargon of the economist. Her attention to literary style has been the secret behind my publishing success.

With the publication of this book, a new guide to economics is now supplied. But will supply create its own demand? Ultimately, it will be up to the reading public to confirm Say's law.

Mark Skousen

Note: Specific page references to the top ten textbooks mentioned in *Economics On Trial: Lies, Myths, and Realities* are listed at the back of the book. Excerpts and longer quotations are referenced at the end of each chapter.

CONTENTS

INTRODUCTION	How Economics Went Wrong	1
CHAPTER 1	What Is Economics Anyway?	14
CHAPTER 2	Costs, Benefits, and Trade-Offs	20
CHAPTER 3	How the Economy Really Works	28
CHAPTER 4	What's Missing in GNP?	38
CHAPTER 5	The Fallacy of the Paradox of Thrift	47
CHAPTER 6	The Magic and Myth of the Multiplier	63
CHAPTER 7	The Truth about Aggregate Supply and Demand	74
CHAPTER 8	The Real Cause of Inflationary Recessions	88
CHAPTER 9	Depression Economics	102
CHAPTER 10	Who's to Blame for Unemployment?	119
CHAPTER 11	The Gold Standard	128
CHAPTER 12	Market versus Government Failure	145
CHAPTER 13	The Growing Tax Burden	158
CHAPTER 14	The National Debt	177
CHAPTER 15	The Inequality of Income	187
CHAPTER 16	Japan and the Four Tigers	198
CHAPTER 17	The Poverty of Socialism	208
CHAPTER 18	The Strange Case of Perfect Competition	238
CHAPTER 19	The Economist as Investment Advisor	255

CHAPTER 20	The Next Economics	274
CHAPTER 21	The Future of Economics	291
APPENDIX	Where to Get the Best Information on Economics	299
REFERENCES		301
INDEX		303

INTRODUCTION

HOW ECONOMICS WENT WRONG

*I am here to report that there is absolutely nothing wrong
with the current state of economics. . . .*
—William Baumol[1]
Economics Professor,
Princeton University

Over a million students study economics each year in college.
Unfortunately, these future businesspeople, consumers, investors, and government leaders are often getting a defective, if
not dangerous, education. It is a tragic fact that many of the
principles taught for the past generation in the university
classroom, the corporate boardroom, and the halls of the legislature are simply bad economics—having led to massive inflation, serious recessions, severe unemployment, huge federal
deficits, wasteful government spending, high tax rates, consumer spending binges, stock market crashes, low productivity
among many workers, and undersaving on a gigantic scale.
Meanwhile, some farsighted countries, particularly Japan and
other Far Eastern nations, have rejected this Western-style economics, adopting instead a completely different approach that
is pro-savings and pro-growth, with low tax rates on investment and minimal government interference. Within one generation, Japan, Hong Kong, Taiwan, and other Pacific Basin
nations have gone from rags to riches and are rapidly taking
over the economic and financial world.

A POSITIVE APPROACH, TOO

The purposes of this book are simple: first, to expose the unsound doctrines taught in today's economics and the poor policies being practiced by most Western governments, and second,

to reestablish the basic principles of genuine prosperity and the beneficial policies governments need to institute in order to secure that prosperity for ourselves and our descendants.

This is not just a book about bad economics. It also makes a case for good economics. In each chapter, after critiquing the current orthodoxy, I present a new way of looking at economic behavior: a new definition of economics, an alternative to aggregate supply and demand curves, a new national statistic that more accurately describes economic activity than does gross national product (GNP), an alternative explanation of inflationary recession, overlooked advantages of a pure gold standard, and a surprising new look at who did and did not predict the Great Depression of the 1930s.

IDEAS HAVE CONSEQUENCES

The ideas developed by Adam Smith, David Ricardo, Karl Marx, John Maynard Keynes, Milton Friedman, and other ivory-tower economists have had major impacts, for both good and bad, on the world in which we live. Many mainstream economists deny that they can be held responsible for the problems the world faces because, they say, political leaders often ignore the sound advice of economists. This may be true in some areas, yet in many ways, the actions of businesspeople and government leaders are greatly affected by the economic doctrines they learn from the academic world. As Keynes concluded on the last page of his influential work, *The General Theory*, "Practical men, who believe themselves to be quite exempt from any intellectual influences, are usually the slaves of some defunct economist."

Sometimes the influence of economists can be highly beneficial, and this has been particularly true in such areas as free trade, deregulation, and privatization. Unfortunately, many other economic dogmas taught by the academic profession have turned out to be defective economics with disastrous results. Many of the problems we face today, including high federal deficits, inflation, excessive tax rates, low savings and capital growth, high consumer debt, and the welfare state can be traced back directly to fundamental errors taught by economists over the past 50 years both in and out of academia. Many of these errors are still repeated today, as my book demonstrates. Bureaucrats and legislators in Western governments and most less developed countries have been greatly enamored by Keynesian economics in particular, which gives theoretical support for inflation, high government spending, deficit financing, and the welfare state. State officials in the Soviet Union, China, and many less-developed countries have in the past been captivated by Marxism–Leninism, which calls for abolishment of private property and the creation of a centrally planned collectivist state. Both kinds of government interventionism have caused serious economic problems from which we continue to suffer.

Only by witnessing firsthand the destructive effects of bad economics have government leaders and businesspeople been forced to abandon the crank policies of the Keynesian and Marxist economists. Academic professors have had to go back to the drawing board to see what's wrong with their economic theories. As Ben Franklin said, "Experience keeps a dear school, but fools will learn in no other."

THE ACADEMIC WORLD VERSUS EXPERIENCE

I've wanted to write a book on economics ever since I took my first course as a freshman in college. My first economics teacher was a graduate student with little practical experience, lecturing on a topic that was supposed to be about how the real world works. For the most part, academic economists are not general practitioners, and in fact many of them eschew the necessity of pragmatic application, dismissing it as unscientific storytelling. They teach what they have learned from textbooks authored by professors who in turn learned economics from a previous generation of textbooks and professors. The vast majority of articles in the professional journals are highly mathematical exercises in pure theory, far removed from practical values. When economists turn to evidence for their theories, they rely on complex econometric models and impersonal statistical research. It is a hapless cycle in academia that has seldom been broken and probably won't be broken any time soon because of the way the system works. Economists, wrote J. B. Say in the early 19th century, are "idle dreamers, whose theories, at best only gratifying literary curiosity, were wholly inapplicable in practice."[2]

Economists with extensive practical experience are seldom hired by universities for two reasons: first, commercial economists make a lot more money in the business world, and second, they are usually not up-to-date on the latest trends in economic theories and analyses. To attract top-notch talent from the business world, universities would have to be willing to pay substantially more in salaries and benefits than they now pay. A massive pay increase might give the theoretical economists more opportunity to test their hypotheses in the real world by giving them more time and means to travel, to consult with businesses and government officials, to participate in the financial world, and to do more research. But there is also the professional jealousy factor, which cannot be assuaged by money—the fact that academic economists, running a closed shop, believe that practical experience may taint a professor's objectivity and purity of thought.

COMMON NONSENSE IN THE CLASSROOM

Somehow my first college instructor instilled in me a desire to study economics. I'm not sure why—he taught it so conventionally—but perhaps it was because he made it so confusing. Many of the concepts he taught just didn't make sense to me.

Maybe it was the "paradox of thrift," the odd idea that savings, though good for the individual, are somehow disastrous for the community. Or the "something for nothing" idea that government could simply spend (or print) more money to make unemployment and recession miraculously disappear. At any rate, it seemed to me that economics professors taught a great deal of questionable economics. I was determined to figure out what was wrong with the way economics was taught and how the situation could be fixed.

WHY I MAJORED IN ECONOMICS

My major was decided in my freshman year. I am the kind of person interested in virtually all subjects, so I wanted to choose a major that covered as many peripheral areas as possible. Economics fit nicely because in it many areas of the social and natural sciences overlap significantly. In business, economics covers finance, management, investments, and statistics. In the social sciences, it includes politics, history, and psychology. Finally, it uses mathematics, a subject I liked and usually excelled in. As Paul Samuelson says, economics is the queen of the social sciences.

My interest in the subject was never diminished. I earned a B.A. in economics in 1971 at Brigham Young University (BYU), an M.S. in economics in 1972 at BYU, and a Ph.D. in economics in 1977 at George Washington University. Most of the professors taught the orthodox methodology, the "neoclassical synthesis." I took every conceivable course in economics and related disciplines, getting mostly A's. In graduate school I was a teacher's assistant and taught several introductory courses. My approach was straightforward and conventional. I had my doubts about economics, but despite nearly seven years of study, I didn't have any answers until after I left college.

Even though I hold a Ph.D. in economics from a well-known university, have taught courses in economics, and have written books and academic articles on the subject, I view myself as an outsider to the profession. I am currently an adjunct professor of economics and finance at Rollins College, a liberal arts college in Winter Park, Florida. I stress the word *adjunct;* I am not a full-time economics teacher. I travel too much and am involved in too many business activities to teach full-time. I am not a purely academic economist.

WHAT THE BUSINESS WORLD TAUGHT ME

After finishing my Ph.D. in 1977, I decided that it was essential to get some practical experience in the business world before teaching economics at a university. I wanted to teach economics eventually, but only if I could draw upon my own experiences to make a point. Being unable to do so would just perpetuate the principal weakness of most textbook economists.

While working on my Ph.D., I was employed as an economic analyst for the Central Intelligence Agency. It was an analytic desk job, thus hardly a business-world experience, but I did learn a lot about the inner workings of the federal government. (I lived 12 years in Washington.)

It wasn't until I became the editor of an investment newsletter in the mid-1970s that I was introduced to the commercial world, the fast-moving arena of assets and liabilities, profits and losses, and entrepreneurship and management—the real world of supply and demand. I was an employee, not an owner, of the newsletter publishing firm, but I could see for the first time the true meaning of savings, capital formation, risk, and economic growth. The firm started as a small operation, but under the agile ability of the owner it quickly expanded into a multimillion-dollar corporation during the financial revolution of the 1970s. I was a firsthand witness to dynamic market changes. During this time, I saw my publisher's success and tried to imitate it by starting my own publishing business. I researched, wrote, published, advertised, and fulfilled special reports and books on financial and economic topics. I hired workers (including my wife), maintained accounting records, acquired tools and equipment, filed tax returns, and engaged in a variety of activities that "professional" economists only write about. By the early 1980s, I, too, had a million-dollar business.

Economics professors can speak only theoretically about entrepreneurship, risk, capital goods, prices, taxes, government regulation, and supply and demand. I experienced all of these. I became a risk taker: some of my promotions and advertising worked; others did not. I became a capitalist: I made profits and sometimes I incurred losses. I have gone into business as a partner in a restaurant, a cattle feeding operation, an oil well, a gold mine, and real estate. I became intimately familiar with what economists call "capital goods"—machines, tools, equipment, and technical know-how. Input and output were no longer academic words to me. I also became a taxpayer and learned firsthand how debilitating taxation can be, both directly and indirectly. What I learned is a far cry from what is taught in the textbooks.

THE WORLD OF HIGH FINANCE

In the 1980s, I decided to strike out on my own as an investment newsletter writer. Understanding the economic principle of comparative advantage and wanting to devote most of my time to analyzing the financial markets and the everchanging economic world, I arranged to have someone else publish my newsletter—Phillips Publishing, Inc., of Potomac, Maryland. The publisher's primary responsibilities are to promote the newsletter, print the copy each month, mail each issue, and try to renew each subscriber. It's a full-time job, requiring entrepreneurial and managerial skills. By going through a publisher, I not only freed up my time to do research and write books, but I also reduced my risk. I no longer take the lion's share of the risk in promoting the newsletter—the publisher takes that—and consequently my publisher gets the lion's share of the profits. I get paid a royalty based on the number of new subscribers and the number of renewals. But my risk is not eliminated by any means. If I don't deliver sound investment advice or an interesting letter, subscribers will not renew and my income will drop accordingly. Therefore, I have continued to be an entrepreneur and a speculator.

The investment world has proven to be fertile ground for using the principles of economics on a daily basis. Every day, new ideas and information become available on which to make an investment decision. Conservative investors and aggressive speculators respond quickly to new supply and demand figures. The financial markets represent economics in action every day.

In this regard, I put my theories and beliefs on the line every month when I write my newsletter and every day when I make an investment decision. Sometimes I'm right and sometimes I'm wrong, and I learn from my mistakes (sometimes painfully). Thousands of individual investors depend on my interpretation of economic and financial events, and they may act on only a single piece of advice. This is not the case in the university classroom, where most students are not yet active players in the marketplace, either in business or investments. They naively accept the professor's provincial views without challenge. It's not their fault; most students have not had enough experience to know whether they're learning sound economics or not.

SEEING THE WORLD FIRSTHAND

As a financial newsletter writer and investment advisor, I have also traveled throughout the United States and the world, lecturing at financial and economic conferences. I have lived in Latin America, the Caribbean, Europe, and the United States, and I have spent considerable time in major cities in Asia, Africa, and other parts of the world. I have been to many third-world countries and witnessed firsthand the effects of runaway inflation, chronic unemployment, confiscatory taxation, and massive government planning. I have also seen the beneficial effects of well-managed economies with low inflation, low taxes, free trade, and high economic growth. Every time I go to a new place, I discover how wrong my preconceptions were about the people and the economy—preconceptions I had learned largely from school or books. In this regard, I'm reminded of a story told to me by Larry Wimmer, an economics professor at BYU. After 20 years of teaching, he finally got the opportunity to go to the Soviet Union. Before leaving, he read all the books he could find on the subject. Yet he was ultimately unprepared for what he witnessed. He told me, "It was amazing—the Soviet economy is much worse than I ever imagined!"

The point I am trying to make is this: I was essentially a product of the purely academic world when I graduated, but over the past two decades I have become a practical economist, with widespread experience in the business and financial world. I have finally reached the point at which I can fairly assess the differences between theoretical economics as it is currently taught and practical economics as it exists in the real world. My conclusion is overwhelming: While I learned some valuable information, the fact is that I had to relearn practically everything I was taught in college!

Many former students of economics feel the same way. I have talked to dozens of successful businesspeople who took economics in college. Many of them said they did well in the course gradewise, but they often came out bewildered, wondering if it all made sense. Only years later did they come to the same conclusion I have come to. Much of textbook economics is a chimera. To paraphrase St. Paul, economics is the science of things hoped for, the evidence of things not seen.

WHAT IS TAUGHT AND NOT TAUGHT

My critique of economics is not meant to cover every aspect of this voluminous area. This work is not a substitute for a textbook. It should be considered supplemental reading. My main purpose in writing this book is twofold: First, to point out the chief omissions made by today's economists, that is, the good economics they often fail to teach in college and in books. Second, to show the fallacies of certain theories frequently taught in economics courses as well as certain misguided policy recommendations. The professors' sins of commission can often be just as bad as their sins of omission.

MY METHODOLOGY

My method of dissecting modern economics is simple. The fairest method would be to survey all of the 50,000 or more economists teaching at universities, or working for government and private enterprise, to find out what they believe. Some surveys have been done in this area. I'm sure that if I had gone this route I would have discovered many talented, creative economists who deviate from the textbook norm and are just as frustrated as I am with the current pedagogy. Nevertheless, I have chosen a less tedious path. I have selected the top 10 textbooks currently being used in the English-speaking countries as a representative sample of modern economic thinking. I realize that there are over 250 economics textbooks published today. But it would be entirely unwieldy and unnecessary to review all of them. Therefore I have limited myself to the top 10. I surveyed major publishers (McGraw-Hill; Harper & Row; Holt, Rinehart & Winston; Harcourt Brace Jovanovich; etc.) at the most recent annual American Economic Association meetings. They then gave me what they considered to be the most popular introductory texts being used. There is no official list, so economists may dispute which texts belong in the top 10.

The list includes Paul Samuelson's text, *Economics,* now coauthored with William D. Nordhaus, even though some publishers believe that it may no longer belong in the top 10. But because it was the principal text from which most students learned economics over the past 30 years and is regarded as the primary ancestor of almost all of the postwar economics textbooks, I have included it in my survey. It was also the textbook I used in undergraduate coursework.

Most of the authors on the list are from the United States, which appears to dominate the textbook arena in the English-speaking world, including Canada and England. (The international editions make only marginal changes.)

The top 10 textbooks are (not in order of sales):

Paul A. Samuelson and William D. Nordhaus, *Economics,* 13th ed. (New York: McGraw-Hill, 1989).

Campbell R. McConnell and Stanley L. Brue, *Economics,* 11th ed. (New York: McGraw-Hill, 1990).

William J. Baumol and Alan S. Blinder, *Economics: Principles and Policy,* 4th ed. (New York: Harcourt Brace Jovanovich, 1988).

Richard G. Lipsey, Peter O. Steiner, and Douglas D. Purvis, *Economics,* 8th ed. (New York: Harper & Row, 1987).

Roy J. Ruffin and Paul R. Gregory, *Principles of Economics,* 3rd ed. (Glenview, Ill.: Scott, Foresman, 1988).

Edwin G. Dolan and David E. Lindsey, *Economics,* 5th ed. (Hinsdale, Ill.: Dryden Press, 1988).

Roger Leroy Miller, *Economics Today,* 6th ed. (New York: Harper & Row, 1988).

Ralph T. Byrns and Gerald W. Stone, *Economics,* 4th ed. (Glenview, Ill.: Scott, Foresman, 1989).

James D. Gwartney and Richard L. Stroup, *Economics: Private and Public Choice,* 5th ed. (New York: Harcourt Brace Jovanovich, 1990).

Martin Bronfenbrenner, Werner Sichel, and Wayland Gardner, *Economics,* 2nd ed. (Boston: Houghton Mifflin, 1987).

THE NEED FOR A BRAND NEW TEXTBOOK

Some people may ask, "Why don't you write your own textbook?" Someday I might. But right now, given the conservative structure of the publishing business, it might be a long, uphill battle to get in print the kind of economics textbook I'd like to see. In many ways, my textbook would be revolutionary. I have talked to several economists who have written textbooks, and they tell me that the process often works against real innovation. All major textbook publishers establish a review committee, which decides what should be included and what should be excluded from textbooks. Pressure is applied immediately to include the standard neoclassical models, no matter how unrealistic they may appear to the author, and to eliminate as unnecessary many of the topics the author may feel are important. The emphasis may shift from economist to economist, but the basic structure—the grand neoclassical synthesis, which consists of a mix of the Keynesian and classical models as developed in Samuelson—must not be eliminated. The central core of economics must not be tampered with since it is the basis of standardized testing. Although there are several nontraditional textbooks (the most well-known being *The Economic Way of Thinking*, by Paul Heyne, and *Economics: An Introduction to Traditional and Radical Views*, by E. K. Hunt and Howard J. Sherman), the textbook establishment is apparently unwilling to take new risks in developing the kind of textbook I would propose.

Still, there is hope. Recently, there has been some rumbling in the academic community about the desperate need for a Samuelson-style revolution in the introductory textbook. Several years ago, the major book publishers cosponsored the Invitational Conference of the Principles of Economics Textbooks with the Joint Council on Economic Education. Speakers included Kenneth E. Boulding, Michael J. Boskin, Joseph E. Stiglitz, Campbell R. McConnell, and Edwin G. Dolan.[3] According to the sponsors, it was necessary to call a time-out and reassess the whole subject matter. Unfortunately, the critics at the conference only quibbled over details in textbook teaching—arguing whether the consumer price index (CPI) truly reflects inflation, whether textbooks are politically diverse enough, or whether books need to be more international. No one attacked any of the core of modern economic concepts, such as the circular flow diagram, the paradox of thrift, national income accounting, perfect competition, long-term equilibrium, elasticity, etc. It is my contention that the core of neoclassical economics is unsound, primarily in macroeconomics but also in certain aspects of microeconomics. If the economics profession is going to come up with an original Samuelson-style text, it must start over rather than engage in patchwork. It is time to start all over, with the kind of *practical* economics found in this book.

AN OBJECTIVE ANALYSIS?

This critique of modern economics should not be deemed politically conservative or liberal. That the teaching of economic science needs radical surgery is true enough, but this is not necessarily a political statement. As soon as one labels a writer, learning stops. When something needs to be changed, I am a liberal. When something is correct as it stands, I am a conservative. This is not meant to be a political book, although my biases will naturally become apparent. This book attempts to analyze objectively the way the economy works, what economists often call positive economics rather than normative economics, the way things ought to be. As such, it is a businessperson's critique of economics, written from the perspective of someone who has a generation of experience in the business and financial world. It is a dispassionate assault on the theoretical economics not in harmony with what is really happening outside the classroom. It is not a question of conservative or liberal economics but rather of good or bad economics. This book is an all-out attack on bad economics.

NOTES

1. William Baumol, "Economics Education and the Critics of Mainstream Economics," *Journal of Economic Education,* Fall 1988, p. 323.
2. J. B. Say, *A Treatise of Political Economy* (1821; reprint, New York: Augustus M. Kelley, 1880), p. xxxv.
3. See the Spring 1988 issue of *The Journal of Economic Education.*

CHAPTER 1

WHAT IS ECONOMICS, ANYWAY?

You may temporarily find yourself unlearning more than you learn, or operating in a fog of confusion.
    —Martin Bronfenbrenner, Werner Sichel,
    and Wayland Gardner
    Economics (1987)

The first thing academic economists may not tell you is an accurate definition of economics. Every definition I've read in modern textbooks is either misguided, unfocused, or incomplete, leaving students confused and uncertain at the beginning of the course.

The top 10 textbooks have a common basic theme in their definitions of economics. They all say, more or less, that economics is the science of scarcity and choice—the existence of "limited resources" and "unlimited needs." A typical definition is made by Ruffin and Gregory:

> Economics is the study of how scarce resources are allocated among competing ends.

The origin of this concept goes back to the British economist Lionel Robbins, who in 1935 defined economic science as the study of "the relationship between ends and means that have alternative uses."[1]

THE QUESTION OF SCARCITY

But are scarcity and choice the real essence of economics? Scarcity itself can have a confusing and uncertain meaning for a student. It may not fit his personal experience. As an individual, he may not recognize this alleged universality of scarcity

14

and unlimited wants. For instance, he may have the means of providing himself with food, clothing, and housing over the next several months. Under the circumstances, his basic wants may already be saturated. If he has one car he may not want another car. On a larger scale, he may recognize that there are already too many cars in Manhattan or on the Los Angeles freeways. In this context, there is no scarcity of automobiles but rather an overabundance. If he has been to any of the major cities in advanced countries, he undoubtedly has noted that the stores are teeming with consumer goods. The shelves are stocked to the hilt, and the storage facilities are full with inventory. The point is that sometimes resources are abundant, not scarce, and needs are sometimes limited, not unlimited. Abundance may be just as important an economic problem as scarcity.

On the other hand, there are many places in the world where scarcity is readily apparent. Many people in developing and socialist countries may be suffering from famine, poverty, and/or shortages. Their needs appear unlimited.

To a businessperson, scarcity means a shortage—goods or equipment that are temporarily out of stock. This is quite distinct from the peculiar meaning used by armchair economists, who define scarcity as the universal fact that all goods that command value are limited in number and have a price associated with them. I'm not denying that this is an important principle that students need to be taught. Everyone needs to understand why goods and services have positive prices. But using the word *scarcity* may not be the best way to describe this principle. To an economist, an item may be available in all the stores and yet be scarce. To an economist, diamonds are especially scarce, which is why they command such a high price, based on the theory of marginal value (which says that one diamond is worth much more than one loaf of bread). But to a diamond dealer, a manufacturer, or even a consumer, diamonds are not scarce at all. They may be high-priced, but not scarce. You can walk into a jewelry store and choose from among hundreds of diamonds, each with a varying price. If the jeweler doesn't have the stone you want, he can get it, probably within 24 hours.

In short, scarcity is not a concept that can form the basis of defining the real world. The economist's definition of scarcity—that all goods are limited and therefore have a price—does not always fit people's perceptions. Several textbook writers admit that there are problems with economic jargon that does not fit common usage, but this does not discourage them from using these terms.

The problem with this scarcity-and-choice definition of economics is that it is largely a static view of the material world rather than a dynamic description of the production process.

THE CONNECTION BETWEEN SUPPLY AND DEMAND

In this sense, the textbook writers miss the real definition of economics by not establishing the crucial connections between resources and wants, production and consumption, and supply and demand. The most they state is that scarce resources are used to fulfill consumer needs. But they don't say *how* this is actually accomplished in the economy other than to say simply that inputs—land, labor, and capital—are used to produce outputs—consumer goods. There is much more to it than that!

The real story of economics is one that takes into account the commonsense knowledge of everyday economic activity. What is it that all workers—miners, manufacturers, clerks, bankers, secretaries, artists, truck drivers, editors, and professors of economics—have in common? In a pedestrian way, they are seeking to earn income. But their material goals are actually much broader than that, even though the average worker may not realize it. They are all seeking to improve the world they live in. How? By altering the present state of things into useful goods and services for the benefit and pleasure of others.

I emphasize the goal of making goods and services *useful.* That's really what economics is all about. Virtually all commodities and products are unusable in their natural or semifinished state. Natural resources are not ready-made, except in an aesthetic way. Raw commodities, semifinished manufactured goods, and even wholesale products are not directly serviceable to the public. Iron ore is of no use to anyone, but a hammer is. Clay is of little value by itself, but bricks can be used to build a house. Wheat must be grown, harvested, made into flour, and ultimately made into bread before it can be eaten. Even wholesale products are not available to the customer until they are conveniently put on the shelves in a retail store. Practically every raw product, except perhaps edible fruit from a wild tree, must be altered or transported in some manner before it becomes usable or consumable. Even an orange needs to be peeled. There may be a few exceptions, such as a meadow in the forest, a lake in the mountains, or a sandy beach, but even most of these require some kind of man-made improvement to maximize their use.

THE TRANSFORMATION PROCESS

Every actor in the economy—whether employee or employer, landowner or lessee, teacher or student—plays a part in the transformation process. They transform raw commodities, capital assets, and wholesale goods into usable consumer products and services.

What do miners do? They dig valuable metals and minerals out of the ground and through various technical means manufacture them into more usable commodities. Iron ore is made into iron, clay into copper, rock into gold, etc.

What do manufacturers do? They take raw materials and transform them into more usable products.

What do artists do? They buy paints, brushes, and boards and create an image for their customers to enjoy.

What do bankers do? They provide a variety of services that allow businesspeople to engage in profitable enterprises and they provide a more convenient way for consumers to pay their bills, borrow money, and fulfill their material desires.

What do teachers do? They inculcate knowledge and skills into students so that the students can more efficiently assist in the production process somewhere along the line, usually after they graduate. Or, teachers may provide knowledge for its own enjoyment.

The list of activities is endless, but the purpose behind these activities is the same: pushing forward the transformation of unfinished goods and services toward final use by consumers. Unfortunately, the textbook definition fails to describe the economic process. Resources are not simply scarce; they are not just used or managed. Resources are changed, transformed, fabricated, reconstructed, edited, converted, and, once in a usable form, consumed and enjoyed by individuals.

Let us then give a more succinct definition of economics:

> Economics is the study of how individuals transform natural resources into final products and services that people can use.

In other words, the basic purpose of economic activity is to turn unfinished, unusable goods into finished, usable goods. This includes repairing and replacing roads, buildings, equipment, and other capital goods. This is the universal phenomenon of economics and is far more central to the meaning of economic activity than scarcity, choice, and using resources. It is a dynamic, not a static, process.

Actually, this more accurate definition of economics was utilized fairly frequently in the previous generation of textbooks before the Keynesian emphasis on spending and consumption replaced the importance of the production process. For example, a text popular in the 1940s, written by Paul F. Gemmill and Ralph H. Blodgett, states: "The problem of economic society is, in large part, to change land—that is, natural resources—into finished goods, and to place those goods in the hands of the persons who will consume them."[2]

IMPLICATIONS OF THIS DEFINITION

We learn some basic principles right away using this approach. The benefit of this conceptualization is that it links land, labor, and capital (the factors of production) with consumer goods—mainstream economists tend to put these into separate little compartments. Now we see that economic activity involves the time-consuming process of transforming natural resources—land—into intermediate manufactured goods—capital goods—and ultimately into directly usable goods and services—consumer goods. At every level and stage of production, labor and entrepreneurship are applied. The direction of economic activity can be diagrammed as follows:

Land ——→ Capital goods ——→ Consumer goods

We also see that economic activity is always a time-consuming process of change. Human action is always dynamic, not static. The natural environment is constantly being altered by work and the production process. "Fixed capital" (machines, tools, equipment) is being used up as it transforms "circulating capital" (intermediate semifinished goods) along the conveyer belt toward final consumption. In this sense, economic growth is always taking place, sometimes faster and sometimes slower than before, if we define *growth* as an effort to convert natural resources and unfinished goods into more usable forms.

This description of economics is far more relevant than the standard textbook definition. The transformation process is taking place in all countries every day, no matter whether the government is socialist, communist, dictatorial, or democratic and no matter whether the economic goods appear to be scarce or abundant. Scarcity and choice—supply and demand—are critical concerns in every economy, but they must be considered at every level of the production process.

NOTES

1. Lionel Robbins, *An Essay on the Nature and Significance of Economic Science* (London: Macmillan, 1935), pp. 16–17.
2. Paul F. Gemmill and Ralph H. Blodgett, *Economics: Principles and Problems* (New York: Harper & Brothers, 1948), p. 219.

CHAPTER 2

COSTS, BENEFITS, AND TRADE-OFFS

Society cannot have its cake and eat it, too.
—Campbell R. McConnell and
Stanley L. Brue
Economics (1990)

Economists rely on two basic diagrams to explain how a simplified economy works and to identify certain characteristics of all economic life. These two concepts are the production-possibility curve (p-p curve) and the circular flow diagram. Unfortunately, both formulas sometimes seriously distort the economic process and leave out essential information. And without a proper view of how the economy works, the student quickly loses any sense of reality in traditional economic thinking.

Let us first analyze the production-possibility frontier, which is used to examine the issues of choice, trade-offs, and opportunity costs in economic life. The p-p curve from Samuelson is shown in Figure 2–1.

In the production-possibility frontier, Samuelson demonstrates the trade-off in a simplified economy between guns and butter, i.e., between military (public) expenditures and civilian (private) spending.

Using Samuelson's example, if an economy is using its fixed resources efficiently, it cannot produce more of both guns and butter. Assuming full employment of resources, if the people want more butter, they must be willing to produce fewer guns. Economists use the p-p curve to demonstrate the important principle of opportunity cost, which states that you must give up one thing in order to do or obtain something else. In

FIGURE 2–1
The Production-Possibility Frontier

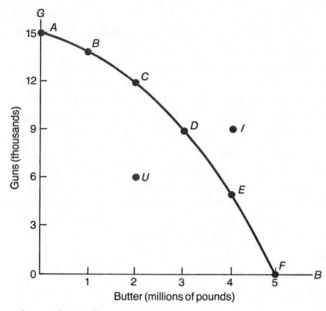

Source: Paul A. Samuelson and William D. Nordhaus, *Economics*, 13th ed. (New York: McGraw-Hill, 1989), p. 28.

the above diagram, the slope of the p-p curve is the opportunity cost of butter in terms of guns.

The concept of opportunity cost is an extremely valuable tool in many areas of business and public policy. For example, suppose the government is considering building a huge interregional highway system at an estimated cost of $100 billion. Supporters of the project may point to all the benefits of this new transportation network. But the economist would ask, "What is the real burden of this multibillion-dollar project? What benefits in other areas are being unfulfilled because funds are diverted to this new highway program?" Opportunity cost is a factor that engineers and politicians often ignore when they promote the development of their own valued projects. The economist is there to announce the real economic cost of such programs.

EXTREME IMPOSSIBILITIES

The production-possibility diagram is a legitimate tool when individuals or groups are deciding between two unrelated choices within a fixed budget. It is true that individuals may make choices between two goods in everyday life, given a limited budget. A consumer may decide whether to spend money on clothing or food. A farmer may choose to plant wheat instead of soybeans. A businessperson may want to save profits rather than spend them. But the p-p curve for an entire nation has serious limitations when it involves two goods that depend on each other, such as investment and consumer goods or military and civilian spending. No nation as a whole chooses exclusively between building automobiles and sending its children to college. No society chooses to use *all* of its resources to make clothing or, on the other hand, to produce food. A nation will always purchase or produce a certain amount of both goods, because each one of them is essential for living.

In short, the two extreme points on the p-p curve of a nation are nonexistent.

GUNS VERSUS BUTTER: THE LIMITED CHOICE

A trade-off between guns and butter does indeed exist. In order for the government to spend more on the military, taxes have to increase, which means fewer funds are available to spend on private consumption and investment. But to suggest that more guns can always be produced by sacrificing more butter is impractical. In reality, as the tax level increases to support a larger military budget, the economy operates less and less efficiently.

Samuelson and other textbook writers seem to have ignored the fact that the defense budget is a burden on society—a sacrifice supported by taxpayers—that is ultimately paid out of private production. You can have butter without guns, but you can't have guns without butter. The most absurd case is at the point at which military expenditures represent 100 percent of the national output. This is a logical impossibility because it implies a 100-percent tax rate on individuals and private enterprise. Obviously, no business or individual can survive if 100 percent of all income is taxed away. They would stop working entirely or go into the tax-free underground. No nation can only produce guns. Even the Soviet Union, a totalitarian regime, can only afford to spend a minority of total output on war goods—estimated to be no more than 15 percent of its gross national product (GNP). Israel provides a classic example of the serious difficulties a country faces when it has a huge military budget—its economy is falling apart.

A more plausible p-p curve between guns and butter would look like Figure 2–2.

In this new p-p curve, we note that at point M maximum civilian production is achieved with no military expenditures. At point N, we give up some civilian spending in order to produce military goods. Point O is where the maximum amount of military goods is produced. Because higher military spending necessitates higher taxation, any attempt to spend more on the military will actually reduce the output of military and civilian goods. At this stage, the economy is suffering from extreme economic inefficiency and is deteriorating rapidly. Finally, we

FIGURE 2–2
More Realistic View of Trade-Off between Guns and Butter

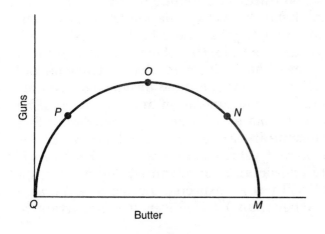

reach point Q, where the people attempt to produce only military goods and no civilian goods. But because military goods cannot be produced without the production of civilian goods, nothing is produced at all. The economy has collapsed.

The new p-p curve may remind some economists of the Laffer curve, a theoretical description of the trade-off between tax rates and government revenues. A similar principle is at work when it comes to attempts by government to expand military or domestic operations too far.

Although the orthodox production-possibility frontier offers some valuable applications, it fails to recognize the limitations individuals and societies face in the choice between essential goods or between public and private expenditures. It sometimes implies that government officials can almost randomly select any point on a p-p curve without suffering serious economic difficulties. In reality, any move away from the voluntary preferences of the individuals who make up the community is a shift away from the productive use of resources.

COMMONSENSE DECISION MAKING

Without resorting to fiction, there are more practical and accurate ways to portray graphically the trade-offs and opportunity costs people face in everyday situations. For example, I have created the diagram in Figure 2–3 to measure the trade-off between present and future consumption.

Suppose an individual is trying to decide whether to continue working or to go on to graduate school and get an advanced degree. Let us examine the choice strictly from a monetary point of view. The decision involves a trade-off between earning a certain amount of annual income today versus earning a substantially higher amount of annual income if he waits four years and obtains an advanced degree. Figure 2–3 demonstrates the opportunity cost of doing graduate work.

Point O is the current year. His income is Y_0. However, if he waits four years and obtains an advanced degree, his upgraded employment will pay an expected income flow, Y_1, at a rate substantially higher than Y_0. However, it is important to

FIGURE 2–3

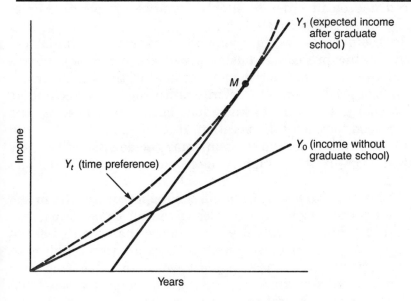

realize that there is another monetary factor in every trade-off involving time—an individual's time preference. Suppose, for example, that the employee discovers that an advanced degree would only increase his income by 1 percent a year. It would hardly seem worth the effort and costs of four more years of graduate school. The curve, Y_t, represents the worker's opportunity cost, the minimum higher return he demands in order to give up the current income stream for four years. It includes the substantial expense of going to graduate school as well as the time involved. Note that the opportunity cost curve gradually slopes upward, a reflection of the compounded interest effect of time.

Point M represents the minimum Y_1 has to reach before the employee will decide in favor of graduate school. If the expected income is higher, his decision to go to graduate school will be much easier, since it would be more profitable. If the expected income flow is below point M, he will continue working rather than go to graduate school, even though the annual income would be higher for a person with an advanced degree.

(All of this assumes, of course, that he does not seek the advanced degree in order to simply enhance his prestige or to achieve other aesthetic goals.)

In the business world, companies undertake a similar decision-making process. A business will adopt new techniques only if they are considered more profitable than the current methods of production. But before instituting a new technique, the company will want to know how long it will take for the new method to reach full operation. If it takes too long to build the plant or machine, the company may decide against the new method even if it is slightly more profitable than the old method.

There are many other examples of opportunity cost in the business world. If you are a salesperson on commission, you know that going on vacation involves more than the cost of the vacation. It also involves foregone income you could have earned if you were at work. If you have a tenant renting your vacation home, you know that using the home for your own monthlong vacation will cost you a month's rent. Finally, the decision by a major corporation to invest in a new project will depend partly on the return it could otherwise earn in the money markets. If money-market instruments (certificates of deposit, commercial paper, etc.) are paying 10 percent, the company is not likely to risk investing in a new venture that is only going to return the same amount. It will hope to reap substantially more, at least 15–20 percent, before making a commitment.

Finally, opportunity cost is extremely valuable in public finance when budgeting for new investment projects. For instance, in the case of the space program, what goods and services and technological improvements are we giving up in exchange for sending astronauts into space?

SUMMARY

In conclusion, the standard textbook depends on production-possibility diagrams that sometimes inaccurately portray what is really going on in the economy. Students would have a much easier chance of grasping the basic concepts of choice, trade-offs, and opportunity costs if textbook instructors would use such practical diagrams as those developed in this chapter.

CHAPTER 3

HOW THE ECONOMY REALLY WORKS

Economics is valuable only if it explains the real world.
—Roy J. Ruffin and Paul R. Gregory
Principles of Economics (1988)

The first task of any economist is to explain what the economy is all about. The circular flow diagram is a major concept used by standard textbooks to describe the economy. Like the p-p curve, the circular flow diagram is oversimplified, leaving out a lot about how the economy actually operates.

The circular flow diagram from McConnell is shown in Figure 3–1.

The circular flow diagram is meant to explain the basic interdependence of production, consumption, and exchange in the economy. The economy is divided into two parts. The first part, the resource market, is represented in the upper part of the diagram. In this sector, businesses hire resources (land, labor, capital, entrepreneurial ability), for which they pay money income (wages, rents, interest, profits). In return, the resources provide the work, capital, and services necessary so that the businesses can make and sell their goods to their customers.

The second part, the lower half of the diagram, is the product market. The businesses sell their products to households, which pay for the consumer goods and services with the income they earned as wage earners, landlords, etc.

The circular flow diagram may appear straightforward and logical, but it has a serious defect. It leaves out the most important part of economic activity! What is missing?

First, the circular flow diagram leaves out the critical element of time. It assumes that everything is done simulta-

FIGURE 3–1
The Circular Flow of Output and Income

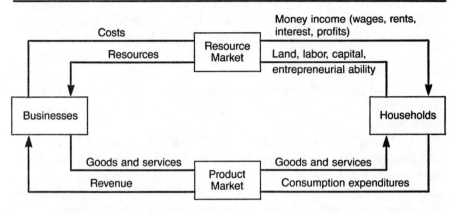

Source: Campbell R. McConnell and Stanley L. Brue, *Economics,* 11th ed. (New York: McGraw-Hill, 1990), p. 45.

neously. There is no waiting in the circular flow model; everything is done at the same time.

The circular flow model of economic behavior can be traced back to John Bates Clark—a turn-of-the-century American economist who envisioned the economy in a timeless dimension of simultaneous production and consumption—and to French economist Leon Walras, who saw the economy in a horizontal fashion where the factors of production are converted instantly into final consumer products.

Neither view is an accurate portrayal of the economy, however. Time is an extremely significant factor in all economic activity. It takes time, often lengthy periods, to produce or consume goods and services. Waiting is a ubiquitous phenomenon: Students take four years or longer before graduating and starting a career. A commercial builder may take two years to construct an office building. It may take 15 years for a landlord to recoup his investment in an apartment complex. It may take seven years of planning and modeling to design a new automobile.

Contrary to Walras's views, final consumer goods are not brought to the market instantly. The manufacturing of each product involves varying periods of investment. Shoes begin with cowhide, which is made into leather and then cut into pieces, and eventually the finished product is on somebody's feet. True, while new shoes are being manufactured, other shoes are being sold in the store. But they are not the same shoes, and the financial situation of the shoe salesperson as well as the shoe manufacturer changes with every new shoe that is brought to the market. The circular flow model assumes equilibrium and does not take into account the dynamic changes in the economy.

In the simplified circular flow diagram, there are no new savings, no financial institutions, no inventories, and no intermediate capital goods of any kind. Even government is left out. It offers no explanation for dynamic change in the economy— for example, shifts in prices, employment, production, bankruptcies, the business cycle, and economic growth. The circular flow model could never explain why some businesses fail and others flourish nor why some individuals earn a high income and others a low income.

THE PURCHASING POWER FALLACY

Ignoring the time element can lead to fundamental errors in economic thinking. For example, one might adopt the so-called purchasing power fallacy by misreading the circular flow diagram. This fallacy says that if workers' income can somehow be increased on its own, their additional purchasing power will allow the workers to spend more, which in turn will expand production and stimulate the economy. This idea was popular during the Great Depression. It is also an argument used to support a minimum wage law. The problem with this popular myth is that it ignores the time element in economic activity. Raising workers' wages and salaries does not automatically increase company revenues just because the workers suddenly spend more. It will, however, increase the company's expenses first and then raise revenues—but only if the company's employees spend their new income on the company's products. Yet there is no assurance that they will do so. The circular flow diagram fails to show this critical microeconomic element of the economy. It simply shows that households buy products from businesses. It does not show that some consumers purchase certain products while others buy different goods. Thus, the workers may well spend their new wages on products not manufactured by their company, or they may save their newly acquired income. The end result would be less profit for the company, resulting in unemployment of the workers.

The only sure way to encourage higher wages and income is for the company first to earn higher profits, out of which it can then pay its workers more. Increased productivity, as measured by profitability, is the key to higher income for workers, and income should only be increased in accordance with increased efficiency.

ECONOMISTS RECOGNIZE LIMITATIONS

Economics writers are only now beginning to recognize the severe limitations and unrealistic nature of the circular flow model. McConnell notes that it does not include the role of government, nor does it include transactions within the business and household sectors. It also assumes constant output and employment. Still, McConnell errs when he says that the circular flow model "lays bare the fundamental operations of pure capitalism."

Baumol and Blinder, as well as Bronfenbrenner, separate out government purchases, savings and investments, and foreign trade. Their reorganized circular flow diagram looks like a plumber's nightmare, but at least it takes into account some critical aspects of economic activity. Lipsey and Steiner refer to these additions as "leakages," as if the economy would work better without savings or foreign trade. Leakage is hardly an appropriate term to apply to an essential ingredient of the economy. Consumption cannot occur without savings. Leakage may be an appropriate term for government, but not for savings or foreign trade.

THE STAGES OF PRODUCTION

If textbook writers have failed to lay bare the fundamental operations of the market with the circular flow model, what model is there that can accurately describe the economy?

A much better approach is to use what I call the stages-of-production model. This model incorporates the fundamental operations of the economy, and students can grasp the concept easily. It also emphasizes the businessperson's perspective of the economy. Most important, it fits perfectly with our definition of economics (see Chapter 1), which states:

> Economics is the study of how individuals transform natural resources and manufactured goods into final goods and services that people can use.

If we could take a short tour of the world economy, what would we see? First of all, we would find all kinds of final durable goods already in service—automobiles on the road, appliances in homes, and machines in offices and factories. All of these goods, previously manufactured, are slowly but surely depreciating, and sooner or later they must be replaced with new products. Second, we would discover a wide variety of consumer goods ready to be purchased by customers—cars in the showroom, food in the grocery stores, clothing in the department store, and so forth.

Activity behind the Scenes

But behind these items in the retail outlets lies a third group, a host of businesses and workers who manufacture, transport, and market these consumer goods and services. Behind the retailer is the wholesaler, behind the wholesaler is the manufacturer, and behind the manufacturer are the resource suppliers, who represent the earliest stage of production.[1] The farmer plants the wheat, the miner extracts the ore and minerals, the tree companies grow the trees, and so forth.

Despite the amazing complexities of production processes, certain generalities can be made about every good and service in demand today: First, it takes time to produce and consume goods and services. There is a period of production, followed by a period of consumption. These periods vary between goods. Trees may take 50 years to be produced and 100 years to be consumed. Automobiles may take 1 year to be made and 10 years to be consumed. Bread may take five months to be produced, and one day to be eaten.

Second, all products go through a series of stages. Every good has an industrial genealogy. Here are several simple examples:

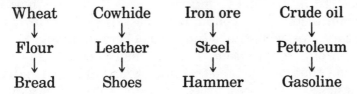

Wheat	Cowhide	Iron ore	Crude oil
↓	↓	↓	↓
Flour	Leather	Steel	Petroleum
↓	↓	↓	↓
Bread	Shoes	Hammer	Gasoline

The industrial process can be generalized as follows:

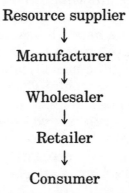

Resource supplier
↓
Manufacturer
↓
Wholesaler
↓
Retailer
↓
Consumer

Third, every stage involves factors of productions—land, labor, capital, and entrepreneurship. Income is paid at each stage (wages, rents, interest, etc.), but the producer/owner takes the greatest risk and can make a profit or suffer a loss. Risk of failure is evident throughout the output chain. The product may not be produced in time, it may not be made properly, or customer demand may suddenly disappear.

Finally, expected value is added at each stage of production. The company will bring together unfinished goods (what economists call working or circulating capital), and through the combined cooperative effort of management, investors, workers and others it will attempt to produce a finished product that will earn more in revenue than it costs. Businesses may endure short-term losses, but long-term profit is essential.

THE STRUCTURE OF THE ECONOMY

A generalized version of the stages-of-production concept can be visualized in graphic form in Figure 3–2. In this figure, we have generalized the economic process into four levels, although there are sometimes hundreds of stages involved in the production of a simple item. The common pencil is a practical illustration that can demonstrate the wide variety of individuals, businesses, and resources that go into the production process. The raw materials that go into a pencil include a cedar tree from northern California, graphite mined in Ceylon, clay from Mississippi, iron ore from Minnesota, and rubber from Indonesia. All of these natural resources are refined in numerous ways before reaching the pencil factory in Wilkes-Barre, Pennsylvania. Then, the pencil manufacturer uses complex machinery to lay the graphite ("lead") into every other slat, apply the glue, and place another slat atop to make a graphite sandwich. The cedar gets six coats of lacquer and is labeled with carbon black. Finally, the eraser (known as "the plug") is attached, and the pencil is ready for shipment. It must go through several marketing channels—agents, wholesalers, and retailers—before it finally reaches the ultimate user, the student.[2] Unfortunately, the way college economics is taught the student seldom visualizes and appreciates this modern miracle of product creation.

The structure of the economy as shown in Figure 3–2, which I have called the aggregate production structure (APS), is extremely versatile. The APS shows the general stages of production that commodities go through and how much time is involved in the economic process. It describes production and monetary processes throughout the economy: goods flow downward toward final use, while money flows upward from consumers to resources owners. It can demonstrate what is currently

FIGURE 3–2
The Aggregate Production Structure

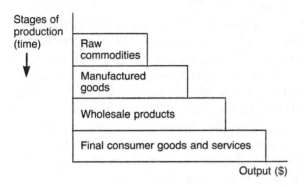

being produced, what is in the pipeline, and what has gone into final goods and services. In a sense, it can represent the past, present, and future of the economy.

THE STRUCTURE OF PRODUCTION IN ECONOMICS

Except for the value-added discussion in the national income chapter, not a single top 10 textbook describes the economy in terms of its stages of production, either on the scale of individual goods (microeconomics) or the whole economy (macroeconomics). Tragically, the stages-of-production concept has become obsolete for mainstream textbook writers. Yet it was taught regularly in the classrooms from 1900 until the 1950s, when the propensity for Keynesian aggregation took over. The commonsense idea that production takes time and that goods pass through a series of stages before reaching consumption was developed to some extent by several schools of thought before this century, particularly by Carl Menger and the Austrians and by William Stanley Jevons and the British school. The time structure of production was taught at Harvard, Princeton, and other well-known universities in the United States prior to the Keynesian revolution. It was used in the most popular U.S.

textbook in the early 20th century, *Principles of Economics,* by the Harvard professor Frank W. Taussig, as well as many other textbooks that lasted through the 1950s.

After the Keynesian revolution, the stages-of-production approach was replaced by a purely aggregational approach to economics, whereby economists explained the world in terms of large aggregates, such as GNP. Fortunately, the time-structure concept has been making a comeback since two of its advocates, Friedrich A. Hayek and John R. Hicks, won the Nobel Prize in economics in the 1970s. More and more professors from all schools of thought are endorsing a return to the idea, including Michio Morshima, Kenneth Boulding, Murray Rothbard, G. L. S. Shackle, and Howard J. Sherman.

Moreover, several disciplines related to economics have adopted a similar approach. They include marketing, which emphasizes "distribution channels," and statistical gathering organizations, which put together industrial output and price indices for various stages (e.g., commodity price index, wholesale price index, consumer price index). In fact, the time-structure description of the economy is essentially the businessperson's approach, since economics is the study of making goods more useful over time. As we shall see in later chapters, this model can be used to analyze a wide variety of problems in economics.

NOTES

1. Some critics have rejected the stages-of-production concept on the grounds that the earliest stage would have to extend back to early man, when iron ore and other raw materials were first extracted. Actually, however, this is not the case. We are analyzing current production, not past economic activity. The beginning of production is when an individual starts a project, not when the equipment he uses was originally built. For a complete analysis of the stages-of-production concept and criticisms made against it, see my work, *The Structure*

of Production (New York: New York University Press, 1990), Chapter 5.
2. Leonard E. Read, founder of the Foundation for Economic Education, was the first to tell the pencil story. His point was not so much to demonstrate the pencil's stages of production, but to prove that a simple item like a pencil is actually so complex that not a single person can make a pencil on his own from scratch. See Leonard Read, "I, Pencil," *The Freeman,* December, 1958. Milton Friedman popularized Read's example in his television series and book, *Free to Choose* (New York: Harcourt Brace Jovanovich, 1980), pp. 12–13.

CHAPTER 4

WHAT'S MISSING IN GNP?

> *GNP ignores intermediate goods, or goods used up entirely in the production of final goods, because to include them would be to double count.*
>
> —Roger Leroy Miller
> *Economics Today* (1988)

There's a lot more missing from GNP than household labor and black market transactions. In fact, according to data revealed in this chapter, the government deliberately ignores nearly 50 percent of economic activity in its GNP data!

GNP and other national income statistics have been a key element in economics textbooks since the early 1950s. Students are told that these are purely objective statistics that describe more or less what is happening in the economy. In reality, national income statistics are highly misleading and purposely leave out one of the biggest sectors of the economy.

THE KEYNESIAN BIAS IN NATIONAL STATISTICS

Economists fail to inform students of economics that the theory behind GNP is highly Keynesian. National income data were developed by Simon Kuznets and the National Bureau of Economic Research in the 1940s. Both were heavily influenced by the Keynesian theory of final aggregate demand. According to Keynes, a nation's prosperity is essentially determined by total *final* spending in the economy—by consumers, investors, and government. This notion of aggregate final demand was in sharp contrast to the classical view that productivity, technological advancement, and savings were the keys to economic progress. Classical economists believed that the aggregate consumer demand was relatively unimportant as an economic catalyst and that a country's standard of living was determined by its productive power. Consumer spending would largely take care of itself. The production process, not consumption, was the most important aspect of economic life.[1]

Under the influence of Keynes, Kuznets and other statisticians created the now-familiar figure of gross national product to represent the final purchase of all goods and services each year. The figure was obtained by using the well-known Keynesian equation,

$$Y = C + I + G$$

where

Y = Gross national product (GNP)
C = Total consumer expenditures
I = Gross investment expenditures by businesses
G = Government expenditures

GNP also includes net exports (exports minus imports), which can have a significant impact on GNP depending on the level of foreign trade.

GNP LEAVES OUT MAJOR PORTIONS OF ANNUAL PRODUCTION

The problem with this consumption approach to national output is that it does not include the total value of all the production that takes place in an economy. GNP takes into account only the production of goods and services sold to final users. It excludes all economic activity associated with the production of intermediate inputs, that is, raw materials, semimanufactured goods, wholesale goods, and other unfinished products (including inventories) that have yet to reach the final consumption stage. GNP includes, under gross private domestic investment, the purchase of all new durable capital goods, such as machines and equipment, because they are treated as final products. But these goods do not include nondurable capital goods or intermediate products such as leather or steel. In short, GNP takes into account fixed capital but not circulating capital. Thus, GNP is not really a gross figure at all, but a net value-added approach.

Neoclassical economists justify this omission by arguing that to include all intermediate goods would be a form of double counting and would overstate total output. Dolan uses the example of a kitchen table that retails for $100 (see Figure 4–1).

The kitchen table goes through three general stages. The timber farm company sells its logs to the sawmill for $15. Its cost (fuel, equipment, etc.) amounts to $5, leaving a profit (value added) of $10. At the second stage, the sawmill company sells its lumber to the manufacturer for $40. Its cost is $15 (Dolan assumes no costs other than the logs), leaving it with a profit (value added) of $25. The third and final stage is when

FIGURE 4–1
Value Added and the Use of Final Products in GNP

Final stage—manufacturing:		
Value of one table	$100	
Less value of lumber	−40	
Equals value added in manufacturing	60 ⟶	$ 60
Next to final stage—sawmill:		
Value of lumber	$ 40	
Less value of logs	−15	
Equals value added at sawmill	25 ⟶	25
Second to final stage—timber farming:		
Value of logs	$ 15	
Less value of fuel, equipment, etc.	−5	
Equals value added in timber farming	10 ⟶	10
All previous stages:		
Value added in fuel, equipment, etc.	$ 5 ⟶	5
Total value added		$100

This table shows why GNP must include only the value of final goods and services if it is to measure total production without double counting. The value of sales at each stage of production can be divided into the value added at that stage and the value of purchased inputs. The selling price of the final product (a $100 table, in this case) equals the sum of the values added at all stages of production.

Source: Edwin G. Dolan and David E. Lindsey, *Economics,* 5th ed. (Hinsdale, Ill.: Dryden Press, 1988), p. 155.

the manufacturer sells the finished table directly to the customer for $100. (Dolan bypasses the wholesaler and retailer.) Its cost is $40, leaving a profit (value added) of $60. If you add up the cost of the value added at each stage, the total comes to $100, equal to the final retail price, whereas, according to Dolan, "Adding together the $100 value of the table, the $40 value of the lumber, the $15 value of the timber, and so on would far overstate the true rate of productive activity (the true value added) in the economy."

THE FLAW IN GNP FIGURES

But the neoclassical economists have overlooked two serious drawbacks of the value-added approach to measuring national output. First, GNP violates the basic principles of business accounting. On an individual company basis, value added is only the bottom line of a company's financial statement. It omits the most important part, without which the company could not even operate. Specifically, businesses must be able to raise sufficient capital (either by borrowing, issuing stock, or self-financing) to pay for the *gross* outlays, not just the value-added portion of doing business. Before it earns a value-added profit, a business must hire workers, buy or lease equipment, stock inventory and working capital, advertise, rent space, and so forth. Businesses cannot ignore the aggregate costs of doing business; therefore, why should economists do so in figuring national output? It is national folly indeed.

If the purpose of GNP is to reflect accurately a nation's economic activity during the year, it must include the total expenditures by consumers, businesses, and government. But by omitting intermediate business input, GNP greatly underestimates actual spending by firms. In sum, GNP does not reflect total spending in the economy. If business firms were asked how much they spent last year, the costs of intermediate input would represent a significant part of total business outlays.

The great drawback to the GNP figure is that it takes the heart out of economic activity. Consider for a moment the purpose of economic action (as defined in Chapter 1): to transform unfinished goods into usable goods and services. Therefore, the heart of economic activity is intermediate input. For example, I recently visited a cannery that makes tomato juice. The ripe tomatoes are put on an assembly line. Workers cut out the stem and remove the skin. Machines crush the tomatoes into a juice. The juice is cooked and poured into cans. The cans are sealed by another machine and placed in large boilers for 30 minutes. After the cans cool, labels are attached and the cans are shipped to their destination. The point is this: all effort along the assembly line is concentrated on the tomatoes, the intermediate good. Throughout the process, it is the tomatoes that are being acted upon. The workers, the machines, the management, and the building all serve as a means to an end: to convert the tomatoes into a more convenient form for consumers, that is, tomato juice. The same approach could be applied to Dolan's kitchen table or any other production process. The intermediate input is the central focus of economic activity. As such, we see how GNP cuts out the heart of the economy by ignoring the intermediate processes and focusing solely on the end product.

GNP EXAGGERATES CONSUMPTION

This brings us to our second criticism. Because they leave out intermediate goods, GNP data grossly exaggerates the level of consumption in the economy. Take a look at GNP in the United States in 1988, stated in billions of dollars:

Personal consumption expenditures	$3,226.0
Gross private domestic investment	765.5
Government purchases	936.3
Net exports	− 93.2
Gross national product (GNP)	$4,861.8

Thus, according to national income statistics, consumption represented 66 percent of GNP in 1988. Other years show similar results. Naturally, this high level implies that the U.S.

economy is consumer-oriented, that changes in consumer spending—not investment or business spending—are the key to economic growth or decline. In fact, according to GNP data, government spending is more important than private investment ($936 billion for government purchases versus $765 for private domestic investment). The overemphasis on consumption is a common misconception found in the financial press and economic commentaries. Especially during the Christmas holidays, the media report almost daily on the outlook for retail sales, suggesting that if holiday sales are up the economy is healthy and sound. Underlying these reports is the notion that if only the Christmas season lasted year-round, the economy could expand even more.

The belief that the economy is consumption-oriented does not square with other data, however. If it were true that the economy were led by consumption, consumer spending should be a principal leading indicator of future economic activity. But according to the U.S. Department of Commerce, final consumer spending is not in the Index of Leading Indicators. (The leading indicator "new orders for consumer goods and materials" is at the manufacturing, not retail, level and emphasizes durable "consumer" goods often used in business.) Consumer spending tends to be a coincidental or lagging indicator, which is to say that consumer spending begins falling during or after a business turndown but not before.

THE GROSS NATIONAL OUTLAYS (GNO): AN ALTERNATIVE APPROACH

An alternative method of calculating the true gross national product is to use the aggregate structural approach developed in Chapter 3. I call this new figure gross national outlays (GNO).

In the simplified Dolan example at the beginning of this chapter (see Figure 4–1), the GNP is $100, representing only the final product (the table). But to measure the total economic activity in producing the table, we must figure GNO. GNO is the value of all expenditures involved in making the table.

Therefore, we add the total value of all stages of production, as follows:

First stage (fuel, equipment, etc.)	$ 5
Second stage (timber farming)	10
Third stage (sawmill)	25
Fourth stage (manufacturing)	60
Final stage (consumer)	100
Total gross national outlays (GNO)	$200

Thus, we conclude that total economic activity in the making of the table is $200, twice the price the consumer actually paid for the final product.

Actual expenditures on intermediate input in the United States can be obtained from input–output tables compiled by the U.S. Census Bureau. Unfortunately, the data is compiled only once every five years from an economic census and then estimated for each year until another census is taken. Even then input–output models are far from up to date. The latest input–output table is for 1982.

Using the latest input–output table, the traditional GNP figure for the United States amounted to $3,166.2 billion in 1982. However, if we add up the value of intermediate input, the total level of intermediate spending comes to $2,745.6 billion. Adding that to GNP, we have a GNO equal to $5,911.8 billion. The breakdown is as follows:

Gross National Outlays (GNO), 1982 (in billions of dollars)

Consumption expenditures		$2,046.4
Business expenditures		3,196.7
Intermediate input	2,745.6	
Gross private investment	451.1	
Government expenditures		641.7
Net exports		27.0
Gross National Outlays (GNO)		$5,911.8
Gross National Product (GNP)		$3,166.2

Source: "Annual Input–Output Accounts of the U.S. Economy, 1982," *Survey of Current Business,* April 1988, pp. 31–46.

According to the above data, GNO was almost double GNP in 1982. Furthermore, under our new definition of gross national spending, consumption represented only 34 percent of economic activity in 1982, compared to 65 percent of GNP. Gross business expenditures, which include outlays for both intermediate input and fixed capital investment, amounted to $3,196.7 billion. Accordingly, intermediate business spending represented 54 percent of real economic activity in 1982, not 14 percent as it appears under the GNP definition. Business spending was almost double consumer spending and four times bigger than government spending.

One of the most interesting sidelights of this new measurement of annual economic output is that the size of government spending is also reduced in scope. Under the GNP definition government spending represents 20 percent of final national output, but under the new GNO definition it reflects only 11 percent of total spending in the economy. However, this figure may underestimate government spending since it does not include the intermediate goods involved in the production of government outlays.

SUMMARY

GNP is a grave distortion of economic activity because it ignores the production of intermediate goods in the business sector. It overemphasizes the role of consumption and government spending in the economy at the expense of business. To understand what is really happening in the world, economists must include the output of intermediate goods in national statistics. Input–output tables should be brought up to date as soon as possible and published annually.

NOTES

1. John Stuart Mill states, "What a country wants to make it richer is never consumption, but production. Where there is the latter, we may be sure that there is

no want of the former." John Stuart Mill, "The Consumer Theory of Prosperity," *Essays on Some Unsettled Questions of Political Economy* (1830). The idea that production, not consumption, is the key element of prosperity is embodied in Say's law, "Supply creates its own demand." Keynes, who believed his "general theory" was a wholesale attack on Say's law, would have it the other way around, "Demand creates its own supply." See John Maynard Keynes, *The General Theory of Employment, Interest and Money* (London: Macmillan, 1936), pp. 18–21.

RECOMMENDED READING

Skousen, Mark. *The Structure of Production*. New York: New York University Press, 1990. Chapter 6.

CHAPTER 5

THE FALLACY OF THE PARADOX OF THRIFT

While savings may pave the road to riches for an individual, if the nation as a whole decides to save more, the result may be a recession and poverty for all.
—William J. Baumol and Alan S. Blinder
Economics: Principles and Policy (1988)

Macroeconomics is without question the most confusing element of a course in economics, and there is no better example of confusion and contradiction in macroeconomic theory than the anti-savings mentality expressed in the so-called paradox of thrift. In fact, the paradox of thrift is an ironic admission that the crude Keynesian model is by its nature self-contradictory.

THE ANTI-SAVINGS MENTALITY

Anti-savings doctrines have existed throughout the history of economics, but they were usually propogated by cranks and heretics (Mandeville, Hobson, Veblen, Foster, Catchings, et al.) Yet after the Great Depression, this heretical view became the mainstream orthodoxy with Keynes leading the way. Paul Samuelson, the author of the first modern textbook on economics, popularized the Keynesian doctrines in his classic text, *Economics,* and all other textbooks have followed suit by devoting large sections to the Keynesian analysis of consumption, savings, investment, taxes, and government policy. Samuelson's book has sold more copies than anyone else's (over 3 million copies) and has been translated into 31 foreign languages.

Samuelson highlighted the paradox of thrift doctrine in his first edition in 1948, and it has been featured in every edition since then. No doubt millions of individuals around the world have been taught this anti-savings dogma, and one wonders how many still believe it and have yet to see a refutation of it. As a result, the anti-savings mentality has led to a deleterious economic policy of the West—taxing savings and investment at high rates while encouraging consumer debt by making interest payments tax deductible. Favorable legislation toward investment has been the exception to the rule. The West has been undersaving and underinvesting on a massive scale for the past 50 years, as evidenced by the deteriorating roads, buildings, and other forms of infrastructure in many parts of the Western world. This is the dark side of the consumer society. Meanwhile, Far Eastern countries and some European nations have adopted an anti-Keynesian, pro-savings attitude and have experienced, not coincidentally, much higher growth rates. But Western policymakers appear to be blind to this historical relationship.

There are many fallacies in Keynesian theory, but the most fundamental error is the notion that savings are bad except in times of "full employment." During a recession or depression, the private citizen's decision to increase savings, get out of debt, and cut back on spending is considered public folly by almost all textbook economists. Lipsey and Steiner state, "In times of unemployment and depression, frugality will only make things worse."

What exactly is this paradox of thrift in the Keynesian model? In times of uncertainty and a potential economic downturn, the acts of saving, reducing spending, and getting out of debt make perfect sense to the individual, but the economist contends that what is true for an individual may not be true for the nation. Samuelson refers to this idea as the "fallacy of composition" in his introductory chapter and says, "Attempts of individuals to save more in a depression may lessen the community's total savings." To demonstrate the deleterious effects of increased frugality, he uses the example of farmers who increase their production of wheat. If one farmer plants more wheat, his income is likely to rise. But if all farmers attempt to plant more wheat, the price of wheat will drop and no one will be better off—in fact, they may be worse off. (Samuelson does not use the case of the farmer in his textbook, but he used it in a telephone conversation I had with him recently.) During the depression, many well-known economists, including Keynes at Cambridge and Taussig at Harvard, went on radio and irresponsibly encouraged people to go out on a spending binge to get the economy moving again. The public did not respond because of a justified fear of going bankrupt, but Keynes and Taussig still argued that they were right in theory.

THE BASICS OF KEYNESIAN THEORY

The basic tenets of Keynesian economics, no matter how unrealistic, are still taught in the classroom. According to Keynes and his followers, the central problem in economics is savings. If savings are invested, there is no problem. But if savings are merely hoarded or if they remain uninvested by financial institutions, there is leakage out of the system, and the economy stagnates. In fact, the crude Keynesian theory of the multiplier assumes that investment is fixed and savings are never invested in the short run. (In more sophisticated Keynesian models, savings may be invested in the long run, but planned investment is uncertain and unstable.) This leakage concept of savings is illustrated in many textbooks. In an earlier edition of Samuelson, the chart shown in Figure 5–1 was used.

To illustrate the paradox of thrift, let us refer to Paul Samuelson's classic example, shown in Figure 5–2. Samuelson states the logic of the paradox of thrift: "If people try to increase their saving and lower their consumption for a given level of business investment, sales (equal to $C + I$ spending) will fall. Businesses will cut back on production. How far will production fall? GNP will fall until people stop trying to save more than businesses are investing."

In Figure 5–2, assuming a marginal propensity to save of one third, the Keynesian multiplier model indicates that every $1 in increased savings will eventually eliminate $3 in income. A $100 billion increase in savings will reduce GNP by $300 billion. Therefore, Samuelson and the Keynesians conclude, the virtue of savings is in reality a vice.

FIGURE 5–1
Savings as Leakage in the Economy

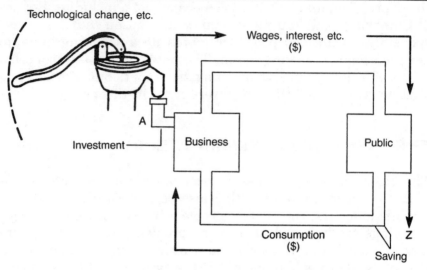

Source: Paul A. Samuelson, *Economics*, 8th ed. (New York: McGraw-Hill, 1970), p. 218.

Two Vital Assumptions

The Keynesian anti-savings doctrine depends on two critical assertions: First, savings and investment are allegedly two entirely separate activities performed by two distinct types of people with little or no link between them. Therefore, individuals could increase their savings, and the savings could somehow not be invested. As a result, consumers buy less and business spends less, causing an economic downturn.

Second, investment under Keynesian theory is primarily a function of business expectations of consumer demand. An increase in consumption will stimulate investment, and vice versa. This is contrary to classical economic theory, which contends that investment decisions are determined by the profit margin of business opportunities. Demand is just one side of the equation. Businesses also consider such factors as the level of interest rates and the costs of production—not just final demand—to determine their profit margins. Nevertheless, ac-

FIGURE 5–2
Saving and Investment Diagram Shows How Thriftiness Can Kill Off Income

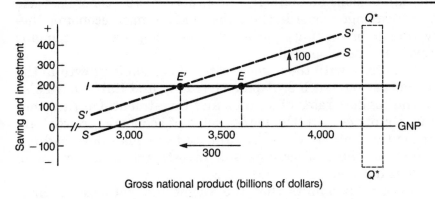

Gross national product (billions of dollars)

Note: Q^* = Full employment output or GNP.

Source: Paul A. Samuelson and William D. Nordhaus, *Economics,* 13th ed. (New York: McGraw-Hill, 1989), p. 184.

cording to the simple Keynesian model an increase in final consumer demand will increase investment, and a decrease in final consumer demand will decrease investment.

ECONOMIC GROWTH AND SAVINGS: THE KEYNESIAN DILEMMA

Actually, however, the paradox of thrift does not prove that thrift is a vice. Rather, it proves that the assumptions in Keynesian economics are fundamentally wrong.

The biggest drawback to the Keynesian anti-savings doctrine is that it runs completely counter to historical evidence. It is in direct conflict with the theory of economic growth, which clearly shows that higher rates of savings go hand in hand with higher rates of productivity and economic growth. Studies by Franco Modigliani, for example, show a strong correlation between a country's savings rate and its compounded annual growth (in per capita disposable income).[1] McConnell reproduces a chart that demonstrates the positive relationship between investment (which depends on business and personal savings) and productivity (see Figure 5–3). It is interesting that Samuelson, McConnell, and other top-10 economists use an anti-savings model in their chapters on macroeconomic theory and a pro-savings model in their chapters on economic growth and development.

Countries with the highest rates of economic growth in the postwar period—such as Japan, Germany, and Italy—have also had the highest rates of savings and investment. On the other hand, countries with the lowest rates of economic growth—including the United States, Britain, and Canada—have had relatively low rates of savings and investment as a percent of national income.

McConnell admits that the Keynesian paradox of thrift violates this relationship and, in the previous edition of his textbook, points to Japan as a classic example. Nevertheless, he joins Samuelson and other mainstream writers in suggesting that increased thrift is only good when "the economy is operating, not in the horizontal Keynesian range, but in the vertical classical range of the aggregate supply curve." The horizontal Keynesian range McConnell refers to is a depression/high unemployment scenario, in which new savings remain uninvested, whereas the vertical classical range indicates full employment, in which new savings are fully invested.

But Samuelson and the Keynesians are still not out of the woods because their full employment explanation does not square with the fact that Germany, Japan, and many countries in the Far East continued to experience high levels of economic growth during periods when resources and human capital were underemployed. Unemployed resources did not appear to dampen their need to fund new investment opportunities.

The Issue of Full Employment

The fact is that full employment is a nebulous and misleading term. There are always unemployed resources, raw materials, and unfinished goods that need to be transformed into usable tools and capital. This is the very nature of economics. There

FIGURE 5–3
Investment and the Growth of Productivity

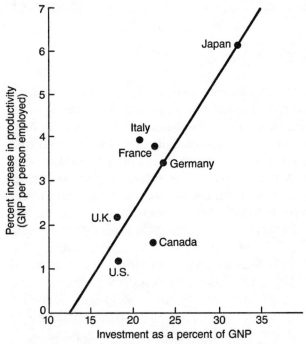

Source: Campbell R. McConnell and Stanley L. Brue, *Economics,* 11th ed. (New York: McGraw-Hill, 1990), p. 424.

are always ways in which capital can be better utilized and workers can be better employed to improve efficiency. Technically, then, there is always unemployment or underemployment, and never full employment.

By full employment, orthodox economists typically mean that most people have a job or can find a job if they want one and that plant capacity is being fully used most of the time. But even then, the Keynesian theory does not resolve the paradox of thrift, despite Samuelson's denial. Let us make the standard full employment assumption. Suddenly, the public decides to save more. According to the crude Keynesian doctrine, this means a reduction in consumer spending. But a cut in consumer spending means a rise in retail inventories and consequently a cutback in business activity, that is, an economic slowdown. Thus, we conclude that the Keynesian theory denies the virtue of savings at all times, even during full employment.

THE FLAW IN KEYNESIAN ANALYSIS

The central problem with the Keynesian model is that it fails to comprehend the true nature of savings and investment in an economic system. The Keynesian model assumes that the only thing that matters is *current* demand for final consumer goods—and the higher the consumer demand the better. But this view fails to recognize another force that is just as strong as current demand—the demand for *future* consumption. Every individual and business must seek to achieve a balance between the demand for current consumption and future consumption. After all, if every attempt to curtail consumption results in a proportional decline in production, as the Keynesian theory contends, then no addition to a nation's wealth could ever occur from increased savings. By the same token, if everyone went on a buying spree at the local department store or grocery store, investment would not necessarily expand. Certainly, investment in consumer goods would expand, but increased expenditures for consumer goods will do little or nothing to construct a bridge, build a hospital, pay for a research program to cure cancer, or provide funds for a new invention or a new production process.

What the Keynesians have overlooked is that the decision to save is an act of time preference, the choice between current spending and future spending. Savings do not disappear from the economy; they are merely channeled into a different avenue. Savings are spent on investment capital now and then spent on consumer goods later.

Everyone cannot be a total consumer, saving nothing. If so, businesses would not have any funds with which to produce consumer goods. It would also be pointless for everyone to save everything, because the purpose of saving is, eventually, to consume. Thus, there is a delicate balance in society between consumption and savings.

People save for a variety of reasons. Their rate of saving varies depending on age and circumstances. Savers always have a goal in mind—to become financially independent, to start a new business venture, to retire, to educate their children, to go on a vacation, to buy a home, etc. Savings are always future-oriented. They may be invested directly by the saver in a business, for example, or indirectly by the saver's investing the money with a financial institution. But money in a savings account does not lie idle, as the simplified Keynesian (depression) model assumes; it is invested into the economy by financial institutions.

It is also important to point out that it is not necessarily true that an increase in savings means, ipso facto, a reduction in consumer spending. In fact, most new savings come about from an increase in income, not from cutting back on spending. Increased savings may come out of higher wages, higher profits, or higher rental income.

But let us take the Keynesian case in which citizens decide across the board to increase their savings and cut back on consumption. True, those businesses engaged in retail sales and the consumer-goods industries would be forced to cut back. But would all businesses fail, as the Keynesians argue? No. As anyone who has been in the business world knows, there are numerous investment opportunities at any time, even during a recession. Banks, lenders, and brokerage firms are always being approached by venture capitalists who have new investment projects that need funding.

Increased savings may mean a temporary cutback in retail sales, but the increase also means that additional funds are now available for investment projects, research and development, capital expenditures, and new processes. Banks, insurance companies, and other financial institutions will have new funds available to lend to entrepreneurs or to form a joint venture on new projects. As new funds become available, interest rates will tend to fall, but even if interest rates are extremely low bankers are noted for finding creative ways to put idle cash to work. (The only exception might be during a monetary crisis, such as in the 1930s, to be discussed shortly.)

Using an altered Keynesian framework, this means that the investment schedule should rise by an amount equal to the supply schedule, as noted in Figure 5–4.

Even the altered Keynesian model still does not do justice to the social benefits of savings. In the modified Keynesian model, when an increase in savings is fully invested, the final equilibrium point, E, is the same as it was before the savings rate increased. But in reality the equilibrium point should be to the right, reflecting an increase in national output. Increased savings that are efficiently invested should increase the real standard of living. Because the new funds are invested in ventures that often involve innovations, improvements in production techniques, and technological change, the end result is an increase in productivity.

AN ALTERNATIVE MODEL

There are many social benefits that an increased savings rate provides that are ignored in the Keynesian model. A more realistic model is the time-structure model (developed in Chapter 3), which is based on the economy's stages of production.

Figure 5–5 illustrates the changes in the time-structure model of the economy due to increased thrift.

Here we see the whole impact of an increase in the savings–investment schedule: First, the increase in savings results in a short-term cutback in retail spending (as indicated by the small shift at the bottom of the structure in Figure 5–5, part A). The consumer-goods industry suffers a *temporary* economic slowdown. However, as noted earlier, under normal circumstances increased savings will not accompany a cutback in consumer spending during periods of economic growth, as Figure 5–5, part B, demonstrates. Savings will normally come from increased income, not retrenchment in consumer spending habits.

FIGURE 5–4
Altered Keynesian Model: Savings and Investment Schedules
Both Shift Upward

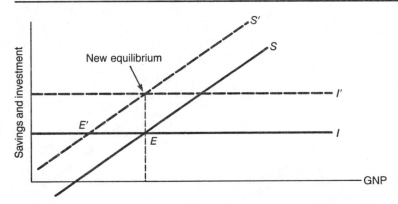

Second, banks and other financial institutions have additional funds to invest in new ventures and projects. The capital-goods industries, especially businesses involved in the stages of production more distant from final consumption, enjoy an economic expansion. Insofar as interest rates decline, the cost of borrowing money declines and the cost of holding inventories falls, especially for those businesses producing products distant from final consumption. Lower interest rates make it possible for businesses to invest in projects with distant payoff periods, including new research, new machines, and new production techniques.

How is it possible that final consumer demand declines temporarily, while most investment demand increases? The answer lies in the reason why people started saving in the first place. An increase in savings indicates a willingness for people to be more future-oriented. They have increased their demand for future consumption. They are capable of waiting longer periods before consuming. Higher savings rates justify lower interest rates and the production of more durable goods and long-term investment projects. Individuals are willing to wait longer. But the wait is worthwhile because the payoff means greater productivity, new technological advancement, and

FIGURE 5–5
Effect of Increased Savings on the Time Structure of the Economy

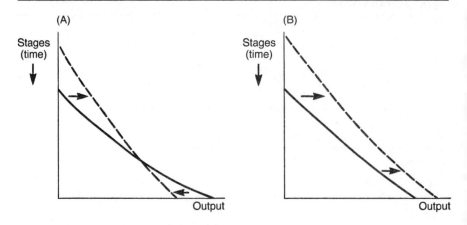

lower costs. These projects often involve new techniques that will increase the quality and life of machines and that will eventually reduce the costs of producing final goods and services.

Third, when these investment projects are completed, the ultimate beneficiaries are the consumers who initially put their savings to work. The benefits of increased savings include lower real prices and higher quality for goods and services. Moreover, the new investment expansion results in higher profits for businesses, which, when the expansion is completed, will result in increased consumer demand. That is why I emphasized that the cutback in consumer demand is merely temporary at the time people start saving more.

In sum, an increase in savings means new inventions; new production techniques; the institution of cost-cutting measures; the replacement of worn-out or outdated equipment and buildings; and, in short, an increased standard of living. Thus we see why savings are an essential ingredient in the theory of economic growth and why this alternative theory of savings and capital formation is completely compatible with historical experience in Japan, Germany, and other countries that have adopted this vision of sacrificing for future consumption. An increase in savings leads to increased production, which in turn results in higher income and a higher standard of living. Historically, savings and consumer spending have tended to rise together as the standard of living increases.

A hypothetical example may be useful in reinforcing the benefits of increased savings. Suppose a community is separated by a river and the only transportation between the two sides is by barge. Travel between the two sections of town is expensive and time-consuming. Finally, the town leaders call a meeting and recommend the building of a bridge. Everyone agrees to cut back on current spending and put their savings to work to build a bridge. In the short run, there is a decline in retail sales, which may temporarily reduce the profits and employment in local department stores. Yet new workers are assigned to build the bridge. In the aggregate, there is no reduction in output and employment at all. Moreover, once the bridge has been built the community benefits greatly from lower travel costs and increased competition between the two sections of town. In the end, the community's sacrifice has been transformed into a high standard of living.

SAVINGS IN A DEPRESSION: VIRTUE OR VICE?

We now return to the conviction expressed by virtually all of the textbook economists that savings are bad during a depression because they are not spent or invested. During the 1930s, Keynesians blamed the continuation of the depression on people's "liquidity preference" for hoarding cash, and on the banks' building "excess reserves" rather than investing. As a result, there was an alleged deficiency in "effective demand." The country was allegedly stuck at an equilibrium level with widespread unemployment. According to Keynes, Say's law— that supply would create its own demand, making overproduction or underconsumption impossible—was proven false, and free-market capitalism would not automatically bring about full employment.

But this stagnation thesis is wrongheaded. Savings will always be invested throughout periods of economic fluctuation unless individuals lose faith in the country's monetary system.

Hoarding and excess bank reserves were the effects, not the causes, of the depression. Moreover, hoarding and cash reserves were temporary phenomena based on individual and business expectations that prices would decline further, thus making investment and consumption more profitable at a future date. Banks held excessive cash reserves in order to protect themselves from potential runs. At some point, when they believed the bottom of the depression had been reached and the monetary system had stabilized, the hoarding and excess bank reserves would dissipate. (Actually the degree of cash hoarding was relatively small during the depression; high bank reserves were more apparent.)

The depression was due to a previously created defective financial system. This system was built upon an inflationary central bank, a fragile fractional reserve banking system, and an unsound gold standard. If the Western countries had established a sound monetary system, the stock market would not have crashed in 1929, banks would not have collapsed on a wholesale basis in the early 1930s, hoarding and excess reserves would not have developed, and the Great Depression would have been avoided. (I discuss how the financial system became unsound—and how it can be fixed—in Chapter 11, which is on the gold standard and the origin of banking.)

Furthermore, increased savings and investment during a crisis might actually mitigate a depressed economy. This view is, of course, completely in opposition to the views in today's orthodox economics textbooks. But here's why it makes sense: Between 1929 and 1933, the capital-goods industry was hit much worse than the consumer-goods industry. Personal consumption expenditures declined from $77 billion to $46 billion, a 40 percent reduction. But gross private investment declined more steeply—from $16 billion to $1.4 billion, a collapse of over 90 percent. Profits and employment in the capital-goods markets declined much more on a percentage basis than did the consumer markets. In such an environment, what effect would an increase in savings have had on the depression? It would have reversed the falling capital markets relative to the consumer markets, stimulating the demand for capital goods (especially if interest rates fell, as they tend to do during a recession or depression) while reducing the demand for consumer goods. Of course, Keynesian economists ask, "Why should a businessperson invest in a new plant just because interest rates are falling if demand for his product is falling too?"

The answer is twofold. First, a businessperson can reduce prices in an effort to recoup the falling demand and increase sales. Whether cutting prices increases or decreases sales depends on what economists call the elasticity of demand for specific products. Under certain circumstances, a firm may be able to stimulate considerable sales by reducing prices, even during a recession. Price cutting may not increase profits, but it could reduce losses.

Second, the businessperson may be able to cut costs sharply, thus offsetting the fall in demand. Investment decisions, you may recall, are not based solely on demand for products, but also on the profit margin itself (price minus costs). Granted, demand and prices may well be falling for the businessperson's products during a downturn, but so likely will his costs be falling. If a company wants to survive a recession or depression, it must be willing to cut costs, to repair old equipment instead of replacing it, or to shift into more profitable enterprises. Moreover, lower interest rates may not only reduce debt service in a business, but may also have secondary effects in reducing the costs of inventory, for example.

Employees' wages may also have to be cut. Keynesians traditionally oppose wage cuts during a recession or depression for fear that such cuts may curtail workers' purchasing power. But they fail to distinguish between wage *rates* and total wage *income*. Wage rates may decline, but if an industry employs more laborers as a result of the wage cuts, total wage income—hence aggregate demand—can actually increase.

The net result is that profit margins can still be achieved in an economic downturn, even if they are at a lower level. Many businesses have survived severe downturns in the economy by following this sound traditional approach. And new savings and investment can help to ameliorate poor business conditions. In conclusion, the old-time virtues of retrenchment, getting out of consumer debt, selling off assets, cutting costs, and increasing savings can allow the nation to start back on the road to recovery. Furthermore, to suggest that individuals go on a spending spree, as Keynes and Taussig did in the depths of the depression, would only make matters worse by reducing the amount of funds flowing to the more depressed capital sector and thereby bankrupting people. In many ways, Keynes and Taussig's suggestion was one of the most irresponsible acts ever performed by major economists; fortunately, not too many people followed their advice.

Samuelson begins his paradox of thrift thesis by denying the virtue of Ben Franklin's axiom, "A penny saved is a penny earned." But now we see that savings are indeed a virtue at all times, not just in times of full employment. On both a theoretical and a practical basis, we can rightfully reclaim the wisdom of the ages. Ben Franklin was right all along.

Incidentally, in the 13th edition of Samuelson's *Economics,* his section on the paradox of thrift has been made optional, with the note that it "may be omitted in short courses." No doubt this is a favorable sign of the times. Perhaps the paradox of thrift concept will soon disappear entirely, or at least be designated as a historical curiosity and an embarrassing excrescence of mainstream economics.

NOTES

1. Franco Modigliani, "Life Cycle, Individual Thrift, and the Wealth of Nations," *American Economic Review* (June 1986), p. 303. This is Modigliani's acceptance speech for the Nobel Price in economics. Modigliani, who has been sympathetic with certain Keynesian policy recommendations, nevertheless argues that "national savings is the source of the supply of capital" and is therefore "a virtuous, socially beneficial act" (p. 297).

CHAPTER 6

THE MAGIC AND MYTH
OF THE MULTIPLIER

Can something be created from nothing?
—William J. Baumol and Alan S. Blinder
Economics: Principles and Policy (1988)

The Keynesian multiplier is a primary instrument in the text-book's toolbox of macroeconomics, which involves the critical issues of national income determination, taxes, and government economic policy. It shows how a certain amount of spending can multiply into many more times itself in national income throughout the economy. For example, $1 billion in private investment or government spending can create $3 billion of GNP. "Can something be created from nothing?" ask Baumol and Blinder. Indeed it can, they respond.

Let's take Baumol and Blinder's example:

> Suppose that Generous Motors—a major corporation in Macroland—decides to spend $1 million to retool a factory to manufacture pollution-free, electronically powered automobiles. Its $1 million expenditure goes to construction workers and owners of construction companies as wages and profits. That is, it becomes their *income*.[1]

But the process does not end there. The construction workers and owners will not simply keep their $1 million in the bank. They will spend some of it. Then Baumol and Blinder assume a marginal propensity to consume (MPC) of 0.8. An MPC of 0.8 means that individuals will spend 80 cents and save 20 cents of each additional dollar they receive. Accordingly, the construction workers and owners will spend $800,000 and save the rest. Baumol and Blinder exclaim, "This $800,000 expenditure is a net addition to the nation's demand for goods and services exactly as Generous Motors's original $1 million expenditure was." Therefore, Generous Motors's $1 million investment has already pushed GNP up some $1.8 million. The process continues. As the shopkeepers receive the $800,000, they in turn spend 80 percent of their new income, adding another $640,000 to GNP.

"Where does it all end?" ask Baumol and Blinder. It does eventually—with GNP $5 million higher than before Generous Motors spent the original $1 million. The multiplier turns out to be 5, based on a geometric progression that is summed up in the following equation:

$$\text{Multiplier} = \frac{1}{1 - \text{MPC}}$$

Baumol and Blinder point out that this is an oversimplified example and that several real-world factors will reduce the true multiplier—inflation, income taxation, international trade, and so forth, which they explain in later chapters. But they don't tell you the real reasons why the multiplier is not what it seems to be.

THE MISREPRESENTATION OF SAVINGS

One of the underlying assumptions inherent in the multiplier concept is that consumption is spending and saving is not. Imagine the horror of the Keynesians if several construction workers or shopkeepers decided to save their income rather than spend it. It could reduce or eliminate the multiplier.

We have exploded this myth about savings in Chapter 5, but it continues to be applied consistently throughout the Keynesian model, resulting in some egregiously misleading and preposterous conclusions. In truth, saving is spending just as much as consumption is, but it is a different kind of spending, certainly a better kind of spending in the sense that savings go in part toward the construction of durable capital goods and the creation of new productions, inventions, lower costs, and higher quality. In brief, savings may offer longer lasting benefits than pure consumption.

But wait, does this mean that the multiplier is no longer less than one, that actually *all* of the $1 million investment by Generous Motors is spent? Indeed, it appears so. Not only do the construction workers and owners spend $800,000 on consumables, but their savings also go to work. The banks and savings institutions lend these new savings deposits to businesses, which spend and invest the remaining $200,000, which starts a multiplier of its own.

We see now that the multiplier is really 1, not 0.8, which means that the spending chain is infinite. Of course, there are a few barriers that keep GNP from reaching nirvana: the time lag, the fact that people and businesses experience delays in their spending decisions, and the "full capacity" limitation on real national output. Nevertheless, this magical theory of the multiplier suggests that a relatively small injection of new spending will work wonders in pushing output up to its fullest potential, especially if the economy is suffering from underemployment.

It might also be added that such a macro theory implies that the investment could be performed by business or by government, and that the money could be spent on anything—Keynes suggested pyramid building in *The General Theory*—and it would have the same multiplier effect. To Keynesians, it's hard to imagine "malinvestment," that is, a bad decision being made by business or government. Management recognizes the possibility of malinvestment in its business decisions—that an investment project can turn out to be too costly or not in demand by its customers. Suppose for example that the demand for Generous Motors's pollution-free electronic car is insufficient. The people reject it as they did Ford's Edsel. As a result, Generous Motors may close the plant, which implies a negative multiplier effect that could certainly devastate the community where the plant is located. But the Keynesian model neglects to acknowledge such a possibility. To them, all spending is good.

On a micro level, there is no doubt a multiplier effect, either positive or negative. A major corporation moving into a small town can create a dramatic initial boom, just as the discovery of gold in California, Nevada, and Alaska created boomtowns throughout the American West in the 1850s. On the other hand, when major companies move out of a small town the effect can be as dramatic in reverse, just as the boomtowns in the 1850s often turned into ghost towns in the 1870s.

THE UNTOLD STORY

But can the multiplier have the dramatic impact Keynesians contend it can on an economywide scale? Under most conditions, the answer is no.

The art of economics is to look at not just what is seen but what is not seen as well. It is not to analyze the effect of an action on just one group but on all groups. It is what Henry Hazlitt, former economics editor of *Newsweek,* calls the one lesson everyone should learn in economics.[2]

Let us return to the Generous Motors example once more. Baumol and Blinder highlight the obvious—Generous Motors's spending $1 million to create a new automobile. But what is the not-so-obvious? Perhaps Generous Motors cut back $1 million in another plant in order to spend these funds on the electric car. On a national scale, such a negative effect could cancel out the multiplier, resulting in no net change. However, the effects would be quite different in the separate communities.

Suppose, however, that Generous Motors does not cut back on any other operations and instead simply adds the electric car project to its budget. The funds to develop the new car cannot appear out of thin air. They probably will come from Generous Motors's bank account, thus causing Generous Motors's account balance to decline by $1 million. Assuming that all other things are unchanged, this means that the bank will have $1 million less on deposit to lend out and will have to cut back its loan commitments. Again, this effect works to negate the positive multiplier.

Of course, the new electric car may be popular with customers, returning a sizable profit that exceeds the profit rate of Generous Motors's other plants, as well as what it was earning on its bank deposits. The net result is positive for the economy, increasing the people's standard of living and causing a net expansion of economic activity. Economic growth does have a positive multiplier effect, but only if the growth is real and not a misallocation of investment capital.

GOVERNMENT SPENDING AND THE MULTIPLIER

The same critique can be applied to the government expenditure multiplier. Textbooks demonstrate that the purchase of goods and services by the government has a favorable impact on national output. In McConnell's case, a $20 billion spending program pushes net national product (NNP) up from $470 to $550 billion, an $80 billion increase. Thus the government multiplier is 4 (see Figure 6–1).

The $20 billion government spending program is the visible act. But what is not seen, and why will NNP not necessarily increase by $80 billion? There are several alternative views.

First, the government program has to be financed, either through taxes or the issuing of bonds. An increase in taxes will introduce a negative multiplier, because private individuals will have less disposable income to spend and save. Issuing bonds may also raise interest rates and curtail private investment, thus instigating another negative multiplier effect.

Second, the government program may compete with a private business, causing the private company to curtail its operations or even to go bankrupt. If the government's program competes with private enterprise—as, for example, in medical care or child care—one spending program may offset the other. It is also quite possible, even likely, that the government program will be less efficient than the private company's operation, thus reducing social well-being.

FIGURE 6–1
Government Spending and the Equilibrium NNP

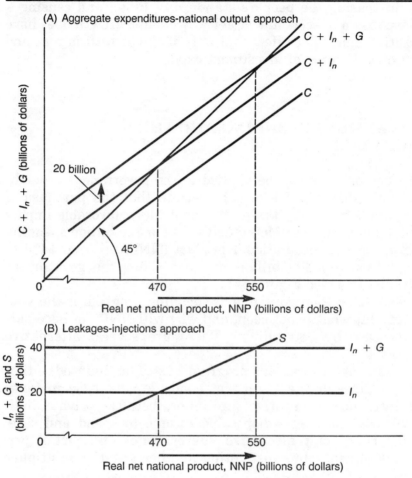

Source: Campbell R. McConnell and Stanley L. Brue, *Economics*, 11th ed. (New York: McGraw-Hill, 1990), p. 259.

Many economists readily acknowledge these drawbacks regarding the government multiplier but continue to present it in the textbooks. McConnell indicates that his example involves numerous simplifying assumptions, such as the ideas that increased government purchases somehow neither depress nor stimulate private spending, that the price level is constant, that taxes are fixed, etc.

THE TWISTED RESULTS OF THE BALANCED-BUDGET MULTIPLIER

Perhaps there is no better example of distortion in Keynesian economics than the balanced-budget multiplier. According to this theory, a tax cut has less impact on GNP than does creating a new government spending program of an equal amount. Or, to put it another way, an increase in government spending would require a tax increase larger than the federal expenditure to offset its effects.

The reason for this appears quite straightforward. Miller states, "During the first round of spending of a tax cut, there is a *leakage* into saving. No such leakage occurs with an increase in government spending." Samuelson states specifically, "When government spends $1 on *G*, that $1 gets spent directly on GNP. On the other hand, when government cuts taxes by a dollar, only part of that dollar is spent on *C*, while a fraction of that $1 tax cut is saved." Once again, we return to the absurd assumption underlying the balanced-budget multiplier that savings are not spent in the short run.

In reality, of course, tax cuts are far more beneficial to the nation than a new government expenditure. A tax cut puts more money into the hands of individuals, who voluntarily decide where to spend and save their money. (Dolan suggests that a tax cut usually benefits savings more than consumption.) Their decisions will mean a greater optimal use of resources than will a government program that forces citizens to use their funds in a manner that may go counter to their wishes. As a corollary, private business activities tend to be more efficient and productive than government programs because those benefiting from the government programs do not pay directly for them.

Second, the fact that part of the tax cut will go toward new savings is an advantage, not a drawback, over government expenditures. Whereas new federal spending may involve questionable projects, transfer payments, or other forms of pure consumption, private savings are likely to go toward investment projects that have long-term benefits involving innovation, greater efficiency, and technological breakthroughs.

In short, the concept of the balanced-budget multiplier is so far removed from reality that it should be relegated to the dark hole of historical economics, only to be resurrected as an example of antediluvian theories.

INFLATION AND THE MULTIPLIER

There is only one possible situation where government policy could have a major multiplier effect on the economy, and that is the case of pure money creation, what economists call an "autonomous" increase in government spending. In this Keynesian case, a government program does not depend on additional taxation or the issuing of bonds in competition with private capital markets to secure its funding. Instead, the U.S. Department of Treasury prints money directly or sells its bonds to the central bank (which in turn pays for the bonds out of its own account, an indirect form of printing money). In this case, the government multiplier may work its wonders for a while. Not only can it create a microeconomic boom in the areas where the new money is spent first, but it is also likely to create a nationwide inflationary boom as the new income is spent elsewhere.

Discussing the creation of fiat money necessitates a shift in the focus of our analysis. In our critique of the multiplier above, we stressed how business investment or government spending affects not just one group but all groups. Now, in analyzing the effects of a new monetary multiplier, we must shift our focus to short-term versus long-term effects. The role of the economist is to look not just at the short-term effects of an action but at its long-term impact as well.

The monetary expansion may cause a positive multiplier effect in the short run, but a negative multiplier effect in the long run. Those who get the new money first will tend to benefit the most, whereas those who get the new money last will tend to be hurt the most. "Who gets the new money first?" is a question every economist should ask, but one that none among the top 10 textbook writers does. New government spending may help one group in the beginning—particularly the companies and workers involved in the federal projects—and hurt another group later on. It may create an inflationary boom that increases wages, production, and a false sense of prosperity at first, but it may eventually turn into a deflationary bust a few years later. It is a well-known fact in business cycle analysis that government-induced inflations do not last, that their multiplier effects eventually dissipate as prices rise dramatically. Sooner or later, government leaders are forced to stop inflating and the boom comes to an end, sometimes with bitter consequences.

In sum, monetary inflation by the central bank, often accompanied by federal deficits, causes a boom–bust business cycle that cannot guarantee a positive multiplier effect in the long run.

WHAT ABOUT THE ACCELERATOR?

The other major instrument in the Keynesian toolbox is the accelerator principle. The accelerator is used to demonstrate the volatility in capital investment expenditures. Because Samuelson is the principal proponent of this doctrine, we will use his example of a textile firm that has annual sales of $30 million, of which $3 million goes toward replacing a textile machine each year.

Now suppose sales rise by 50 percent, from $30 million to $45 million. Assuming a constant capital-output ratio, the number of machines must also rise 50 percent. Therefore, to keep up with sales, the textile company buys 11 machines, 1 to replace the worn-out one and 10 new ones to make more textiles. We see now that the accelerator acts like the multiplier:

a 50 percent rise in sales creates a 1,000 percent rise in capital investment!

However, what happens if sales level off? If sales hold steady, net investment will quickly fall to zero, and gross investment will fall back to only one machine. As Samuelson states, "A drop to no growth in sales will result in a 90% drop in gross investment and a 100% drop in net investment."[3]

The overall conclusion by Samuelson: "Changes in output may become magnified into larger changes in investment."

THE OTHER SIDE OF THE STORY

Many economists have criticized the accelerator principle and have dropped any discussion of it in their textbooks. Lipsey and Steiner use an example similar to Samuelson's, but they impose severe limitations on its application. For example, increased sales regarded as temporary may not induce new purchases of machines. The company may simply work its machines and employees overtime. Machines may be repaired rather than replaced. Moreover, inventories serve to buffer the fluctuations in demand.

But no one seems to acknowledge the most serious defect in the accelerator principle, which is that, like the multiplier, the accelerator ignores the other side of the story. If sales for the textile company rose by 50 percent, it is quite probable that sales declined 50 percent for another group of companies, or perhaps that consumer interests changed so that people decided to buy more clothes and fewer televisions or compact disc players instead of cassette decks. In either case, while sales increased in this particular textile company they may well have declined in other markets. As a result, while new investment may accelerate in one company it may decelerate in others. Samuelson and the Keynesians fail to recognize this possibility. They assume that sales will rise or fall in the aggregate.

Again, the only situation in which the accelerator principle might apply in the aggregate is in the case of an exogenous monetary inflation. When new money is introduced into the economy, certain businesses are affected first, and their sales and capital outlays will undoubtedly rise dramatically during the expansionary phase of a business cycle. Of course, during the contractional phase the accelerator principle works in reverse.

SUMMARY

In conclusion, we see that two popular Keynesian devices, the multiplier and accelerator, have severely limited uses in economic analysis. On any economy-wide basis, the government-induced multiplier and accelerator may well have no long-term positive impact on economic growth.

NOTES

1. William J. Baumol and Alan S. Blinder, *Economics: Principles and Policy,* 4th ed. (New York: Harcourt Brace Jovanovich, 1988), p. 186.
2. Henry Hazlitt, *Economics in One Lesson,* 2nd ed. (New York: Arlington House, 1979 [1946]), pp. 15–19. Hazlitt's story, "The Broken Window," is a classic attack on the claim that war and destruction are good for the economy. Unfortunately, his works have been largely ignored by the profession. Instead of responding to his lucid criticisms, mainstream economists usually proclaim, "But he's not an economist!"
3. Paul A. Samuelson and William D. Nordhaus, *Economics,* 13th ed. (New York: McGraw-Hill, 1989), p. 216.

RECOMMENDED READING

Friedman, Milton. *Capitalism and Freedom.* Chicago: University of Chicago Press, 1962. His chapter on fiscal policy raises serious questions about the efficacy of government spending.

CHAPTER 7

THE TRUTH
ABOUT AGGREGATE SUPPLY
AND DEMAND

*Macroeconomics has undergone enormous changes during
the last decade.*
—James D. Gwartney and Richard L. Stroup
Economics: Private and Public Choice (1990)

The deep recessions of 1973–75 and 1981–82 changed the way
mainstream economists think about macroeconomics. Prior to
the 1970s, they were convinced that inflation could only be a
problem if the economy was at full employment. According to
their Keynesian theory, price inflation could not occur when
there was unemployment. Economists relied on the so-called
Phillips curve, which hypothesized that there was an inverse
relationship between price inflation and unemployment. If
prices rose, unemployment would decline and vice versa.

But the economy-wide impact of the energy and food crises
in the 1970s changed all that. Suddenly, inflationary recession—or stagflation, as some economists call it—reared its ugly
head. It was a world turned upside down as unemployment and
consumer prices were both rising at the same time. The Phillips curve was knocked off its course. Economists had to come
up with a new theory to explain the concomitant rise in consumer prices and fall in real output.

Until the 1970s, the orthodox economists virtually ignored
the supply side of macroeconomic issues. The original Keynesian economics focused entirely on final aggregate demand,
with its emphasis on consumption, government spending, and
tax policies. Monetarist economics has also been demand-
oriented—with money being the principal focal point—based

on the idea that the economy could be controlled through the money supply. Peter Drucker refers to Milton Friedman, the chief spokesman for monetarism, as fine-tuning Keynes. In essence, Friedman contends that if a nation's money and credit are stabilized at a steady rate, the economy will take care of itself—a statement with which Keynes would probably not argue. Neither Keynes nor Friedman comment much about productivity, technological change, or the benefits of increased savings, although certainly Friedman would favor policies to encourage them.

In the 1980s, the mainstream economists came up with a new creation to explain inflationary recession: the aggregate supply (*AS*) and aggregate demand (*AD*) curves. *AS* and *AD* curves look familiar to students who have been taught supply and demand for individual products, a concept that is usually introduced early in the microeconomic section, the theory of the individual firm.

Demand curves for individual products are downward-sloping because, other things being equal, if the price for a commodity declines, customers will tend to buy more of it. By "other things being equal" we mean that prices of other goods and people's incomes remain relatively constant.

On the other hand, supply curves for individual products are upward-sloping because, other things being equal, if the

FIGURE 7–1
Supply and Demand for an Individual Commodity

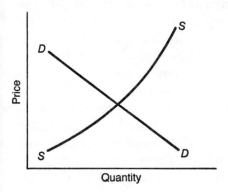

price for a commodity rises, increased profits will induce producers to expand output. Again, the assumption is that the
prices of other goods (and costs) are not rising at the same
time. Figure 7–1 illustrates the standard supply and demand
curves for an individual commodity.

Of course, supply and demand schedules for individual
goods are difficult to draw. It is one of the practical tasks of
business economists to estimate them. In the classroom, they
serve a useful theoretical purpose in explaining certain laws
in economics, the effects of changing economic conditions for
individual goods and services, and the impact of such government policies as rent controls and farm subsidies.

THE MISSING LINK BETWEEN MICRO
AND MACRO

However, there appear to be a number of serious roadblocks in
going from supply and demand analysis of individual products
to supply and demand analysis for the whole economy.

Economists are well aware of the difficulty of moving from
micro to macro supply and demand. One can talk about the
general demand for money, since the stock of money as the universal medium of exchange can be regarded as the total demand for all goods and services. In this sense, aggregate
demand exists, but it does not necessarily exist as a downward-
sloping curve.

There is even less justification for an AS curve than for
the AD curve. How can you aggregate the supply of all commodities in any real sense? Every commodity is distinct. You
cannot add quantities of apples and oranges. The most you can
do is add the monetary value of apples and oranges, which is
what macroeconomists do. Production can be measured by adding together the revenues obtained by each producer. But then
we have returned to the "demand for money" concept, which we
defined as aggregate demand. Are AD and AS inseparable?
(French economist Leon Walras thought so—in individual markets there could be excess demand or excess supply, but in the
whole economy they cancel each other; ergo, AS equals AD.

This is known as Walras' law, which is similar to Say's law, "Supply creates its own demand.")

Mainstream economists have developed an *AS* schedule that shows a positive relationship between the general price level and real national output. Figure 7–2 shows the typical view of *AS* in relation to *AD*. Note how the *AS* and *AD* curves look very similar to supply and demand curves for individual products.

DO THE AS–AD DIAGRAMS FIT REALITY?

It is obvious that textbook writers have taken a fancy to the *AS–AD* diagrams. They are simple to understand and appear to be powerful tools. There are a maze of them scattered throughout the text to illustrate a wide variety of economic

FIGURE 7–2
AS in Relation to AD

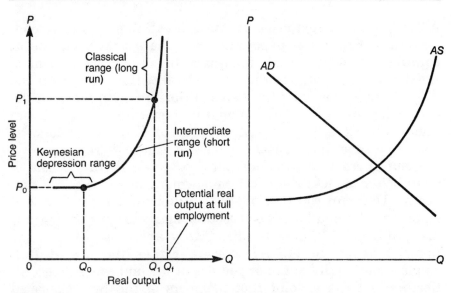

Source: From *Economics*, 4/e by Ralph T. Byrns and Gerald W. Stone, p. 311. Copyright © 1989, 1987 by Scott, Foresman and Company. Reprinted by permission.

phenomena, such as "demand-pull" and "cost-push" inflation, stagflation, Keynesian depression policy, etc.

Unfortunately, they are often misleading and inaccurate in their description of economic reality. Let's look at several examples.

Deflation and Real Economic Growth

For example, according to Figure 7–2, real production can increase without any rise in the price level in the depression range. Once the economy gets out of the depression, there is a positive relationship between prices and real production.

Yet this is not always correct. Historically, there are many examples of gently falling prices and sharply higher real output, for example, in the 1890s, in the 1920s, and to some extent in the 1950s. This historical fact makes it hard to fathom a positively sloped *AS* curve. There is no theoretical reason why real output cannot increase in the face of deflation, since real output depends on increasing profit margins, not price alone.

Equilibrium at Less than Full Employment?

All of the top 10 textbooks use the *AS–AD* diagram to demonstrate the Keynesian hypothesis that the economy can be at equilibrium at less than full employment, or even at massive unemployment. Judging from the fact that almost all the *AS–AD* diagrams start from an equilibrium point between the depression area and maximum full employment, it appears that orthodox economists have accepted Keynes's theory, at least as a short-term phenomenon (see Figure 7–3).

But there is a fundamental problem with this thesis of equilibrium at less than full employment in the *AS–AD* diagrams: How can you have macro equilibrium at less than full employment when labor and resource markets exist in flagrant disequilibrium? It is self-contradictory and demonstrates the inner flaws of the *AS–AD* curves. Either you are at full-employment equilibrium, or you are at unemployment disequilibrium. This is a point that members of the New Classical School have raised, and it's an important one.

FIGURE 7–3
Potential Output, Actual Output, and the GNP Gap

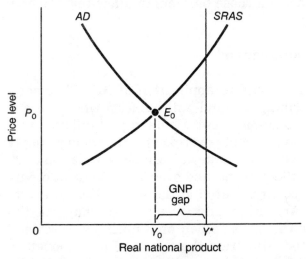

Source: From *Economics*, 8th edition by Robert G. Lipsey et al, p. 476. Copyright © 1987 by Robert G. Lipsey et al. Reprinted by permission of Harper & Row, Publishers, Inc.

Even in microanalysis of supply and demand, disequilibrium cannot in any way be regarded as an equilibrium position. A rent control law creates a housing shortage, but the shortage is not an equilibrium condition—housing starts to deteriorate, black markets arise, etc. Farm subsidies cause surpluses in agricultural commodities. The status quo is never maintained—surpluses grow even larger, and the costs of the farm program soar. In the case of chronic labor unemployment, millions of workers cannot remain unemployed indefinitely. The burdens of unemployment insurance, welfare, and other social costs are just too great to allow the status quo to continue. Eventually, something must give way. Wages must fall, new investment must begin, and the unemployed must be put back to work.

How anyone in the economics profession can think in terms of macroeconomic stability when millions of citizens are out of work and when huge amounts of capital goods lay idle is beyond me. Recession, or even depression, cannot be a lasting condition; the barriers to full recovery must be removed, and it is incumbent upon economists in business and government to focus on breaking through those barriers to allow the economy to function properly.

Inflation at Full Employment

Another example of inaccurate application of *AS–AD* macro-economics is in describing demand-pull inflation when there is full plant capacity and employment. Demand-pull inflation typically occurs when governments overexpand the money supply so rapidly that prices begin to take off. Runaway inflation of 20 percent, 50 percent, 100 percent, and even 1,000 percent occurs frequently in many countries around the world. Recent examples include Brazil, Argentina, and Israel. It even happened in the United States in the 1970s, albeit on a much lower scale.

How do economists illustrate the effects of high monetary inflation accompanied by high government expenditures? Lipsey and Steiner use the graph shown in Figure 7–4. According to this graph, an increase in autonomous federal expenditures or monetary inflation does not increase real output or income but only raises prices. Economists refer to this region as the classical range, where an increase in either the quantity of money or government spending will have no effect on the economy's real productive capacity. While prices may indeed increase, even dramatically, real output remains the same. The graph in Figure 7–4 demonstrates this "crude" quantity theory of money, purporting to show that rapid monetary inflation only raises prices in the long run and does not affect real output.

Unfortunately, there is something unreal about it. Galloping inflation, or even trotting inflation, does have a negative impact on real production, both in the long run and in the short run. Perhaps the publishers of economics textbooks ought to send their writers to see firsthand the effects of runaway inflation. I have been to many Latin American countries suffering from chronic inflation. I was in Rio de Janeiro recently when the inflation rate was 500 percent per annum and rising. No new construction was going on, while existing buildings

FIGURE 7–4
Effects of High Monetary Inflation

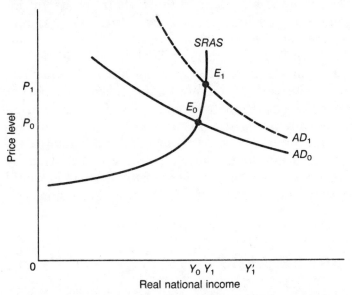

were crumbling. Poverty and crime appeared everywhere. Tourists were warned not to take their valuables with them to the beaches. There was no long-term planning. Brazilians were spending most of their time thinking up ways to unload their worthless currency as quickly as possible or to transfer assets abroad. Yet the textbook writers point to a dot on a graph and call this "equilibrium."

In countries with rapid inflation, real output is on the decline. Capital is gradually being consumed. Buildings, roads and other forms of the infrastructure are slowly but surely deteriorating. The only semblance of rational economic activity is occurring where transactions are tied to the U.S. dollar, which represents their only tie to a secure medium of exchange. Black markets are in abundance. Capital flight and secret foreign bank accounts are common. Every day, ordinary workers spend more time playing games to get rid of their depreciating currency than they do in productive labor. Instead of investing in the stock and bond markets and bank certificates of deposit, investors seek to protect their assets by investing in gold and precious stones, hoarding dollars, and sending money outside the country.

My point is this: When a nation's leaders engage in massive inflation, real productive activity is neither stable nor rising—it is falling sharply. A sharply rising price level is not cost-free. In short, the economists should show chronic inflation causing a backward-bending supply curve.

The textbook economists could theoretically demonstrate a reduction of real output accompanying runaway inflation by shifting the *AS* curve back as the *AD* curve rises. This would be similar to their explanation of inflationary recession, our next subject.

INFLATIONARY RECESSION

Keynesian economists believe that the *AS–AD* diagram has rescued them from defeat in the 1970s. Back then, Keynesian economics was facing a serious theoretical crisis. The 1970s witnessed dramatically the problem of coexistent inflation and recession. According to the crude Keynesian theory, stagflation should not happen; the Phillips curve implied that rising prices resulted in lower unemployment. But in the 1970s, we experienced rising prices and higher unemployment at the same time.

The *AS* and *AD* curves came to the rescue in the early 1980s. The original Keynesian model, which analyzed the economy solely in terms of depression conditions, ignored the supply side of the economy. Now the *AS–AD* model included the supply side, accounting for shifts in the supply due to the energy and agricultural shortages. The supply shifts were caused by "supply shocks," particularly the energy and agricultural crises of the mid-1970s and the escalation of oil prices once again in 1979–80. From 1973 to 1975, consumer prices rose 26 percent, while real GNP fell 3 percent. From 1980 to 1982, consumer prices increased 30 percent, while real GNP dropped 1 percent. Miller illustrates how the supply shocks shifted the *AS* curve backward (see Figure 7–5).

The Keynesian explanation sounds reasonable at first. But then one realizes that an inflationary recession involves much more than falling production and rising prices. The *AS–AD* diagram has one major deficiency. It can only show the consumer price level, or the average price index. It cannot illustrate systematic changes in the prices of commodities, manufactured products, or wholesale goods. For example, according to the U.S. Department of Commerce, in 1975, at the bottom of the 1973–75 recession, the average price of finished consumer goods rose by 9.58 percent, but crude materials rose only by 0.41 percent, and raw commodities fell by 17.63 percent. In 1982, another recession year, finished consumer goods rose by 3.58 percent, crude materials fell by an average of 2.89 percent, and spot commodities fell by 14.43 percent. We see then how incomplete the *AS–AD* diagram is and how modern

FIGURE 7–5
***AS* Curve Shifts Backward**

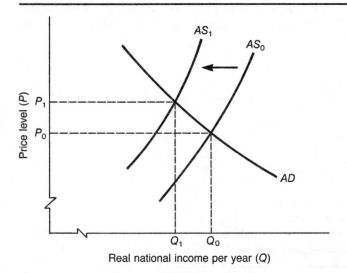

Real national income per year (*Q*)

Source: From *Economics Today*, 6th Edition by Roger Leroy Miller, p. 239. Copyright © 1988 by Harper & Row, Publishers, Inc. Reprinted by permission of the publisher.

economists will have an almost impossible task in explaining the more complex aspects of a stagflation through the use of their aggregate diagrams.

A MORE REALISTIC DIAGRAM
FOR STAGFLATION

The time-structure approach introduced in Chapters 3–5 offers a much more complete description of the inflationary recession. Recall from Chapter 3 how the economy's structure can be divided into four generalized stages of production. Categorized by their distance from final use, they are:

1. Raw commodities stage.
2. Manufacture stage.
3. Wholesale stage.
4. Retail consumer stage.

Figure 7–6 reproduces this diagram from Chapter 3.

For convenience purposes, let us call the model for the economy's stages of production the aggregate production structure (APS). The APS of the economy can illustrate the differing effects stagflation may have on the economy. It's important

FIGURE 7–6
Stages of Production

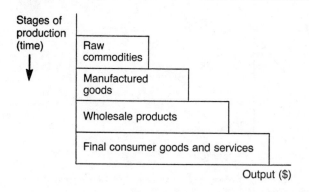

to realize that the APS is quite distinct from the *AS–AD* model and that it is based on a more natural description of economic activity. Unlike the *AS–AD* schedules, the downward-sloping APS triangle is not an imaginary creation. Every stage on the APS represents the real monetary output of firms producing goods and services at that particular stage of production during the year. (We noted the real numbers for GNO—a measurement of the APS—for 1982 in Ch⁻ .,ter 4.)

As you will recall, the vertical axis of the APS represents time, or the length of production, from final use. The further away from the point of origin, the longer the period of production from final use. Thus, output related to the extraction of raw commodities would be the highest stage of production on the APS, while consumption output would be at the lowest stage, near the horizontal line.

The horizontal line represents nominal output, based on the gross revenue of each producer. Since price and quantity are linked together on the horizontal axis, the APS cannot measure real output precisely, although relative changes between stages will indicate expanding and contracting markets.

Using this basic background, let us examine how the APS illustrates an inflationary recession. In Figure 7–7 we see that the APS schedule has shifted so that the raw commodities sector has lost the most revenue. The manufacturing sector has also lost revenue, but less than the commodity sector. The wholesale sector shows virtually no change, whereas the final retail sector indicates a slight rise. The diagram is drawn so that output has declined overall. Thus, the dynamic shift in the APS meets the definition of an inflationary recession—falling production with rising consumer prices—with the added caveat that prices of "higher-order" goods may be falling.

INTRODUCING A NEW MACROECONOMICS

The APS is a highly useful tool for analyzing macroeconomic events because it is, in a sense, a halfway house between micro and macro. The APS does not combine all production into one

FIGURE 7–7
A More Complete View of Inflationary Recession

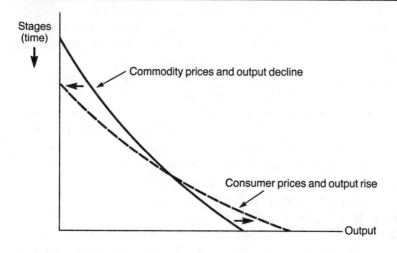

aggregate supply, as Keynesians and other economists do with their *AS–AD* curves. It does not have a single index for all prices or total output, but it has several price and output indices, categorized according to their time distance from final consumption.

On the other hand, the APS is not entirely micro either; it does not disaggregate itself into individual firms. Rather, it aggregates only those firms situated within a stage of production. Firms producing within the same stage of production are aggregated, whereas firms in another stage of production are put into another category. In short, *intra*stage output is aggregated, but *inter*stage output remains disaggregated. Thus, the APS is a perfect mix of micro and macro, leaving time as the principal factor to measure against output.

For centuries, economists have argued over the missing link between micro and macro economics. How can the supply and demand for individual goods be aggregated for the whole economy? The debate has intensified in the past 30 years, as many critics complained that Keynesianism lacks a micro foundation for its macroeconomics. Nobel Prize winner Kenneth J. Arrow says it is a major scandal that economists have been unable to link micro and macro economics. However, I believe that the APS as outlined in this book constitutes the missing link that economists have been searching for.

RECOMMENDED READING

Skousen, Mark. *The Structure of Production*. New York: New York University Press, 1990, Chapter 6.

CHAPTER 8

THE REAL CAUSE OF INFLATIONARY RECESSIONS

Conventional monetarist or Keynesian approaches offer little insight into why high rates of inflation and unemployment might occur simultaneously.
— Ralph T. Byrns and Gerald W. Stone
Economics (1989)

Since the world is likely to continue experiencing a series of inflationary recessions, students of economics ought to know how it is possible to having rising prices in the face of falling demand, a circumstance that, until the 1970s, conventional economists denied could happen.

As I pointed out in Chapter 7, modern economists usually explain the phenomenon of stagflation as a result of unexpected supply shocks, such as an energy crisis. In addition, mainstream economists assert that an inflationary recession can occur if the economy expands beyond the natural rate of GNP. Prices gradually rise and real GNP falls. I would like to suggest that inflationary recessions can happen without either an external supply shock or overexpansion of the economy. In this chapter, I argue that inflationary recessions are indeed a universal consequence of inflation-induced business cycles.

My contention is based on a theory of inflation developed originally by two Austrian economists, Ludwig von Mises and Friedrich A. Hayek, and the great Swedish economist, Knut Wicksell. It is a pity that neither the Austrian nor the Swedish thinkers are given more than cursory mention in today's introductory economics.

Moreover, the Austrian–Swedish theory of the business cycle fits the perspective of the businessperson and investor better than any other theory. It is applied economics at its best.

Their particular explanation of the inflationary cycle emphasizes the microeconomics of the business cycle—how inflation affects specific businesses, investments, and prices—and not just the economy in general or the price level. By taking the micro approach to inflation, Mises and his student Hayek were among the few economists in the 1920s to predict the economic crisis of the 1930s.

THE NATURAL RATE OF INTEREST

According to Wicksell, there exists a natural rate of interest that reflects a society's time preference. Wicksell tried to explain why the level of interest rates differs between countries. Inflation is certainly a major factor, but even in countries where inflation rates are similar, Wicksell concluded, differences in interest rates are principally due to the consumption/savings habits of individuals in separate countries. If a country has a high level of savings and capital formation, the large supply of investment capital will keep interest rates relatively lower than in a country with a poor rate of savings. In Figure 8–1, the natural rate of interest occurs where the supply of voluntary savings equals the demand for investment. Wicksell argued that nations could attempt to reduce the market rate of interest below the natural rate, but such a situation could not last. Eventually, the market rate must return to the natural rate, reflecting a nation's consumption/savings ratio.

But nations often attempt to imitate the low interest rates and high economic growth of more successful countries by expanding the domestic money supply in an effort to push down the market rate of interest and thus promote economic growth. But this creates a false prosperity and an artificially low interest rate. Mises showed that under a gold standard, a country's policy of inflation cannot last. The specie-flow mechanism operates in such a way that gold starts flowing out of the country and will continue to do so unless the country stops inflation, devalues its currency, or abandons the gold standard entirely. When the state stops inflating, an inflationary boom must eventually end in a deflationary bust. The Great Depression

FIGURE 8–1
The Natural Rate of Interest

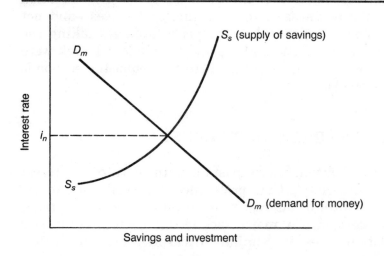

Savings and investment

was caused in large measure by the fact that Western governments, especially that of the United States, artificially lowered interest rates in the 1920s while remaining on the gold standard. As gold started to flow out of the United States, the Federal Reserve stopped inflating in 1929, and the world suffered a stock market crash and massive economic collapse. There were many other reasons why the depression was so severe and endured for so long, but central bank policy was the principal culprit.

INFLATIONARY BIAS IN THE WEST

Since the Great Depression, world governments have erred on the side of inflation. Everyone fears another deflationary collapse. By eliminating the gold standard or weakening it sufficiently, it is possible for a government to inflate for a long period of time before a crisis occurs. In fact, by going off the gold standard entirely and by creating a powerful central bank, a government can inflate for much longer periods of time and at much higher rates. The historical evidence is clear: the 20th century, largely under the influence of central banking, has been one of high inflation. According to Michael David Bordo, wholesale prices in Great Britain and the United States had a slightly deflationary secular trend between 1800 and 1913. But since the creation of central banking in the early 20th century, wholesale prices have trended sharply upward.[1]

Central banking has succeeded since the Great Depression in two of its goals: avoiding deflation and escaping depression. But it has not avoided inflation, and it has not escaped severe recessions. In fact, central banks are the cause of both. Let us see why.

Who Gets the Money First?

None of the top 10 textbook economists asks the all-important question, "When the government inflates, who gets the new money first?" The reason economists don't address this issue is because their approach is too aggregative. Both Keynesians and monetarists tend to write about the general price level, not individual prices, and national output, not individual firms or industries. They need, however, to focus on the business-person's micro approach in the tradition of Wicksell and Mises.

This new money is created directly by central banks and indirectly by the treasury. If the government runs a deficit, the treasury sells bonds to individuals, institutions, and banks. Central banks create new money by buying treasury securities from the banks and other institutions and paying for the bonds with cash from their own account (known as open-market operations). They can also expand credit by lowering the discount rate or by reducing the reserve requirement on checking or savings accounts.

The textbooks generally do a good job with their chapters on money and banking, explaining in great detail the engine of inflation. But what they don't teach very well is the grave distortion of both prices and production that inflation can cause. Most textbook writers preach that inflationary expansionism has few ill effects unless full employment has been reached. But inflation can be damaging even in times of unemployment. The followers of Mises and Wicksell have stressed very emphatically how this credit boom creates an artificial economic boom, particularly in the capital-goods markets.

Distortion in the Capital-Goods Industries

Who gets the new money first? The primary beneficiaries of inflation are commercial banks, financial centers, and large corporations requiring long-term financing. Investors know that financial centers such as New York, London, and Tokyo benefit greatly from a new investment boom. That is a principal reason why real estate has done so well in these cities.

Business economists are also well aware that long-term projects gain the most from low-interest loans. New projects involving heavy machinery, construction, and research benefit tremendously from new financing. The financial advantages accruing to the capital-goods industries can be clearly illustrated using the APS (see Chapter 7).

As Figure 8–2 indicates, the capital-goods markets expand much more rapidly than the consumer-goods industries in the early stages of credit expansion. But it is not just commodity producers and manufacturers that benefit initially from the new money. A boom in stocks, real estate, and other asset-related investments typically accompanies an inflationary expansion.

Why the Boom Cannot Last

Not all economic booms are artificial. If it represents a genuine use of private and public savings to create capital formation and to finance technological improvements and innovative production techniques, a boom can last indefinitely. The economic miracles of West Germany and Japan in the postwar period are classic examples.

But the injection of new fiat money into the business system creates its own seeds of destruction. Changes in the money supply are not neutral, either in the short run or the long run.

FIGURE 8–2

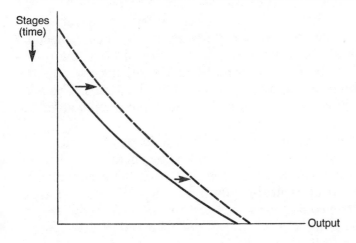

While stimulating some sectors, they seriously damage others, depending on the degree of inflation.

An inflationary boom is a form of macroeconomic disequilibrium. As the boom spreads, wages and other forms of income rise, and the new funds are spent according to traditional time-preference patterns. If the new funds represented genuine savings, the boom could last, because the increase in the savings rate would reflect a willingness for people to wait for the long-term production process to be completed. But because society has not in fact changed its willingness to wait, the boom is cut short as consumers impatiently demand consumer goods before the new production processes are complete. The capital-goods boom quickly turns into a consumer-goods boom. Consumer-goods businesses compete against the capital-goods businesses for the available credit supply. Interest rates, previously declining, now start to rise.

Rising interest rates spell trouble for the capital-goods industries, particularly those involved with long-term projects that depend on additional bank financing or with new long-term projects. The end result is an economic recession, or perhaps even a depression in certain parts of the country if the credit crunch is severe enough. In any case, the hardest hit sector of the economy is the capital-goods market.

Ludwig von Mises calls incomplete investments, for which there is insufficient demand, malinvestments. Businesspeople would agree with that description and can point to many examples, such as the overinvestment in the oil industry in the late 1970s, which turned into an oil bust in the 1980s. The APS diagram in Figure 8–3 describes the recessionary phase of the cycle.

We can see from Figure 8–3 why a form of inflationary recession is always in evidence during the contraction phase of the business cycle. During a typical deflationary recession, the prices and output of capital-goods industries fall more sharply than those of the consumer-goods industries. (We noted this in Chapter 7.) During every major deflationary depression or recession in the 20th century, the prices for producer goods and raw commodities fell more than the prices for final consumer goods.

But in terms of mathematics, we can view the relationship between investment and consumption differently. If investment industries' prices fall more than consumer industries' prices, this is the same as saying that consumer industries' prices rise

FIGURE 8–3
Deflationary Depression

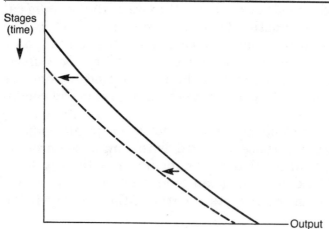

relative to investment industries' prices. Even though all prices fall, the recession can be regarded as a relatively inflationary one for consumption in the sense that consumer prices fall less than producer prices.

The only reason economists have not noticed this relationship in the past is that virtually all prices have fallen during recessions. But in the 1970s, consumer prices started rising during a recession in absolute terms and not just relative terms, and the economists suddenly noticed this "new" phenomenon, which is really not so new after all.

Why did consumer prices rise during the recessions of the 1970s and 1980s? Because monetary inflation by the central banks was markedly higher than in previous periods. The money supply expanded by as much as 15 to 20 percent in the United States in the 1970s and 1980s, compared to 5 to 6 percent in the 1950s and 1960s, as Figure 8–4 indicates.

Central bank policies in other countries also became more inflationary in the 1970s and 1980s. The money supply seldom declines at all on a year-to-year basis in any advanced nation anymore. If it did, we would suffer a deflationary recession or depression.

Thus, the only difference between a deflationary recession and an inflationary recession is a matter of degree. The relative pattern remains the same in both types of recessions.[2]

THE ENERGY CRISIS AND STAGFLATION

In this light, it is worth reexamining the contention by mainstream textbook economists that the energy crisis was an exogenous supply shock unrelated to the aggregate demand side of the economy. In fact, the energy crisis was more related to the demand side than previously considered. Notice that the OPEC-imposed energy crunch occurred directly after serious monetary inflation occurred in the United States and other countries in the late 1960s and early 1970s. Oil prices rose sharply from 1973 to 1974, after having been relatively stable for decades. Oil prices subsided for a while during the mid-1970s, following a monetary contraction, and then took off

FIGURE 8–4
Monetary Inflation

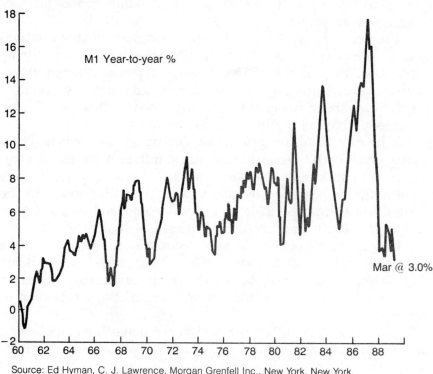

M1 Year-to-year %

Mar @ 3.0%

Source: Ed Hyman, C. J. Lawrence, Morgan Grenfell Inc., New York, New York.

again in 1979–1980. But directly prior to this energy crisis was another massive inflationary binge in the United States and other Western countries. Perhaps this is more than coincidence.

In this regard, note that oil is a crude natural resource far removed from final consumption. As the Austrian theory of inflation suggests, the higher-order goods such as oil should increase in price more than consumer goods during a massive inflation and fall more than consumer goods during a recession. Indeed, after the 1980 oil crunch and the monetary contraction of the early 1980s, oil prices plummeted and the hundreds of malinvested oil rigs and equipment became idle.

OTHER FACTORS INFLUENCING
THE ECONOMY

The ill effects of monetary inflation can be postponed or miti-
gated by other factors occurring simultaneously. For example,
the price of some raw commodities may not rise much during
a monetary inflation, perhaps because substantial new supplies
are coming on the market. Another factor may be an increase
in private savings during a credit crunch, when capital is desperately needed, which could therefore postpone an economic
downturn. Another possibility is that tariffs, quotas, and other
trade barriers may be lowered or eliminated, which could reduce prices and stimulate new production. Finally, tax rates
may be lowered, which could also mitigate the ill effects of a
recession by stimulating more efficient use of resources. Of
course, taxes and tariffs could also be raised, which would
make the recession worse.

WHAT'S MISSING IN THE PHILLIPS CURVE?

All standard textbooks discuss an alleged inverse relationship
between unemployment and the rate of inflation, the Phillips
curve. Figure 8–5 illustrates this relationship.

Prior to the 1970s, Keynesian economists defended their
inflationary policies by pointing to studies by A. W. Phillips,
who found that in Britain, wages historically had risen when
unemployment was low and had fallen when unemployment
was high. (In the modern interpretation, wage changes are presented by price changes.) However, as Figure 8–6 indicates,
since 1970, the relationship has completely fallen apart. The
Keynesians explain this breakdown by referring to the ill effects of supply shocks. As Alan S. Blinder states,

> That inflation and unemployment rose together following the
> OPEC shocks in 1973–74 and 1979–80 in no way contradicts the
> notion of a Phillips curve trade-off . . . . When A. W. Phillips
> discovered his curve in the late 1950s, and for more than a dec-
> ade thereafter, fluctuations in aggregate demand dominated the

FIGURE 8–5
A Hypothetical Phillips Curve

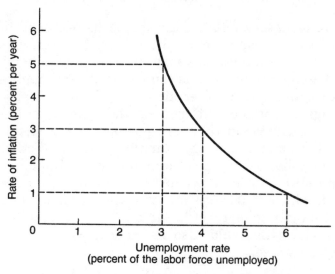

Source: From *Economics Today,* 6th Edition by Roger Leroy Miller, p. 396. Copyright © 1988 by Harper & Row, Publishers, Inc. Reprinted by permission of the publisher.

data . . . . But from, say, 1973 until, say, 1981, fluctuations in aggregate supply . . . dominated the data.[3]

However, there is more to the breakdown of the traditional Phillips curve than simply relating it to supply changes. As the Austrian–Swedish theory of the business cycle suggests, an inflationary expansion can create an artificial economic boom and thereby reduce unemployment. Thus, it is perfectly possible to witness rising prices and falling unemployment during a boom. However, this situation cannot last, especially if the inflationary boom is excessive. Eventually, the boom in production and employment must collapse as individuals voluntarily reestablish their time preferences. We therefore conclude that in the short run, higher inflation reduces unemployment but that in the long run it causes higher unemployment. The Phillips curve misinterprets what is happening in the economy, thus demonstrating the flaws inherent in basing theory solely on historical studies.

FIGURE 8–6
The Phillips Curve—Historical Reality

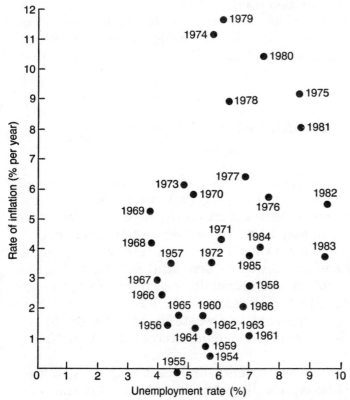

Source: From *Economics Today,* 6th Edition by Roger Leroy Miller, p. 397. Copyright © 1988 by Harper & Row, Publishers, Inc. Reprinted by permission of the publisher.

THE FICTION OF POTENTIAL GNP

Economists are fond of their term *potential GNP,* by which they mean what national output would be if full employment existed. They refer to the serious waste and human suffering rising from this GNP gap. But what they do not seem to understand is that unemployment of capital and workers is an unavoidable, necessary effect of mismanaged macro policies. The previous boom that brought about full employment was a malinvestment that could not be sustained. The artificial boom requires a bust. Therefore, it is inappropriate to refer to an inflationary economy operating at full capacity as an economy that has achieved its potential.

Economists would do well to consider more appropriate ways to measure potential GNP that could be achieved through major tax reform and the elimination of other barriers to economic growth.

MORE INFLATIONARY RECESSIONS TO COME

Governments have unintentionally guaranteed that the most recent economic crisis will not be the last. Recession is inevitable once the central banks start on the road of credit expansionism. The crisis may be postponed but not eliminated.

Economics professors usually regard recessions as anathema, but they can be viewed as beneficial acts that clean out the malinvestments in the economic system previously created by fiat money inflation. Recessions make businesses more cost-conscious and governments less wasteful. It is fortunate that citizens have been willing to endure recessions from time to time.

Unfortunately, governments and central banks, fearing worsening conditions, usually panic at some stage of the recession and start reinflating. Thus begins another round of a boom–bust cycle.

Is it possible that the garden-variety recessions of the recent past could turn into something more sinister, such as a massive deflationary depression like that of the 1930s? Orthodox economists think not, but as we have seen they've been wrong before. We will examine depression economics in Chapter 9.

NOTES

1. Michael David Bordo, "The Gold Standard: Myths and Realities," in Barry N. Siegel, ed., *Money in Crisis* (San Francisco: Pacific Institute, 1984), pp. 212–13. The

wholesale price index for the United Kingdom and the United States are reproduced in Figures 11–3A and 11–3B.

2. The first economist to observe the universality of an inflationary recession was Murray Rothbard, dean of the neo-Austrian school. In the second edition of his work, *America's Great Depression,* he wrote: "The prices of consumer goods always tend to rise, relative to the prices of producer goods, during recessions. The reason that this phenomenon has not been noted before is that, in past recessions, prices have generally fallen . . . . The result of the government's abolition of deflation, however, is that general prices no longer fall, even in recessions. Consequently, the adjustment between consumer goods and capital goods that must take place during recessions, must now proceed without the merciful veil of deflation. Hence, the prices of consumer goods still rise relatively, but now, shorn of general deflation, they must rise absolutely and visibly as well. The government policy of stepping in to prevent monetary deflation, therefore, has deprived the public of one of the great advantages of recession: a falling cost of living." *America's Great Depression,* 2nd ed. (Los Angeles: Nash Publishing, 1972), p. xxvi.

3. Alan S. Blinder, *Hard Heads, Soft Hearts* (Reading, Mass.: Addison-Wesley Publishing, 1987), p. 42.

CHAPTER 9

DEPRESSION ECONOMICS

*However, given our current knowledge of macroeconomics,
most economists believe that the likelihood of another Great
Depression is remote.*
— James D. Gwartney and Richard L. Stroup
Economics: Private and Public Choice (1990)

Most neoclassical economists, from Milton Friedman to Paul
Samuelson, believe that a full-scale depression can't happen
again. But it is a curious fact of history that the established
economists of yesterday also heralded the "New Era" of the
1920s as "depression-proof." With one exception, to be discussed shortly, no economist representing any of the major
schools of thought predicted the 1929 stock market crash or the
subsequent economic cataclysm in the 1930s. It was one of the
dark chapters in the history of the economics, yet not a single
major textbook admits the failure of the established economics
profession to predict the worst economic event in history.

IRVING FISHER AND THE
NEW ERA OPTIMISTS

Yale professor Irving Fisher, the most famous American economist, was an incurable New Era optimist who believed that
the Roaring Twenties would usher in a new and better world.
He was also a promoter extraordinaire of the stock market.
The foremost monetary theorist in his day and an advocate of
the quantity theory of money, Fisher argued in favor of the
long-term neutrality of money, that is, that monetary inflation
would merely raise prices and have no long-term ill effects.
Modern monetarists hold to a similar position. With the Federal Reserve in control of the money supply, Fisher believed,
the business cycle would be a thing of the past.

Because Fisher believed that nothing can be seriously wrong with the economy as long as consumer prices remain stable, his principal monetary goal was price stabilization. Since consumer prices did not rise in the late 1920s, Fisher did not expect a stock market crisis or economic bust. He denied any "orgy of speculation" on Wall Street, even though the average stock had more than tripled in value in only seven years. When Boston financial advisor Roger Babson warned investors of an impending crash in early September 1929, Fisher disagreed, saying, "stock prices have reached what looks like a permanently high plateau." His monetarist theories completely failed him, and both his reputation and financial status were destroyed in the 1930s. He never recovered.[1] Surprisingly, in their textbook, Byrns and Stone omit this fact from their biography of Fisher, whom they call the "premier American theorist of the early twentieth century."

The Harvard Economic Society, relying on macroeconomic aggregates to predict the economic future, fared no better. The Harvard economists expected a correction in the market, but no business depression. After the crash, the economic society stated, "Despite its severity, we believe that the slump in stock prices will prove an intermediate movement and not the precursor of a business depression."[2]

Wesley C. Mitchell, the uncontested authority on business cycles in the 1920s and a founder of the National Bureau of Economic Research (NBER), joined Fisher in his New Era optimism. In 1929, Mitchell wrote the final essay of a NBER report on the outlook for the economy and, despite some concerns, concluded that there was little evidence of an unhealthy boom, and that therefore any violent relapse would be unlikely.[3]

THE MISINTERPRETATION OF KEYNES

John Maynard Keynes correctly predicted the disastrous results of Britain's return to the gold standard at an overvalued sterling exchange rate in 1925, but he was unable to sense any financial or economic danger in the late 1920s. In 1927, he told the Swiss banker Felix Somary, "We will not have any more crashes in our time."[4] In late 1928, Keynes delivered a paper on inflation in the United States. Reviewing data on the cost of living and business credit, he concluded that there was nothing that could be called inflation yet in sight. The stock market, he said, would not suffer a severe slump unless it was discounting a depression, which he regarded as unlikely because of the powers of the Federal Reserve Board.[5]

Financially, Keynes was hurt badly by the crash, losing three fourths of his net worth, although he recovered fairly quickly.

AUSTRIAN ECONOMISTS PREDICT DEPRESSION

It is an interesting yet little-known note in history that the Austrian economists—including Mises, Hayek, and Somary—fully expected a stock market crash and depression. Although they did not attempt to pinpoint a specific date when these events would occur, they nevertheless believed that a depression was inevitable. The Austrian school taught that fiat money inflation causes an imbalance between production and consumption, and that a depression is the only cure for this imbalance. Mises and the others rejected Fisher's price stabilization notion, arguing that an economic contraction would happen whether consumer prices were stable or not. Therefore, the Austrians were not fooled by stable prices in the late 1920s, as were the monetarists.

As early as 1924, Mises predicted that the Austrian bank Credit Anstalt was going to crash. It fell in 1931, pushing Europe into a full-scale depression. Hayek, a student of Mises, was more precise in his timing. As director of the Austrian Institute of Economic Research, he published several articles in early 1929 in the institute's monthly reports, contending that the American boom would collapse within months because the Federal Reserve had decided to stop feeding the inflation. The Austrians stressed that the international gold standard would prevent the inflation from lasting forever. Hayek notes, "The Federal Reserve was not only unwilling but was unable to continue the expansion because the gold standard set a limit to the possible expansion. Under the gold standard, therefore, an inflationary boom could not last very long."[6]

Felix Somary, a Swiss banker and diplomat who was an economics student along with Mises at the University of Vienna, was prophetically pessimistic prior to the depression. In fact, according to contemporaries, Somary prophesied the stock market crash, remained gloomy throughout the depression era, and foresaw World War II as an inevitable consequence of the peace treaties after 1918. As early as 1926, he predicted that the stock market boom would end with the bankruptcy of governments and the destruction of banks. In 1928, he warned a group of economists that, even though commodity prices were not overinflated, stock prices were, and the huge disparity between loan rates and yields on stocks was an unmistakable symptom of a crash. His speech was *not* well received. He said afterward, "Here among my acquaintances were representatives of at least a dozen economic theories, but not one of them had an inkling of the nearness of the greatest crash of our generation."[7] After the stock market debacle, Somary remained pessimistic and, as a manager of a Swiss bank, withdrew all the bank's deposits from England, Germany, and Italy. But in June 1932, he published a small pamphlet entitled *Turning Point?*, in which he suggested that the worldwide depression had possibly bottomed out. The stock market started recovering from that point on, but the depression didn't end until several years later.

In the United States, the sound-money banking school led by E. C. Harwood and Benjamin Anderson, among others, warned that the Federal Reserve's inflationary policies would cause a crisis. The only economist and financial advisor to predict both the stock market crash and the depression was E. C. Harwood, a professor of military science at MIT and founder of the American Institute for Economic Research in Great Barrington, Massachusetts. Developing a monetary theory closely paralleling that of the Austrians, Harwood believed that bank credit inflation was the cause of financial fluctuations and the business cycle. Noting the net export of gold in 1927, he concluded that the credit expansion by the Federal Reserve had to

come to an end. By February 1929, he was warning his readers
about the grave dangers in security speculation. After the
crash, he did not expect a quick return to prosperity, and even
suggested in an article for the November 29, 1929 issue of *The
Annalist,* which was published by *The New York Times,* that
banks would fail in wholesale lots.[8]

Given the superior record of the Austrian and sound-
money schools during the critical 1929–33 period, one would
expect them to receive more notice in the textbooks.

THE DEPRESSION AND THE BATTLE
OVER MEN'S MINDS

What happened that caused economists of the 1930s to reject
the one school of thought that actually predicted the debacle?
The established economists in the 1930s at first listened to
Hayek and the Austrians but finally rejected as too extreme
their laissez-faire cures of cutting taxes, tariffs, and government spending, and of encouraging prices and wages to fall
sufficiently to bring back full employment.

Then Keynes's new doctrine—outlined in his complicated
work, *The General Theory* (1936)—took the profession by storm
in the late 1930s. Keynes turned the world on its head, aiming
to overturn classical economics. Prior to Keynes, classical economists favored the traditional Western values of thrift, the gold
standard, free trade, balanced budgets, and the preference of
long-term benefits over short-term expediency. Even as the battle fronts for World War II were forming, there was a quiet
battle for men's minds being waged whose results were at least
as significant. By developing a theory that justified unconven-
tional policies whenever there were unemployed resources,
Keynes was able to convince the profession to reject the virtue
of thrift, to substitute fiat money for gold, and to favor short-
term anti-depression measures such as deficit spending and inflation no matter what the long-term consequences were. The
Great Depression provided fertile ground for Keynes's wholesale attack.

THE LESSONS OF THE DEPRESSION

Today's economics writers, still dressed in Keynesian clothes, say they have learned the bitter lessons of the depression. What are those lessons? Primarily, they maintain, that free-market capitalism cannot provide full employment and a stable economic environment. Since capitalism is inherently unstable, government must therefore intervene and keep it from falling off the edge. For example, Baumol and Blinder state:

> The worldwide depression also caused a much-needed revolution in the thinking of economists. Up until the 1930s, the prevailing economic theory held that a capitalist economy, while it occasionally misbehaved, had a "natural" tendency to cure recessions or inflations by itself. The roller coaster bounced around but did not run off the tracks.
>
> The stubbornness of the Great Depression shook almost everyone's faith in the ability of the economy to right itself . . . Keynes discarded the notion that the economy always gravitated toward high levels of employment, replacing it with the assertion that—if a pessimistic outlook led business firms and consumers to curtail their spending plans—the economy might be condemned to stagnation for years and years.[9]

Baumol and Blinder end by suggesting how government actions might prod the economy out of its depressed state. Lipsey and Steiner add, "Keynes argued that the unemployment was due to too little aggregate demand and his remedy was to raise demand, not cut wages."

Who's at Fault: The Free Market or the State?

In short, the textbooks teach that the cause of the depression was not government but the capitalist system and that the cure is not the free market but state action.

But the facts indicate the opposite to be true. Governments and their inflationary conduits, the central banks, deliberately violated that free-market monetary mechanism, the international gold standard, by expanding the monetary base beyond specie reserves after World War I. Under the international gold standard, it meant an inevitable contraction in the money supply at some point and therefore a recession.

But the 1930 recession need not have turned into a full-scale depression. It happened because of major blunders committed by an activist government, not the market. After the stock market crash, the U.S. Congress more than doubled income tax rates and raised import tariffs by 50 percent in early 1930 (see Gwartney and Stroup, p. 327). President Herbert Hoover called in business leaders and demanded that they maintain wage rates even though prices had started to fall. This was a pre-Keynesian strategy that backfired as unemployment rose sharply after 1930; had wages been permitted to fall gradually, millions of people would not have found themselves losing jobs in bankrupt companies.

In 1931, the Federal Reserve took strong deflationary measures by raising the discount rate sharply to reverse a potential gold drain. On top of that, the government-created banking system in the United States was highly unstable, due to a fragile fractional reserve system. This meant that one or two major bank failures could quickly spread throughout the country, creating massive hemorrhaging of the monetary system. This is precisely what occurred. As Milton Friedman and Anna Schwartz point out in their ground-breaking work, *A Monetary History of the United States,* the inept Federal Reserve allowed the collapse of one half of the commercial banks in the United States, resulting in an unprecedented decline of the money stock by over one third during the period 1929 to 1933. Friedman and Schwartz state, "The monetary system collapsed, but it clearly need not have done so."[10]

The point is this: If government leaders had not acted so ineptly in regard to monetary and banking policy, the depression would never have occurred and the economy would not have stagnated. The Keynesian analysis of the depression is wrongheaded. The free market does not run the economy off its tracks unless it is pushed or unless the tracks are misplaced. Once off the tracks, it takes time to get back on. The blame for every period in economic history characterized by either runaway inflation or a massive depression can be placed squarely on the engine of interventionist government policies.

Keynes blamed the depression on hoarding, excessive bank reserves, and uninvested savings, which, he asserted, caused a massive deficiency in aggregate demand. He criticized Say's law, the classical theorem that denies a deficiency in aggregate demand. But Say's law makes sense if the monetary system is sound and stable, which it would be under a noninflationary commodity standard (to be discussed in Chapter 11).

Keynes's attack on savings and the virtue of thrift rings hollow. Savings are always invested and never leaked out unless people feel threatened by the instability of banks, the primary intermediaries between savers and investors.

Holding cash, what Keynes labeled "liquidity preference," is a short-term phenomenon that signifies a dramatic increase in the demand for money when there is either a great deal of uncertainty about the financial soundness of banks or expectations of lower prices. Take away the fear of monetary bankruptcy, and hoarding would quickly disappear.

IS GOVERNMENT SPENDING A CURE FOR THE DEPRESSION?

Let us now consider the Keynesian thesis that government deficit spending can get us out of a depression. Virtually all economists are unanimous in recommending a deliberate policy of increasing government spending as a way out of a depression.

Using the *AS* and *AD* curves, Ruffin and Gregory illustrate the standard effect of increasing government expenditures during a depression (see Figure 9–1).

During the Great Depression, the U.S. government began a series of new spending programs to stimulate economic activity and reduce unemployment. Keynes criticized President Roosevelt for not doing enough. Studies by Keynesians conclude that the federal deficits in the 1930s were relatively small and therefore had a minimal impact on the economy. Indeed, Professor C. Cary Brown of MIT concludes, "Fiscal policy seems to have been an unsuccessful recovery device in the 'thirties—not because it did not work, but because it was not tried."[11]

FIGURE 9–1
Keynesian Aggregate Supply with Bottlenecks

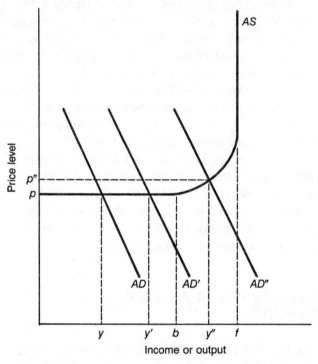

Source: From *Principles of Economics,* 3/e by Roy J. Ruffin and Paul R. Gregory. Copyright © 1988 by Scott, Foresman and Company. Reprinted by permission.

However, the APS's diagram of the U.S. economy provides another possible interpretation as to why deficit financing *per se* may be impotent. As you recall, the APS is altered during a depression so that the capital-goods industries are much harder hit than the consumer-goods industries (see Figure 9–2).

The Keynesian prescription during a depression is to increase government spending, particularly through expenditures for welfare, public works, etc. Because in a depression private investment is weak, they argue that the only way investment can be stimulated is to increase consumer demand through government spending. Unfortunately, this means that

FIGURE 9–2
Change in the Economy during a Depression

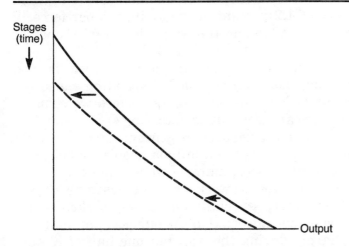

the Keynesian policy is working at the wrong end of the production process. As Figure 9–2 indicates, it is the higher-order capital goods market (especially the heavy manufacturing industries) that is hardest hit. The effort to stimulate final consumer demand will do very little for the early stages of production and, in fact, may encourage natural resource producers and heavy industries to reduce their output and switch to the consumer-goods industries where demand is more dependable. So, while unemployment falls in the consumer markets, it may rise even more in the higher-order capital markets. This would be especially true if the higher deficits raised interest rates.

DID WORLD WAR II END THE DEPRESSION?

Virtually all economists accept the view that World War II got us out of the depression. The period 1940 to 1945 saw Keynesian economics in action. As Lipsey and Steiner comment, "Once the massive, war-geared expenditure of the 1940s began, income responded sharply and unemployment evaporated. Government expenditures on goods and services, which had been running at under 15 percent of GNP during the 1930s, jumped to 46 percent by 1944, while unemployment reached the incredible low of 1.2 percent of the civilian labor force."[12] Perhaps this means it's too bad the war didn't start sooner or last longer.

Is there any truth to the Keynesian claims that war is good for the economy and that mammoth deficit spending ended the depression? Let us look behind the figures before we come to any conclusions. Appearances can be deceiving. The boom during World War II may not have been as genuine as it is thought to be. The civil unemployment of 8 million people was negated by 8 million new military jobs, many of whose applicants were killed or maimed. The average work week increased by 20 percent, as many employees, especially engineers, worked weary 14-hour days, seven days a week. On the surface, national output increased sharply during the war, but one half of it went toward the war effort. Two years' worth of national income, $230 billion, was spent on artillery shot away, ships sunk in the sea, supplies abandoned to rust in the jungles of the South Pacific, and wages paid out to members of the armed forces.

The standard of living declined during this time, despite higher nominal incomes. According to the U.S. Department of Commerce, per capita income actually declined in real terms during the period 1940 to 1945. Americans gave up many of the pleasures of life. Construction of private housing, automobiles, and appliances came to a standstill. Sugar, coffee, meat, and other food products were often in short supply and, despite price controls and rationing, prices still rose an average of 30 percent during the war. Businesspeople were fined and jailed for violating price control and rationing regulations. Taxes increased dramatically and permanently. The only clear winner in the war was the government, which never fully relinquished its emergency power and size after 1945. As Randolph Bourne aptly states, "War is the health of the state."

Furthermore, Keynesians cannot use World War II as a clear example of the ability of government spending to pull us out of a depression. Other things were not held equal during the war. For example, the money supply increased by 20 percent a year, doubling during the war. Therefore, economists cannot prove that it was solely fiscal policy (or solely monetary policy) that caused an economic recovery. I would also add a third major factor: the unprecedented rise in personal and business savings rates during the period 1941 to 1945. Personal savings as a percentage of disposal personal income rose to as high as 25 percent in 1944, due to patriotic zeal and the lack of consumer goods. The same thing happened in Britain. In Chapter 5, I noted the advantage of increasing savings rates. Sacrificing current consumption for future consumption will result, ceteris paribus, in an expansion in the capital goods industries, lower interest rates, and eventually an increase in income and consumption, as was seen in the postwar era.

In sum, we must not conclude that war is good for the economy, nor that increased government spending is a counter-cyclical cure for depression. Ultimately, economic malaise must be overcome by freeing the human spirit and by adopting the virtues of thrift, hard work, entrepreneurship, and capital formation. Above all, the government must provide a stable monetary and fiscal environment. Regarding World War II, Stuart Chase sums it up best: "The conclusion here is not that chronic warfare is the cure for chronic depression, but a more hopeful one. People must have a *goal* to stir them to activity; something big to do, to make sacrifices for. Then their latent powers really come out."[13]

CAN IT HAPPEN AGAIN?

The ultimate question is, "Are we headed for another world depression as in the 1930s?" Even conservative Milton Friedman joins the orthodox ranks when he says the economy is depression-proof. Giving a speech in Sweden in 1954, Friedman argued that government leaders now understand the basic inner workings of the economy and have the technical tools to prevent a full-scale collapse. He referred to several institutional changes that make such an event inconceivable, such as federal deposit insurance; abandonment of the gold standard; and the growth in the size of government, including welfare payments, unemployment insurance, and so forth. Most important, authorities have learned how to avoid a monetary collapse.[14]

Yet avoiding a monetary deflation does not necessarily mean avoiding a depression. Certainly many countries, especially in Latin America, have suffered inflationary depressions, and the West has gone through several severe inflationary recessions. In essence, Friedman's "built-in stabilizers" have simply removed the barriers to currency depreciation. Inflation rather than deflation has been the problem of the post-depression world, as the wholesale price index chart indicates (see Chapter 11). And it is a mistake (committed in the *AS–AD* diagrams) to think that monetary inflation only raises prices without distorting real output.

While the United States and other advanced nations have certainly been depression-resistant over the past 50 years, they are not depression-proof. A financial accident could precipitate a panic that could destabilize the world's monetary system and bring about an economic collapse, even as governments desperately attempt to inflate us out of the crisis. It is important to note that although government policy controls the *macro*economic sphere, it does not control the *micro*economics of the financial world. The international financial markets are still largely laissez-faire. In the face of growing uncertainty and potential instability, institutional investors, large corporations, and individual speculators could withdraw suddenly and unexpectedly from major positions in securities, bonds, and other investments. That is, in essence, what happened on October 19, 1987, the worst stock market crash in 200 years, an event that most establishment economists said could not happen again.

There could also be a run on the dollar, just as there used to be runs on gold. Federal deposit insurance, which Friedman said would eliminate the possibility of future bank failures, has actually destabilized the U.S. banking industry even more by creating the illusion that bank deposits are risk-free and customers do not have to be concerned about the quality of a bank's portfolio. The number of bank and thrift failures has increased dramatically in the United States over the past decade. Banks still operate under a fragile fractional reserve system, where the reserve requirement is only 3 percent for savings accounts and 12 percent for checking accounts, which means that if all depositors decided to withdraw their money on the same day, only 3 percent to 12 percent would receive their funds. In this respect, nothing has changed since the 1930s. If the public ever loses confidence in the monetary system and tries to convert deposits into cash, the banks would be just as vulnerable to wholesale bankruptcy as they were 60 years ago.

Monetary inflation causes all kinds of price and production distortions. The world economy suffers from an increasing macroeconomic disequilibrium. Such macroeconomic instability is not inherent in the free market, as Marxists and Keynesians contend, but is caused by government intervention in the monetary sphere. Once a country heads down the inflationary path, it is difficult to reverse course. The rate of monetary expansionism has been gradually increasing in the United States and other Western nations. The money supply used to grow at a rate of 2 to 3 percent a year in the early 1960s. Now it usually increases at double-digit rates.

In short, the economy is not depression-proof. Although governments have been remarkably successful in averting disaster since the Great Depression, the war is not over. As long as the financial/banking system is built on a volatile, destabilizing inflationary policy coupled with a fragile fractional reserve banking system and laissez-faire financial markets, the possibility of financial chaos and a subsequent economic cataclysm should not be discounted.

When and if another economic debacle does come, it probably will not be predicted by most economists. Because they do not think it is possible, they are blind to the warning indicators. Moreover, they do not have the tools nor the theories with which to forecast it. One of the most telling signs of trouble within the established economics profession is its apparent incapacity to come up with an econometric model that forecasts depressions. In the September 1988 issue of *American Economic Review*, three econometricians from Harvard and Yale argued that the Great Depression was unforecastable, even after using modern time-series analysis of the data. They reviewed the work of Irving Fisher and the Harvard Economic

Service, both of which failed to anticipate the crash and depression, and concluded that Yale and Harvard "would be justified in appearing optimistic about the economy on the eve of and in the months following the Crash."[15] They added that none of the major theories of the depression imply that the depression could have been predicted. Friedman and Schwartz place the blame on mistakes made by the Federal Reserve Board, which they say could not have been anticipated, even by Irving Fisher. Unfortunately, the authors ignored the Austrian contribution, which clearly foresaw the economic collapse based on the facts that the Federal Reserve promoted a capital-goods boom in the 1920s that could not last, and that the international gold standard could not coexist alongside a weak banking system.

It is certainly not comforting to know that today's sophisticated econometric models are based on the same methods and data that could not predict the last great economic cataclysm. In light of the most recent stock market crash, it appears that now more than ever the profession desperately needs a new macroeconomic forecasting model. Is it not time to seriously consider the analytical tools developed by the one school which predicted the last great depression?

NOTES

1. For a review of Fisher's career, see Irving Norton Fisher, *My Father Irving Fisher* (New York: Comet Press, 1956), especially pp. 242–65. Despite Fisher's blunders, most neoclassical economists consider Fisher "one of the greatest, if not the greatest, and certainly one of the most colourful American economists." *Who's Who in Economics,* 2nd ed., ed. Mark Blaug (Cambridge, Mass.: MIT Press, 1986), p. 273.
2. Harvard Economic Society, *Weekly Letters,* especially November 2, 1929 (Cambridge, Mass.: Harvard University Press).
3. William E. Stoneman, *A History of the Economic Analysis of the Great Depression in America* (New York:

Garland Publishing, 1979), p. 20. See also Wesley Mitchell, "A Review," *Recent Economic Changes in the United States* (New York: McGraw-Hill, 1929), pp. 890–94, 909–10.

4. Felix Somary, *The Raven of Zurich,* translated by A. J. Sherman (London: C. Hurst & Co. 1986), pp. 146–47.

5. John Maynard Keynes, *The Collected Writings of John Maynard Keynes,* vol. XIII (London: Macmillan, 1973), pp. 52–59. Also see Charles H. Hession, *John Maynard Keynes* (New York: Macmillan, 1984), pp. 238–39.

6. Interview with Friedrich A. Hayek, *Gold & Silver Newsletter,* June 1975 (Newport Beach, Calif.: Monex International). Lionel Robbins refers to Hayek's prediction of the depression in America in the Foreword to Hayek's *Prices and Production,* 1st ed. (London: George Routledge & Sons, 1931).

7. Copies of Somary's speeches and warnings are reprinted in Somary's autobiography, *The Raven of Zurich.* Somary's gift of prophecy was not fool-proof, however. Before he died in 1956, he predicted the U.S. was about to enter another depression.

8. Harwood's articles are summarized in his book, *Cause and Control of the Business Cycle,* 5th ed. (Great Barrington, Mass.: American Institute for Economic Research, 1957). The editor of *The Annalist* deleted Harwood's sentence suggesting widespread bank failures, fearing that it would cause a panic. See Jagdish Mehra, *Keynes vs. Harwood: A Contribution to Current Debate* (AIER, 1985), p. 12.

9. William J. Baumol and Alan S. Blinder, *Economics: Principles and Policy,* 4th ed. (New York: Harcourt Brace Jovanovich, 1988), pp. 84–85.

10. Milton Friedman and Anna Schwartz, *A Monetary History of the United States, 1867–1960* (Princeton, N.J.: Princeton University Press, 1963), p. 407.

11. Quoted in Richard G. Lipsey, Peter O. Steiner, and Douglas D. Purvis, *Economics,* 8th ed. (New York: Harper & Row, 1987), p. 573.

12. Lipsey, Steiner, and Purvis, *Economics,* p. 573.

13. Stuart Chase, *For This We Fought* (New York: Twentieth Century Fund, 1946), p. 49. For a revisionist view on the critical importance savings played during World War II, see my article, "Saving the Depression: A New Look at World War II," *Review of Austrian Economics,* 2 (1987), pp. 211–26.

14. Milton Friedman, "Why the American Economy Is Depression-proof," *Dollars and Deficits* (Englewood Cliffs, N.J.: Prentice Hall, 1968), pp. 72–96. The "built-in stabilizers" discussed by Friedman are also emphasized in modern textbooks. See for example Byrns and Stone, *Economics,* 4th ed., p. 147.

15. Kathryn M. Dominguez, Ray C. Fair, and Matthew D. Shapiro, "Forecasting the Depression: Harvard versus Yale," *American Economic Review,* September 1988, p. 605.

RECOMMENDED READING

Friedman, Milton, and Schwartz, Anna J. *The Great Contraction, 1929–1933.* Princeton, N.J.: Princeton University Press, 1963.

Rothbard, Murray N. *America's Great Depression,* 4th ed. New York: Richardson and Snyder, 1983.

CHAPTER 10

WHO'S TO BLAME FOR UNEMPLOYMENT?

Unemployment is considered a social evil that must be kept at an 'acceptable' level.

—Roger Leroy Miller
Economics Today (1988)

Since the Great Depression, the fear of losing one's job has remained a deep concern. According to a recent survey, becoming unemployed is the greatest fear people face, next to death itself. (Other major fears include an IRS audit and giving a public speech.) The trauma of being unemployed is highlighted by the top-10 textbook economists, most of whom devote a separate chapter to the subject. They cite horror stories from *Brother, Can You Spare a Dime?* and *Hard Times,* both oral histories of the 1930s. Other writers note studies on the emotional and psychological trauma of losing a job.

Since the end of World War II, it has become a national policy in most nations to ensure full employment of their citizens. Communist countries seek to guarantee employment of all workers, no matter how underemployed or misemployed. In Europe and the United States, full employment is a national goal. The Employment Act of 1946 and the Full Employment and Balanced Growth Act of 1987 committed the federal government to the central goal of full employment. If the private sector cannot provide enough work, the government is obligated to spend more money to hire more workers. McConnell declares, "The government's obligation is to augment private spending so that total spending—private and public—will be sufficient to generate full employment."

Certainly unemployment can be a serious problem in the economy from time to time. It is a great tragedy to see large amounts of capital and human resources left idle for months if not years. Fortunately, however, human capital is much more adaptable to changing economic conditions than is physical capital. Machinery, equipment, and tools are usually very specific in their use and often cannot be transferred easily to other uses (e.g., an oil rig can only be used for one purpose). But human capital is always nonspecific. Workers can perform a variety of tasks and can be retrained to accomplish other jobs more fitting to the new economic situation. Nevertheless, the flexibility of labor does not eliminate the difficulties of changing jobs or finding new work.

UNEMPLOYMENT IN THE FREE MARKET

Why is private industry unable to always employ everyone who wants to work? Why is work sometimes scarce?

Certainly, a certain amount of unemployment is a regular characteristic of the free market. The dynamics of the market economy involve improvements in technology, sudden changes in consumer preferences, competition between domestic and foreign companies, and shifts in population. Therefore, it is natural to expect some workers to be displaced, transferred, fired, and retired as businesses come and go, expand and contract. The economics textbooks do a good job of describing the types of socially necessary unemployment— what they call seasonal, frictional, and structural unemployment. Most economists now accept the notion that there exists a certain natural rate of unemployment that government fiscal and monetary policy cannot eliminate, however painful it may be for individuals, for it is from this pool of labor that workers in new occupations are taken. Many Keynesian economists favor institutional changes designed to lower the natural rate, but such changes are difficult at best.

THE MARKET AS A JOB DESTROYER

One characteristic of the labor market often overlooked by academic economists is the extent to which the market is a job destroyer as well as a job creator. As labor economist Richard B. McKenzie has declared, "Economic progress has two legs. One is eliminating jobs with new technologies, the other finding new tasks for workers."[1] And it is not just innovation that makes tasks obsolete but foreign competition as well. This may seem to be an evil by-product of the market, but McKenzie raises the unrecognized advantages of job destruction, which he contends may be a useful measure of economic success. His defense of job destruction is not a justification for government-mandated job elimination through protectionist legislation or minimum wages. Rather, he argues that job elimination in the marketplace is a necessary element of dynamic economies and goes hand in hand with job creation. He refers to a General Accounting Office study that shows that regions with high rates of plant closings are also regions with high rates of plant openings and many expansions of old plants. According to McKenzie, the net effects of this job destruction–creation activity are better working conditions, more enjoyable jobs, and a higher standard of living. He summarizes, "The day the country no longer has to face adjustment problems will probably be the day its people can no longer look forward to a better economic future."[2]

In China, where the government is under a mandate to provide 100 percent employment, no jobs are destroyed, with the result that farms still use water buffalos instead of plows and new buildings are excavated by hundreds of workers instead of a single earthmover. In many cases, five Chinese workers are assigned to do the work of two.

A national goal of full employment should not bind us to the dangerous notion that any job is better than no job at all. If economic progress means anything, it signifies the gradual disappearance of drudgery, thankless tasks, repetitious work, and tedious jobs. The Marxists may have been the first to emphasize the problems of alienation, exploitation, and poor working conditions in the labor market, but evidence is growing that these problems are being eliminated more rapidly under capitalist societies than under Marxist regimes. Progress means an increase in the number of challenging work opportunities, jobs that not only pay well but are also exciting and fulfilling. The expansion of the service economy in the United States and other developed nations should be viewed as an advancement in the country's standard of living, not as a loss in its competitive edge with foreigners in the manufacturing sector. It's a question of comparative advantage.

Even the level of unemployment, if truly voluntary and not forced by lack of marketable skills, can actually be a reflection of a higher level of living standards. By unemployment, I do not mean being idle, but rather engaging in a variety of part-time activities and avocations. Surely it is a sign of prosperity when one half of the population or more can "retire" from regular working hours and enjoy a high standard of living through freelance work or self-employment.

WHO IS TO BLAME FOR CYCLICAL UNEMPLOYMENT?

According to mainstream economists, the free market suffers from a more serious form of unemployment, known as cyclical unemployment. Just as the market is characterized by major cycles in business activity, so is it characterized by severe unemployment from time to time, far above the expected natural rate. Such unemployment is involuntary in the sense that individuals willing to work cannot find gainful employment. Moreover, such unemployment in the capitalist system can last indefinitely, according to critics, as it seemed to do during the 1930s. In such cases, these economists argue that only the government is in a position to be the "employer of last resort," just as it must be the "lender of last resort" when private financial institutions run into trouble.

My contention, however, is that cyclical unemployment is caused primarily by government policies, not by the free market. If individuals are allowed to operate fully and without state interference, cyclical unemployment should not be a serious problem in the marketplace.

HOW GOVERNMENT CAN CREATE UNEMPLOYMENT

There are numerous examples of government-caused unemployment. They include monetary inflation and deflation, employment taxes, and minimum wage legislation.

Monetary Inflation and Deflation

Government initially creates an artificial inflationary boom in employment opportunities (especially in the capital-goods industries) but then forces a credit crunch and recession, which in turn means massive layoffs as the economy seeks to reestablish an equilibrium level. We noted in Chapters 8 and 9 how the government's boom–bust policies were a major cause of cyclical unemployment during the Great Depression as well as during the postwar recessions, and how other federal policies (increasing taxes and tariffs, pressuring industries not to reduce wages, etc.) kept unemployment high for many years.

Another side effect of monetary inflation is that it increases the cost of living, which in turn forces people to work overtime, take on part-time work, or require more members of the household to work in order to maintain their lifestyle. In 1950, only 12 percent of mothers with children under age 6 worked. Today, 57 percent do. Of all mothers with children under age 14, two thirds are now in the workforce. Women are not just working because they want to be liberated from household tasks, since many of the jobs they take are low-paying clerical and secretarial jobs. They are doing so because inflation has made it virtually impossible for a family to survive on one income.

High Employment Taxes and Mandatory Employee Benefits

Academic economists may theorize about the causes of unemployment, but if you really want to know why unemployment is a persistent problem in an area, just ask local businesspeople, "What deters you from hiring more workers?" They may offer several explanations, but one frequent answer will be the high hidden costs of labor, caused in part by taxes and compulsory benefits. Employers would be much more willing to hire workers if they did not have to pay social security, unemployment compensation, health insurance, child day care, and other mandatory benefits in addition to corporate income taxes. The employee may think primarily in terms of take-home pay, but the employer must consider the total cost of hiring a worker, which may add 30 percent or more to the base salary when all benefits and government programs are included. Making extensive use of independent contractors has been a way of reducing these costs, but there are severe limitations to this method, and the government is constantly cracking down on such circuitous methods. The end result is that government-mandated employee benefits discourage businesses from hiring more workers.

Minimum Wage Legislation

Government-imposed minimum wages do provide some valuable benefits, primarily to union workers and other laborers whose services are still in demand after the minimum wage is raised. But the minimum wage is an ineffective, if not counterproductive, way to ensure a minimum standard of living for low-income workers. Companies devise ways to circumvent the minimum wage, such as laying off workers; becoming more discriminatory in hiring new employees (often discriminating against minorities); adopting mechanized instead of labor-intensive production processes; and using underground, sub-minimum hiring methods. As most of the writers of the top-10 economics textbooks point out, minimum wages reduce job opportunities for the uneducated, the young, and the inexperienced. Undoubtedly, minimum wage legislation—along with the factors of compulsory employment taxes and benefits, noted above—has contributed to the high rates of unemployment among teenagers and minorities.

Meanwhile, for those workers lucky enough to be hired or remain employed, the benefits are enhanced. Even employees who get paid more than the minimum wage benefit because companies' wages and salaries are based on relative differentials. If the new-entry workers' basic compensation is increased, firms are under pressure to raise wages and salaries across the board for workers in higher positions as well. Thus, one can see how the minimum wage can increase the cost of labor substantially, not just among low-income earners.

On January 14, 1987, *The New York Times* ran an editorial with a startling headline: "The Right Minimum Wage: $0.00." It stated flatly, "The idea of using a minimum wage to overcome poverty is old, honorable—and fundamentally flawed." The editorial went on to say that the minimum wage simply raises the costs of labor, amounting to a hidden tax on the jobs of those at the lowest rung. As an anti-poverty program, the minimum wage accomplishes just the opposite of what it is meant to do.

THE IMPACT OF KEYNESIANISM ON WORKER PRODUCTIVITY

Traditionally, Keynesian economists have blamed the capitalist system for extended unemployment. They say that the government is the solution to, not the source of, the unemployment problem and that the state must provide a policy of hiring workers when private enterprise is unable or unwilling to do so. As a result of this doctrine, the government has suffered from overexpansion and excess bureaucracy. In 1930, there were a little over 0.5 million federal employees. Today there are 4.2 million, including 1 million military personnel, who represent approximately 4 percent of the labor force in the United States. This percentage may be viewed as small compared to the size of government spending as a percentage of the economy, but it is still a significant burden. The size of federal employment is an even more serious problem in socialist countries. In addition, it is important to consider the number of people in jobs created primarily to deal with the government, such as tax accountants, attorneys, and lobbyists. As Peter Drucker comments,

> Does anyone, for instance, believe that tax accountants contribute to national wealth or to productivity, and altogether add to society's well-being, whether material, physical or spiritual? And yet in every developed country government mandates misallocation of a steadily growing portion of our scarcest resource, able, diligent, trained people, to such essentially sterile pursuits.[3]

During an economic downturn, there is no effort to reduce the number of government workers for fear of exacerbating the recession. If anything, the central government hires more workers and puts them to work building symbolic pyramids. As Nobel Prize-winning economist James Buchanan has demonstrated, the federal government is becoming an autonomous power that always seeks to aggrandize itself through more legislation, an increased budget, and more employees. Thus, for example, government workers are no longer called "public servants," but "federal employees." This form of Keynesian jobism has led to high levels of inefficiency and bureaucracy. There seems to be little or no check to government expansionism. Even Samuelson notes, "If the government builds too many dams, too many bombers, too many fancy government office buildings, there is no profit-and-loss statement by which the economic worth of these projects can be calculated."

The state has become an ungovernable, bloated monstrosity incapable of running its affairs in a business-like fashion. Noting the sickness of government, Peter Drucker believes that most governments no longer attract good people: "They know that nothing can be done; government is a dead-end street."[4]

SUMMARY

What should the government do to maintain high levels of employment?

First, it must eliminate the barriers it has erected that deter the employment of individuals, including minimum wage laws and compulsory benefits. It should reduce employment taxes as much as possible.

Second, government officials should reject the Keynesian notion that big government and a large workforce are necessary to maintain macroeconomic stability. They must recognize that such a policy is counterproductive and burdensome to society. Efforts should be made to privatize government services as much as possible so as to increase the efficiency and growth rate of the economy and eliminate the bureaucratic power of federal agencies. Third, the government needs to adopt a stable monetary system that does not create an artificial boom–bust cycle in the business world. That is the subject of Chapter 11.

NOTES

1. Richard B. McKenzie, *The American Job Machine* (New York: Universal Books, 1988), p. 9.
2. Ibid., p. 15.
3. Peter F. Drucker, *The Frontiers of Management* (New York: Harper & Row, 1986), p. 14.
4. Peter F. Drucker, *Innovation and Entrepreneurship* (New York: Harper & Row, 1985), p. 263.

RECOMMENDED READING

Sennholz, Hans F. *The Politics of Unemployment*. Spring Mills, Penn.: Libertarian Press, 1987.

CHAPTER 11

THE GOLD STANDARD

How absurd to waste resources digging gold out of the bowels of the earth, only to inter it back again in the vaults of Fort Knox, Kentucky!

—Paul A. Samuelson
Economics, 8th ed. (1970)

Judging from the number of pages in the top 10 textbooks devoted to gold and the origin of money, the interest of mainstream economists in the gold standard and "real money" is practically nil. Two of these textbooks do not even mention the gold standard, despite its critical role in economic history and despite resurging interest in government policy and personal investment strategies. Economists apparently have taken little notice of the dramatic increase in the minting and trading of legal-tender gold and silver coins as a de facto return to a specie standard, or of the fact that central banks are monitoring the price of gold to reflect worldwide economic instability. Some analysts believe that gold will play a key role in the Soviet Union's efforts to make the ruble convertible. Economics textbooks may number 1,000 pages, but they spend 5 pages or fewer discussing gold, usually in the international section or an appendix, and then almost always in a negative light.

THE NEED FOR A MONETARY ANCHOR

To determine the need for a commodity standard in today's economy, consider this question: What would be the ideal economic environment? Most people would agree on the following national goals:

1. Stable, low interest rates, perhaps in the 2 to 3 percent range.
2. Little or no inflation or perhaps even a gently falling price level.
3. Low unemployment and the possibility of finding or changing a job with little trouble or waiting.
4. Steady economic growth and a rising standard of living, without the threat of recessions or depressions.
5. Widespread freedom to work, think, and act independently without force or fraud.

Is this dream world possible? Sudden external shocks and occasional crop failures cannot be predicted or avoided from time to time, but the five goals listed above are at least conceivable. We are certainly a far cry from achieving these five goals, even in the so-called free world. Nevertheless, it is my contention that a genuine gold standard could help us to achieve many of these macroeconomic objectives. The purpose of this chapter is to demonstrate the benefits of the gold standard as an ideal monetary standard and as a superior alternative to the textbook-endorsed fiat money standard.

I am not suggesting that the historical gold and silver standards the West lived under between 1821 and 1971 achieved the five lofty aims listed above. They were in many ways pseudocommodity standards with large fiduciary elements in them, and this defect rendered them incapable of solving international crises. The textbooks do an excellent job of pointing out the serious weaknesses in the historical gold standards, but they are obstinately silent on the potential strengths of a genuine 100 percent gold-backed currency.

THE MEANING OF A GENUINE GOLD STANDARD

How would a pure gold standard work? It would offer several properties: First, pure gold bullion measured in troy ounces would serve as the official monetary unit of account in every country. Second, gold would normally circulate as a general medium of exchange. Gold bullion would form the basis of very large transactions. Gold coins would be used for medium-to-large purchases. Silver, copper, and token coins would be involved in smaller transactions.

Third, money substitutes would be commonly used as a convenient alternative to bullion or coins. These would include paper banknotes, token coins, and checking accounts ("demand deposits") as means of payment. However, a pure gold standard would require all currency, coins, and checking accounts used for final payment to be fully backed by bullion or full-bodied coins in bank vaults or other secure storage facilities. Money substitutes would be treated as warehouse receipts; printing of additional banknotes or lending demand deposits (known as "fractional reserve banking") would be considered a fraudulent practice. In short, a pure gold standard is a 100 percent banking reserve system.[1]

A 100 percent reserve system would not put the banks out of business, as some critics have maintained. Banks, of course, would charge monthly fees for their checking services. Moreover, they would continue to act as financial intermediaries, loaning money from time deposits and savings accounts. Time deposits and savings deposits would have to be genuine, with severe penalties for early withdrawal.

Fourth, national currencies (dollars, pounds, francs, etc.) would be defined as specific weights in gold bullion. Exchange rates between individual currencies would be fixed by definition. Samuelson uses a historical example: "Thus, Queen Victoria chose to make her coins about ¼ ounce of gold (the pound) and President McKinley chose to make his unit 1/20 ounce of gold (the dollar). In that case, the British pound, being 5 times as heavy as the dollar, would naturally have an exchange rate of $5 to £1."

THE ORIGIN OF MONEY

Samuelson's example needs to be amplified in the context of the origin of money. Unfortunately, modern textbooks do not tell the story of money as the older principles books did. Only a few have a page or two briefly outlining the history of money, and none of the top 10 explain where pounds, dollars, and francs originated.

The decision by governments to use ounces of gold to define their national currencies was not an ad hoc decree just to create a monetary system from among many substitutes. In fact, all national currencies originated historically as units of weight for gold or silver. The original British pound sterling signified one Saxon pound of standard silver. The official American dollar was adopted because the Spanish dollar circulated widely in the 18th century, but before then the dollar came from well-minted private silver coins in the valley of St. Joachim in Bohemia in the 16th century. The word *dollar* came from *Joachimsthaler, thaler* meaning valley, *thaler* eventually becoming *dollar.* Other currencies such as the German mark and French franc were also originally commercial weights used in business transactions. Silver formed the basis of all currencies because it was more plentiful than gold and was used commercially throughout the Western world. Gold gradually replaced silver as the unit of account in the 19th century when the yellow metal was discovered in large quantities in the United States, Australia, and South Africa.

Thus, all monetary units initially came from varying weights of metal, primarily silver, used specifically in commercial trade. In general, all commodities are bought and sold by their units of weight—bushels of wheat, pounds of butter, and so forth. Gold and silver are no different. When someone in the marketplace had silver and needed wheat, he exchanged bushels of wheat for ounces of silver. The precious metals emerged naturally from the marketplace as the medium of exchange because of their unique properties and advantages over barter. They were relatively scarce, indestructible, and stable in value. They were easily divisible into pounds, ounces, and grams, thus easily portable and convenient for day-to-day as well as large transactions.

In sum, a pure commodity standard does not emerge from the goldbug's make-believe world, nor is it simply a creation by government edict. Neither is it just another alternative monetary system, equal in choice to any other system, as Bronfenbrenner suggests. The gold (or silver) standard is historical, cultural, and logical in the natural development of money. As Carl Menger clearly states, "The origin of money [is] entirely natural. . . . Money is not an invention of the state. It is not the product of a legislative act. Even the sanction of political authority is not necessary for its existence. Certain commodities came to be money quite naturally, as the result of economic relationships that were independent of the power of the state."[2]

The naming of different national currencies (dollars, pounds, marks, etc.) has caused a great deal of confusion in the mind of the student of economics. The world would have been better off monetarily if all countries on the gold standard had simply used ounces or grams of gold as their *numéraire* rather than names of currencies. After all, if Queen Victoria defined the pound sterling as ¼ of an ounce of gold and President McKinley defined the dollar as ¹⁄₂₀ of an ounce of gold, then in fact, ¼ of an ounce is simply traded for ⁵⁄₂₀ of an ounce. It is the same as saying that 12 inches is one foot. However, governments maintained the veil of a national currency in order to maintain the capability of inflating their currency (a constant temptation) while still operating behind the facade of a gold standard.

ADVANTAGES OF A GENUINE GOLD STANDARD

Ignoring for now the reasons why governments have slowly moved away from the gold standard, we can discuss the benefits of adopting a pure gold standard.

No Monetary Deflation

First, under a pure gold standard the money supply is unlikely to decline. It is inconceivable that a monetary collapse could occur under a 100 percent gold standard, as happened in the period 1929 to 1932, when the money supply held by the U.S. fractional reserve system fell by one third. Using a pure gold standard, banks would be required to maintain a 100 percent specie reserve, which would eliminate the fear the public might have regarding the solvency of banks. Why would panicky depositors want to withdraw their money when the total amount owned is stored safely in the bank's vaults? Thus, bank runs would be senseless. Moreover, the government could not blunder in reducing the money supply because the monetary stock would consist entirely of gold bullion or coins.

Unlike other metals used for industrial purposes, gold is hardly ever consumed. It simply changes form. The amount of gold unrecovered in industry, lost in the sea, or buried in somebody's backyard is relatively small. The ring worn today may have been mined in the times of Caesar. Throughout history, the total stock of gold has never declined from year to year. The amount of world gold stocks increases every year by 1 to 4 percent, depending on annual production. Of course, annual production of the yellow metal rises and falls, but because of gold's relative indestructibility the total aboveground stocks have never diminished. This is demonstrated in Figure 11–1, which shows world gold production from 1800 to 1932 and the gold stocks held by all governments between 1810 and 1932, during which time the Western world was officially on some kind of gold standard and several major gold rushes occurred. Note how line **a** never declines. Annual production, as measured in Figure 11–2, sometimes declines but it is always adding to total world stocks.

Price Inflation Unlikely

Second, price inflation would be highly unlikely over the long run under the gold standard. Figures 11–3A and 11–3B, which show wholesale prices in the United States and Britain from 1810 onward, demonstrate that average prices tended to decline slightly overall under the classical gold standard, even when there was not a 100 percent gold backing of the currency. Prices did occasionally move up sharply but only during a war, such as the Civil War in the United States, during which the United States temporarily went off the gold standard and issued fiduciary greenbacks.

The reason behind the slight deflationary trend is that since 1492 annual gold output has never increased the total

FIGURE 11–1
World Gold Stock and Gold Production, 1800–1932

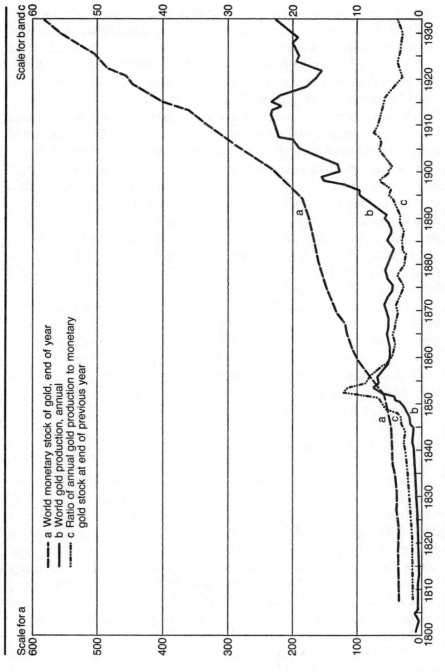

a World monetary stock of gold, end of year
b World gold production, annual
c Ratio of annual gold production to monetary
  gold stock at end of previous year

FIGURE 11–2
World Gold Production

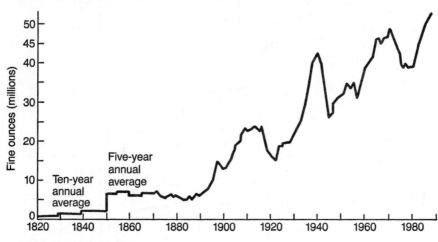

Source: United States Mint.

supply of gold by more than 5 percent in any one year. Prior to the California gold discoveries in 1848, annual increases in the gold supply seldom exceeded 1 percent. The gold discoveries in California and Australia in the 1850s added substantially to the supply of gold, creating a temporary price inflation, especially in the West. Miners extracted more metal in the next 20 years than they had in the entire previous 350 years. Nevertheless, annual production never augmented the world's supply of gold by more than 5 percent in any one year. Moreover, the opening of new mines in South Africa in the period 1890 to 1910 only boosted total gold supplies by 3 to 4 percent per annum. Since 1910, annual increases in the stock of gold have varied between 1 and 2 percent.

In the past decade, although gold production has increased by 20 percent per annum, mining companies have had difficulty increasing the aggregate gold stock by more than 1 to 2 percent per annum. Under the circumstances, it is easy to see why price inflation is highly unlikely under a pure gold standard on a worldwide scale. In fact, a slight deflationary pull on prices is more likely. This is not necessarily bad. Declining

FIGURE 11–3A
Wholesale Price Index, United Kingdom, 1800–1979

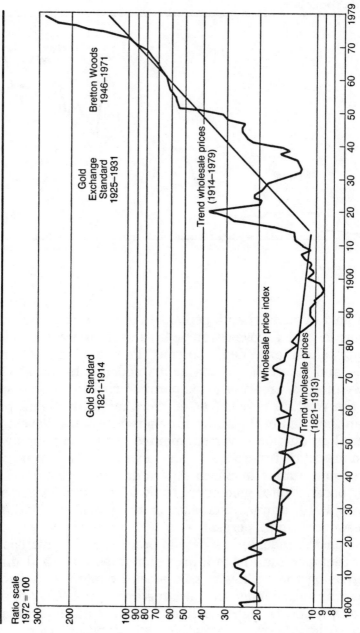

Note: Prepared by Federal Reserve Bank of St. Louis.

Source: Reprinted with the permission of the Pacific Research Institute for Public Policy. From: Bordo, David. "The Gold Standard." In *Money in Crisis*, edited by Barry N. Siegel. San Francisco: Pacific Research Institute, 1984.

FIGURE 11–3B

Wholesale Price Index, United States, 1800–1979

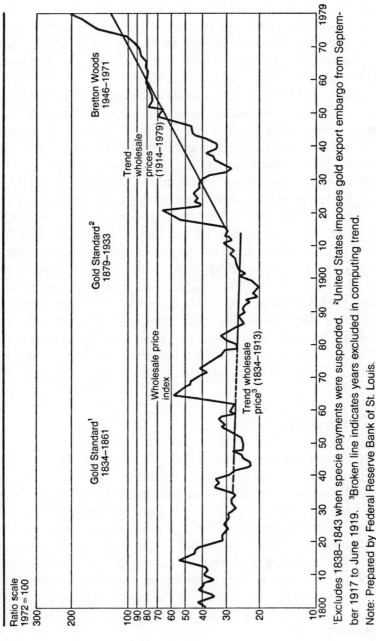

Ratio scale
1972 = 100

Gold Standard[1]
1834–1861

Gold Standard[2]
1879–1933

Bretton Woods
1946–1971

Wholesale price
index

Trend
wholesale
prices
(1914–1979)

Trend wholesale
price[3] (1834–1913)

[1]Excludes 1838–1843 when specie payments were suspended. [2]United States imposes gold export embargo from September 1917 to June 1919. [3]Broken line indicates years excluded in computing trend.

Note: Prepared by Federal Reserve Bank of St. Louis.

Source: Reprinted with the permission of the Pacific Research Institute for Public Policy. From: Bordo, David. "The Gold Standard." In *Money in Crisis*, edited by Barry N. Siegel. San Francisco: Pacific Research Institute, 1984.

prices do not necessarily mean a depression. Profit margin is what counts, and if lower costs can offset lower prices, then businesses can continue to thrive. In fact, there have been many periods when a slightly falling price level has been accompanied by rapid economic growth, such as in the 1890s, 1920s, and to some extent in the 1950s.

Although there may be little or no inflation worldwide under a pure gold standard, what about rising prices in areas where a new gold rush is occurring? This can be a problem. For example, the California gold rush made the United States a major gold producer for the first time, which had a pronounced effect on its money supply. During the period 1849 to 1854, for example, the total amount of U.S. currency increased at an annual rate of 13.9 percent at a time when all U.S. currency consisted of gold coins or paper money backed by gold bullion. Thus, it is possible to experience a short-term inflationary impact under gold rush conditions. Bronfenbrenner is correct when he states, "Inflation has by no means been eliminated under gold standards." But such price inflation would tend to be short-lived. Moreover, because gold discoveries raise the monetary stock to a new permanent level, prices are likely to settle at a higher level than before the inflation began without creating a deflationary bust when the new gold rush is over.

No Depression

Third, a depression is not likely to occur under a pure gold standard. There are several explanations for this. First, as indicated earlier, a reduction in the quantity of money is highly unlikely; the quantity of money can only increase gradually. Second, a gold-induced inflation is likely to raise prices to a permanently higher level. There will, of course, be a period of adjustment during and immediately after the gold rush, after which prices are likely to stabilize at the higher level. There is no reason to expect a violent boom–bust business cycle under a stable gold system in which the money supply increases and does not decline.

In this respect, there is quite a distinction between gold inflation and fiat money inflation. Under a genuine commodity standard, no one can create money out of thin air. Money can only be obtained through the exchange of goods and services, not through increased printing. Under a pure commodity system, increased printing would be counterfeiting, which is not only illegal for individuals but for the government as well. Gold miners, of course, do produce new money, but gold production is not cost-free. Huge capital resources are required to explore, develop, and transport the precious metal to its users. This is the principal reason that the stock of gold increases at such a slow rate.

But with paper money unbacked by any commodity, the cost of fueling inflation is relatively cheap. A new banknote costs only a few pennies to print and is then valued at $100. Such printing is legal counterfeiting, and it is relatively cost-free. Thus, whereas the money supply under gold can increase by 5 percent a year, the money supply under a fiat money system can increase by 10 percent, 30 percent, 100 percent, even 1,000 percent—and under certain extreme circumstances there can be an infinite expansion (as in the case of Germany in the early 1920s). As such, government-created inflation can cause serious disturbances in the economy by transferring wealth to one group at the expense of another, stimulating one sector of the economy while depressing another, or creating a boom–bust business cycle as described earlier.

In short, an increase in the quantity of fiat money distorts the market by creating value out of nothing, whereas an increase in full-valued gold reflects the market's structure of production and natural, voluntary time preferences.

No Need for Central Banking

Fourth, a pure commodity standard requires minimal state functions. The role of the government might be limited to certifying coins of a fixed weight or perhaps to minting coins themselves. These have been long-standing functions of the Treasury, although it is also conceivable that private firms

could be granted licenses to mint coins, just as private companies mine the metal. The law would prohibit the Treasury from
issuing banknotes without the full backing of specie.

In any case, there would be no need for such central banks
as the Federal Reserve, the Bank of England, the Bank of
France, or any discretionary authorities at all. Because central
banks were created primarily to manipulate the money supply,
set reserve requirements for banks, and to intervene in other
ways, their role would be relatively useless under a pure gold
standard. In the early 19th century, President Andrew Jackson
and other opponents of fiat money recognized this fact and
fought against the establishment of a national bank in the
United States. Unfortunately, their influence was short-lived.

THE CASE AGAINST GOLD

A number of criticisms have been launched against a pure gold
standard over the centuries, many of which are contained in
the economics textbooks. Let us review the main criticisms.

First, gold is too costly. One economist's virtue is another
economist's vice. Defenders of gold argue that it is precisely
because the extraction of gold is so expensive that gold is scarce
and therefore ideal as a monetary standard. Opponents argue
that a gold standard imposes too heavy a burden on society in
terms of resources. The quotation by Samuelson at the beginning of this chapter reflects this idea of costly waste. Ruffin
and Gregory echo Samuelson's sentiments in stating, "It also
seems unwise to dig up gold and then turn around and bury it
again in Fort Knox, all for the purpose of restraining the
growth rate of the money supply." Obviously, printing paper
money is much cheaper than mining gold. Economists of virtually all schools—including Adam Smith, David Ricardo, John
Maynard Keynes, and Ludwig von Mises—have criticized the
gold standard for being too expensive and a waste of resources.

However, the flaw within this argument is that even without a gold standard the costs of gold mining and storage do not
disappear. Roger Garrison makes this point in a brilliantly argued article entitled "The Costs of a Gold Standard."[3] Even af-

ter the rejection of the gold standard, huge resources are still being devoted to the exploration, extraction, and refining of precious metals. In fact, the dramatic increase in the market price of gold has encouraged an even greater use of resources for this purpose as individuals and institutions seek to hedge against inflation in an uncertain economic climate. Even government minting and trading of gold and silver coins have increased tremendously since the early 1970s. Milton Friedman, who used to side with those who considered the gold standard too expensive, has reversed his position and now thinks that the only drawback to a free-market gold standard is that it is a political, not an economic, problem.[4]

Second, the gold supply cannot keep up with the rate of economic growth. Economists contend that this is one of gold's most serious problems. According to Lipsey and Steiner, historically, "the world's supply of monetary gold did not grow fast enough to provide adequate reserves for the expanding volume of trade." Yet this may not be as serious a problem as these critics insist. The economy adjusts to this inelasticity of gold, as economists call it, by allowing prices to fall. Deflation and depression do not automatically go hand in hand. Recall that the Great Depression was intensified by a 30 percent reduction in the money supply. But when the money supply is increasing, albeit at a rate lower than the rate of economic growth, there is no reason that gradually declining prices should necessarily be a drag on society. As noted earlier, there have been periods when industrial nations have had real economic growth accompanied by slight deflation. It is clear that a gold standard would not provide a stable "monetarist rule," whereby the money supply would expand at a steady rate close to the rate of economic growth. But at the same time I see no justification for supporting price stabilization as some kind of ideal monetary goal.

Third, the establishment of a gold standard would make the world too dependent on South Africa and the Soviet Union, the major gold producers. "Do we want to have a monetary system under which our money supply and price levels are determined by the size of Soviet grain harvests?" asks McConnell.

Frankly, this argument is overblown because of the large aboveground supplies of gold, which are held principally by noncommunist countries. Currently the Soviet Union produces approximately 18 percent and South Africa 34 percent of world gold output. Since current production is only increasing the total world stock of gold by 2 percent a year, the Soviet Union's contribution represents only about one third of 1 percent of total world stocks. South Africa's share is larger but still adds less than 1 percent to total world supplies each year. Of course, the Soviet Union and South Africa could create havoc by dumping gold on the market, but why would they under a pure gold standard? It would only be to their disadvantage.

HISTORICAL PSEUDO GOLD STANDARDS

The only situation in which the Soviet Union and South Africa could cause a monetary crisis is in the case of a gold *exchange* standard, whereby governments agree to buy or sell gold at a fixed rate, similar to the type of gold standard the world employed prior to 1971. But this is a pseudo gold standard, not anywhere close the 100 percent gold standard we are discussing here. Over the centuries, governments found ways to inflate the money supply and reduce the size of gold reserves. The arguments against the historical gold standard are largely correct. Mingled with a high level of fiduciary elements, the pseudo gold standard did not eliminate inflation, did not prevent depressions and economic crises, and failed miserably as an international monetary standard in the 1920s and 1930s. But the arguments against the historical gold standard should not be used against a legitimate gold standard. The gold standard must be pure, or very close to pure, to work feasibly over the long run.

THE RETURN TO GOLD

Undoubtedly, there would be a series of obstacles to any attempts to return to a pure gold standard. The United States and other advanced nations could go back to a gold exchange standard, but that would just bring back the same kinds of monetary crises as those that occurred in the past. As Samuelson warns, "The cruel dilemmas of macroeconomics—the large social costs of disinflation or of unemployment—would not magically disappear with the wave of a golden wand." A genuine gold standard, however, with 100 percent bank reserves for currency and demand deposits, would eventually induce the stable economic environment we seek. But getting there would be difficult. For one thing, a return to the gold standard would mean a mammoth windfall profit for gold holders and mining companies. Another problem is how to determine the definition of the dollar and other currencies in terms of ounces of gold. Yet another difficulty is how to devise ways to keep government officials from circumventing the pure specie standard over time. Historically, they have clipped coins, inflated the currency, and slowly developed ways to remove the checks on inflation. I do not pretend to have solutions to these problems, nor do I expect the world's governments to adopt a pure gold standard voluntarily. But if indeed a 100 percent gold standard is as ideal as the theory seems to indicate, it may be worth paying the high price for the ticket into monetary heaven. The ideal opportunity to reestablish a legitimate gold standard would come when the world suffers through a major monetary upheaval. At that point, going back on the gold standard would not create a crisis, but rather it would resolve it. In short, there is an increasingly growing case, both theoretically and politically, for what mainstream economists have erroneously called a "barbarous relic."

NOTES

1. Some hard-money economists advocate a "free banking" arrangement in which banks could issue unbacked currency and lend out demand deposits. As long as these arrangements were fully disclosed to customers, being notified that banknotes and checking accounts from this bank were not the customers' property but were merely credits, the bank would not be acting in bad faith. However, in order for free banking to work, all obstacles to

bank competition would have to be removed so that any bank that became too speculative by issuing excessive banknotes beyond specie would come under pressure to retrench. Free-banking advocates contend that such an arrangement would result in a fairly hard-money monetary system. However, if banks remained uncompetitive, free banking might easily degenerate into "wildcat" banking. For a discussion of these issues, see George Selgin, *The Theory of Free Banking* (Washington, D.C.: Cato Institute, 1988).

2. Carl Menger, *Principles of Economics* (New York: New York University Press, 1976), pp. 261.

3. Roger Garrison, "The Costs of a Gold Standard," in *The Gold Standard,* ed. Llewellyn H. Rockwell, Jr. (Lexington, Mass.: Lexington Books, 1985), pp. 61–80.

4. Milton Friedman and Anna J. Schwartz, "Has Government Any Role in Money?," *Journal of Monetary Economics* (January 1986), pp. 37–62. A pure gold standard, based on 100 percent bank reserve for demand deposits, might appeal to the monetarists, since it would establish a relatively stable monetarist rule, prohibit deflation of the money supply, and eliminate the need for a discretionary monetary authority.

RECOMMENDED READING

Paul, Ron and Lewis Lehrman. *The Case for Gold.* Washington, D.C.: Cato Institute, 1982.

Rothbard, Murray N. *What Has the Government Done to Our Money?* Norato, Calif.: Libertarian Publishers, 1981.

Siegel, Barry N., ed. *Money in Crisis.* San Francisco: Pacific Institute, 1984.

Skousen, Mark. *Economics of a Pure Gold Standard.* 3rd ed. Auburn, Ala.: Mises Institute, 1990.

CHAPTER 12

MARKET VERSUS GOVERNMENT FAILURE

Most people's moral and practical sense argues for some state intervention to mitigate the disastrous results that the market deals out to some.
—Richard G. Lipsey and Peter O. Steiner
Economics (1987)

The top 10 textbooks go to great lengths to categorize the shortcomings of the free-enterprise system. A whole section of economics has been developed around the theme of market failure. Market economies are accused of causing severe business fluctuations, distributing income unequally, encouraging monopolies, allocating resources inefficiently, destroying the environment and not providing for public goods such as national defense.

We have already dealt with some of these alleged shortcomings. For example, we have demonstrated that severe business fluctuations are not initiated in the free market but are instead caused primarily by government instability in monetary and fiscal affairs. Some of the other market problems, such as natural monopolies, will be discussed in Chapter 18.

THE EXTERNALITY PROBLEM

Economists make a major point of the alleged imperfection of the market in its failure to capture the full benefits and costs of a particular economic activity. They call it the "externality problem" in the free market. The externalities can be either beneficial, as in the case of a homeowner whose property value is enhanced by a neighbor's newly landscaped yard, or deleterious, as in the case of the same homeowner whose other neighbor parks broken-down cars in his front yard.

Baumol and Blinder use an example involving the effects of a planting a garden to make their point about beneficial externalities: "For example, a homeowner who plants a beautiful garden in front of her house incidentally and unintentionally provides pleasure to her neighbors and to those who pass by—people from whom she receives no payment."

This is certainly a case of misguided thinking. Perhaps Baumol and Blinder have never planted flowers and plants in their front yard, for if they had they would know that the homeowner can be very definitely compensated both financially and socially for such an act of beautification. My mother is famous in her community for having magnificent flower gardens surrounding her home. She has won awards for the meticulous way in which she maintains her gardens and for the beauty of the irises and other flowers she grows. She is compensated in two ways. First, the value of her homes (she has built four homes in her community) has increased significantly because of her efforts. Her homes have sold more quickly than and at a premium to comparable homes. Real estate agents in any part of the world will tell you that enhancing the outside environment of a home increases its selling price. Second, my mother enjoys a high reputation in the community, and her life has been more rewarding both socially and culturally because of her flower gardens. The fact that her neighbors also enjoy the benefits of her flowers does not diminish her own asset.

It seems curious to me that economists raise the externality issue regarding every beneficial act of an individual in an effort to justify some form of government subsidy. Are Baumol and Blinder suggesting that my mother should be given an annual check from her community representing the pleasures that neighbors and passersby receive when they see and smell her flowers? That would be silly, no doubt, but such an argument is virtually the same one used to support the idea that because society benefits from a crop of well-educated children, the government should subsidize education.

PUBLIC EDUCATION AND PRIVATE MARKETS

Often, economists argue that the private market systematically underestimates the social benefits of education. According to Gwartney and Stroup, "Education adds to students' productivity, preparing them to enjoy higher future earnings, [making them] better citizens, more competent voters. . . . [They] may even commit fewer crimes." The authors contend that therefore the "private market demand curves understate the total social benefits of education." Figure 12–1 illustrates the benefits of a government subsidy to education.

Two points need to be made in response to this case for government intervention: First, the authors fail to take into account the fact that externalities are not always good in high schools and colleges. Economics is just one example where the teaching of false concepts has left a whole generation of students with muddled thinking; students are taught by Keynesians, for example, that consumption is good and saving is bad. Many teachers in high schools and colleges ridicule traditional religious and cultural values, and encourage sexual promiscuity, disrespect toward authority and parents, and so forth. One could just as easily argue that a lot of modern schooling is socially harmful and wasteful, and thus should not be subsidized.

Second, a government subsidy does not appear from nowhere. To subsidize one field is to tax another. Thus, using government funds to raise the level of education beyond what individuals voluntarily desire can only mean that individuals are deprived of other activities they personally deem more important. These other activities may include nonschool education—such as on-the-job training, independent research, travel, and spending and investing—which in many ways may be far more beneficial than formal education. Furthermore, economists may not take into account the tremendous costs of creating a government agency to oversee the subsidization of education.

In sum, I see no justification for government subsidization of education on the grounds of beneficial externalities for the same reason I see no reason that the government should im-

FIGURE 12–1
Adding External Benefits

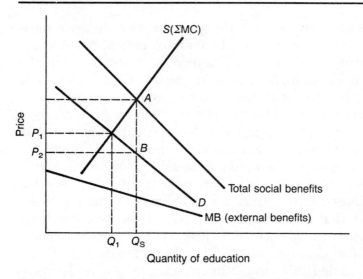

Quantity of education

The demand curve *D*, indicating only private benefits, understates the social benefits of education. At output Q_1, the social benefit of an additional unit of education exceeds the cost. Ideally output should be expanded to Q_s, where the social benefit of the marginal unit of education would be just equal to its cost. A public subsidy of *AB*, per unit of education, would lead to this output level.

Source: Exhibit 2 from *Economics: Private and Public Choice*, Fifth Edition, by James D. Gwartney and Harold L. Stroup, p. 720, copyright © 1990 by Harcourt Brace Jovanovich, Inc., reprinted by permission of the publisher.

pose uniform standards of dress and personal hygiene simply because they may affect the social welfare of others. We are a society of individuals who have common, and uncommon, values.

AIR AND WATER POLLUTION

Detrimental externalities such as air and water pollution are serious problems, and all of the top 10 textbooks include extensive material on such problems. Environmental economics is a popular course on campuses these days. Most economists place the blame for pollution and other negative externalities on the businesses that do the polluting. That seems appropriate until one recognizes that some form of government failure is almost always present in each case. The problem always involves a "common property" situation. No one owns the air, so businesses emit pollution into the air cost-free. Everyone (the community) owns the stream, lake, or ocean, and therefore businesses dump wastes into the water cost-free. Fish populations are depleted to the point of extinction because the body of water where the fish live is owned by the public. Endangered species reach the point of extinction because they are not owned by anyone. (Why were buffalo threatened with extinction but cattle were not?) Trees are chopped down by "rapacious capitalists" and never replenished because the trees exist in a national forest.

But the free market can solve many of these problems if the government would grant private ownership to these now-public entities. When large forests become the property of major tree companies, the forests are converted to tree farms when suddenly there is a major incentive to replace trees that have been cut down. The Nature Conservancy in Hawaii, an 8,500-member nonprofit organization, has protected more than 43,000 acres in Hawaii. Private ownership can conserve endangered species. Private fisheries have developed ways to maintain an optimum fish population in privately owned lakes and streams. Property rights have been established for oyster beds in the Chesapeake Bay. In short, when private ownership exists, the businessperson has a stake in the future and thus an incentive to replenish, repair, and renew what the business uses. Fortunately, some economists (such as Gwartney and Stroup) have pointed out how enforcing property rights can usually solve the public externality problem.

It is much more difficult to delineate the boundaries of private ownership in the case of air and water pollution. Bodies of water could be turned over to private companies with a strong public interest that in turn could prohibit water pollution by firms. But what if a lake is owned by the polluter?

The government solution to environmental problems is almost always long on costs and short on benefits. A crusading Congress seldom has an incentive to weigh the costs of a clean air bill or other environmental action. As Robert Crandall, a senior fellow at Washington's Brookings Institution, says, "When you're carrying out a crusade, you don't ask what's the cost of the religion."[1] For example, the Clean Air Act of 1977 required new power plants to install expensive scrubbers to reduce sulfur emissions. It cost the industry $3 billion, even though a much cheaper solution using low-sulfur coal would have achieved the same results. Why scrubbers? Because the United Mine Workers and high sulfur-coal producers successfully lobbied Congress.

One way to reduce pollution and force companies to develop technological methods of reducing emissions is by imposing fines or taxes. Charges on emissions and effluents provide a strong economic incentive to reduce or eliminate pollution. Instead of Congress imposing stiff pollution controls on automobile manufacturers, they could add fines to the retail price of each car, where the fine would increase for cars that pollute more. Or fines could vary depending on location—they would be higher in cities, lower in rural areas or states. Another solution is for local governments to sell marketable permits, which in effect would charge firms for the property right of pollution. These solutions have one major drawback, however; they transfer funds away from the private pollutor and to the government. Such funds should be used to develop ways to reduce or eliminate pollution; instead, they become general government revenues. But at least there is a tax incentive to reduce pollution.

The more profitable a company and the more prosperous a nation, the easier the pollution problem can be solved. In my travels around the world, I have noticed that the less wealthy a nation, the more pollution there is in its inner cities. I have witnessed widespread pollution and destruction of the environment in many Third World countries, Eastern Europe, the Soviet Union, and other nations under the control of socialist regimes. In short, in order for a firm to "do good" in fighting pollution and achieving other social goals, it must do very well monetarily. Therefore, a much better solution to stopping pollution would be to give a tax advantage to those who develop new production methods that will make the air or water cleaner.

PUBLIC GOODS AND THE FREE RIDER PROBLEM

Economists point to "public goods" and the "free rider problem" in discussing the theory of market failure. National defense is a logical example. Citizens who do not voluntarily pay for national defense will receive national defense whether they pay for it or not.

But does the existence of free riders mean that national defense can never be provided by private firms, such as large insurance companies? Certainly, there are many examples of nongovernment organizations that offer services and still allow free riders. Religious organizations, for example, offer church services and activities that are paid for by voluntary contributions. There are always a number of churchgoers who for one reason or another are unable or choose not to make a donation or pay a tithe. Yet they are not turned away, and the church continues to be supported by the majority of its members. Church leaders frequently encourage all members to contribute something, but they know they cannot compel them to do so.

Fire Protection in the Free Market

Fire protection is another example used by government advocates as a standard public good that must be paid for by taxes and provided by the government. If private companies provided fire protection, homeowners who failed to pay for the insurance would still be protected. If a fire broke out, the fire fighters would still come to rescue the uninsured homeowner in order to protect surrounding homes.

Nevertheless, a study of fire departments in the United States by Robert W. Poole, publisher of *Reason* magazine and author of the book *Cutting Back on City Hall,* indicates that the traditional tax-funded fire department operates in only a minority of American communities. The majority of communities have some form of private fire protection service, either through volunteer departments, private subscription services, or private contracting with government. The most famous privately run fire department is Rural/Metro Fire Department, Inc., an Arizona-based subscription service that also provides security and police service. It has achieved outstanding success in both efficiency and technological advancement. If a nonsubscriber's house catches fire, the company's policy is to protect life and property first, and ask questions later. The state of Arizona grants Rural/Metro the right to send nonsubscribers a bill for its services. Poole notes, by the way, that privately provided fire services generally cost less than publicly provided services.

Road Services

Another example of a public good is road services. In response to the question of whether a private firm could provide a road system for Los Angeles, covering its cost by collecting tolls, most economists would answer no. It would be too expensive. They would recommend a gasoline tax as a cheaper alternative.

Perhaps a good case can be made for public ownership of local roads in a community, but not freeways in Los Angeles. Perhaps economists should come out to witness firsthand what it's like driving on the Los Angeles freeways if they think a gasoline tax would solve the problem. I go to Los Angeles several times a year, and must endure the misfortune of driving there. Every time I think I'd like to move to southern California, I get on the freeway and quickly remind myself why I would never move there. Despite five- and six-lane highways, traffic is often stuck by 3 P.M. It is stop-and-go (mostly stop) during morning and afternoon rush hours. Long ago, the highway department established stoplights at the entrances to the freeways to control traffic flow. I seriously doubt that under the present circumstances tollbooths would delay traffic anymore than it is already delayed under government control. However, by charging higher prices during peak hours or providing higher-priced special speed lanes, private tollbooths could sharply reduce traffic in Los Angeles.

The Strange Case of the Lighthouse

For years, economists have used the lighthouse as a classic example of a public good. Samuelson argues that lighthouses must be owned and operated by the government because "lighthouse keepers cannot reach out and collect fees from ships." McConnell says, "There is no economic incentive for private enterprises to supply lighthouses," because they cannot collect the fees to pay for their operation. "In short," concludes McConnell, "here is a service which yields substantial benefits but for which the market would allocate no resources."

Regrettably, Samuelson and McConnell choose an improper illustration to make their case. The case of the lighthouse is a classic example of how economists often make assertions without checking the facts or doing any comprehensive research. If they had done some research, they would know that lighthouses were originally built and operated for a profit by private enterprises! According to the economist Ronald H. Coase, who conducted a major study of the lighthouse industry in Britain, shipowners and shippers would petition the Crown to construct a lighthouse and to levy specified tolls on ships benefiting from its services. "The lighthouses were built, operated, financed and owned by private individuals, who could sell the lighthouse or dispose of it by bequest."[2] Later, lighthouses in England and Wales were turned over to the quasi-public Trinity House, a private organization with public duties, to continue the service. The lighthouse companies were able to charge for their services through tie-in agreements with the port authorities. Ships were charged fees for docking at the port and for other services, which included the use of the lighthouse. Ships that did not dock may have used the lighthouse's services without paying (the free rider problem), but their number was not sufficient to keep the lighthouse from earning a profit. In any case, it is significant that the system apparently favored by Samuelson and McConnell, that of financing lighthouses out of general taxation, has never been tried in Britain.

THE ROLE OF BUSINESS IN PROVIDING PUBLIC SERVICES

One major omission committed by textbook writers is mention of the growth in social services provided by large private companies. As a nation becomes more prosperous, expanding businesses are able to take on many needs normally met by the state. Fringe benefits are no longer so much on the fringe; they can represent a large percentage of an employee's income. Medical insurance, life and disability insurance, paid vacations, recreational facilities, and educational expenses are just some of the benefits provided by individual firms to supplement and even replace government programs.

Moreover, public goods such as roads, security, and fire protection are being offered by major corporations in resorts, theme parks, shopping centers, housing developments, and condominiums. This is an area that needs to be explored and encouraged by economists.

PRIVATIZATION

One of the major disappointments in today's textbooks is the lack of any discussion of the new trend toward the privatization of government services. Of the top 10 textbooks, only a couple spend any time at all discussing this vital subject. Dolan begins his discussion of the role of government by citing the case of a county jail run by a private company, Corrections Corp. of America, in Panama City, Florida. Unfortunately, no other textbook is as enlightening.

Perhaps one justification for this grave omission is that most of the writers are from the United States, which has far fewer socialized industries than Britain, France, and other countries. Still, there are numerous examples of government programs that could be privatized in the United States. Randall Fitzgerald, in his comprehensive work *When Government Goes Private,* lists a wide variety of government services that could be turned over to private enterprise, which would result in lower costs and greater efficiency. They include the postal service, the court system, public education, mass transit, bridges, the water supply, surplus federal lands, airports, the national weather bureau, railroads, the interstate highway system, and the Tennessee Valley Authority.

No top 10 textbook includes any treatment of privatization in Great Britain under Prime Minister Margaret Thatcher, surely the most exciting new trend in the British economy since World War II. Even critics are now starting to admit that Britain's recovery is in part due to the bold new efforts by Thatcher to denationalize state industries that deal with such things as aerospace technology, automobiles, telecommunications, radio, chemicals, oil, ferries, and hotels. (One wonders, with all the difficulties facing the government in regard to its basic duties, why the state would get involved in running so many businesses in the first place—no doubt much of it was politically motivated.) Since the advent of privatization, the profitability of such companies has soared, costs have been cut, service has improved, and for the first time in their lives citizens of all income levels own stock in major British companies.

Perhaps one reason that mainstream economists are reluctant to discuss the increasing popularity and success of privatization is that it replaces the theory of market failure with that of government failure. Suddenly, the success of privatization threatens the large and ubiquitous role of the government as advocated in most textbooks, in which the authors have traditionally emphasized market failure as justifying the need for strong government policy. But privatization implies that the government can be reduced substantially in size without hurting the economy. Economic growth could explode as public services are denationalized and transferred to the private sector. Imagine government spending declining and the private economy expanding—this is just the opposite of what Keynesian-oriented textbooks have taught for the past 40 years. The neo-Keynesians have usually favored the free market on a microeconomic scale but have opposed market solutions on a macroeconomic level. They are averse to reducing the size of government because they view a large state as essential for macroeconomic stability.

An appropriate way to discuss privatization would be in relation to John Kenneth Galbraith's thesis that private consumption is well-fed while the public sector remains starved. Most of the top 10 textbook writers discuss Galbraith's thesis, which is elucidated in his bestseller, *The Affluent Society*.[3] With great enthusiasm and poetic prose, Galbraith accurately describes the disparity between the public and private sector but then blunders in his solution to the problem by suggesting that the public sector is underfinanced, which implies that the government needs to increase taxes even more. The source of public indigence lies in the fundamental flaw of government programs—their lack of competition and incentives. The solution is not to transfer more private wealth to the public sector but to return as much as possible of the public sector to the private sector.

NOTES

1. Quoted in "Market-Driven Environmentalism: Can We Have a Cleaner Environment and Pampers Too?" *Forbes*, March 5, 1990, p. 96. This cover story, written by Gretchen Morgensen and Gale Eisenstodt, offers free-market alternatives for solid waste, emissions, acid rain, and many other environmental problems.
2. Ronald H. Coase, "The Lighthouse in Economics," *Journal of Law and Economics* 17 (October 1974), pp. 357–76.
3. John Kenneth Galbraith, *The Affluent Society* (Boston, Mass.: Houghton Mifflin, 1958).

RECOMMENDED READING

Cowen, Tyler, ed. *The Theory of Market Failure: A Critical Examination*. Fairfax, Va.: George Mason University Press, 1988. An excellent compilation of articles by Paul Samuelson, Harold Demsetz, James Buchanan, Ronald H. Coase, and Robert W. Poole, Jr., among others.

Fitzgerald, Randall. *When Government Goes Private: Successful Alternatives to Public Services.* New York: Universe Books, 1988. A comprehensive blueprint for increasing efficiency and reducing costs in government through privatization.

CHAPTER 13

THE GROWING TAX BURDEN

Many doctors, artists, celebrities, and business executives, who enjoy their jobs and the sense of power or accomplishment that they bring, will work as hard for $150,000 as for $200,000.
    —Paul A. Samuelson and William D. Nordhaus
    Economics (1988)

When I took my first economics course in college, the instructor repeated this question posed by Samuelson in his textbook: "Do high tax rates discourage work, saving, and risk taking?" The instructor, echoing Samuelson, suggested that an executive would not necessarily be deterred by high graduated income taxes because while some people may work less, other people may work harder in order to make their millions. His argument was that progressive income taxes—no matter how high—would not necessarily retard productivity as long as the executive's after-tax income rose with each additional pay raise. Suppose, for instance, that a business executive earns $150,000 a year and is in the 90 percent tax bracket. (Tax rates went that high in the late 1960s.) He is offered a new position for $200,000 a year. He will take the job, concluded the instructor, even though 90 percent of his raise goes to the government, because his take-home pay would still increase by $5,000.

I tell this story because it is a classic example of the distorted ivory-tower thinking of university economists. At the time, none of the students had any practical knowledge to counter the instructor's argument. None of us had yet been in a real-life situation as a business executive and taxpayer making $200,000 a year. To us, $5,000 seemed like quite a work incentive.

But now, after spending two decades as a businessman, investor, and taxpayer, I can state without equivocation that

Samuelson and fellow defenders of high tax rates do not know what they are talking about. The tax burden is much heavier than most professors realize, and high marginal tax rates do indeed seriously distort economic decisions and incentives.

THREE IMPORTANT LESSONS

Taxes and Productivity

I learned three important lessons as a taxpayer in the business world. First, high marginal tax rates were a major deterrent to productive effort. Let's use an artist as an example. Suppose she is a successful artist and has done so well in the past year that she has reached the 90 percent tax bracket. In November, a potential customer offers her $20,000 to paint a portrait. Even though it may be the normal rate she charges for a portrait, I can assure you that she won't be willing to do it for that price (except perhaps as a personal favor, or unless the customer is someone she especially wants to paint). Why? Because the customer is really asking her to do it for only $2,000, not $20,000. She knows that 90 percent of the revenue from the project will go to the tax authorities and that she will keep only $2,000. She is not going to spend the time and effort for such a small amount. Unless the client offers her more—a lot more—she will turn him down.

I have seen this happen over and over again in the business world. Intelligent entrepreneurs, including writers, doctors, and small-business owners, simply will not waste their talents at below-market prices. They will take more time off, work on alternative projects, or engage in methods of avoiding the tax. In short, high marginal tax rates reduce productivity. Some professionals may continue working because of nonmonetary rewards, but most people won't.

High Taxes Make It Hard to Act Rationally

The second lesson I learned is that when marginal tax rates are extremely high, many businesspeople will do practically anything to get out of paying them. They have a hard time thinking rationally when it comes to high taxes, especially if they are antipathetic to the federal government. At the end of the year, they will invest thousands of dollars in the craziest tax shelter schemes imaginable without any due diligence in order to reduce their tax liability.

High-income taxpayers do not think in terms of keeping 10 percent if they are in the 90 percent tax bracket, or even 50 percent if they are in the 50 percent bracket. "Even at 30 percent, the state is taking too much," the company president may say. Why? Because the tax bill often turns out to be the highest bill of any accounts payable. High-income taxpayers think in terms of absolute costs, as any businessperson would. Millionaire businesspeople will often argue with suppliers over a $3,000 invoice. They are trained to save money wherever they can, and they will do so to reduce their bill to the IRS. At the end of the year, the company president will review the fiscal year and determine his current tax liability. Say it is $50,000. It does not matter so much that he is keeping $150,000 in retained earnings or personal savings. The idea of writing a check to the government for $50,000 is abhorrent. Anything he can do to avoid it will be worth it, he thinks. Some would say this is simply greed at work; others see it as a standard business attitude.

I have consulted with wealthy people who were determined as ever not to send too much to the nation's capital. One man sold a piece of real estate for a long-term capital gain of $5 million at a time when the capital gains tax rate was a low 20 percent. Nevertheless, he was expected to write a check to the IRS for $1 million dollars, and he was determined not to do it. "But you get to keep $4 million!" I exclaimed. It did not matter. He wanted to know how he could shelter his capital gain from the IRS to avoid the tax.

In another case, I consulted with a woman who had silver in a Swiss bank account. She wanted to sell the silver and bring back the money (about $20,000) without reporting it to the IRS. I tried to talk her out of it.

I asked, "How much of the $20,000 is a profit?"

She answered, "About half."

"Did you hold the silver for more than a year?"

"Yes," she replied.

"Good," I told her. "Then you're in luck. It's a long-term capital gain. You only have to pay a maximum tax of $2,000."

She was still reluctant. "I don't know; $2,000 is a lot of money."

"Yes," I assured her, "but you get to keep $18,000."

I'm not sure I convinced her to pay the tax, but the point is that many people have a hard time thinking rationally when it comes to taxes. That is why tax shelters and tax-deferral methods, such as taking early deductions and postponing income, have been so popular. That is also why some taxpayers create phony deductions, fail to declare all of their income, create secret foreign trusts or bearer corporations, or open up Swiss bank accounts. The underground economy has grown tremendously under a high tax system.

My first-year teacher in economics said that studies by economists had found no visible evidence that high tax rates had discouraged people from working, saving, or taking risks in a business. The reason, I discovered, is this: the high tax brackets were deceptive. The tax code in the late 1960s was so full of loopholes that I don't know anyone who paid those rates. Yes, people were in the 90 percent tax bracket, but they arranged their affairs through various financial structures and shelters so as to avoid paying much in absolute terms. In the late 1970s, when the highest tax bracket was 70 percent, and again in the early 1980s, when the highest federal bracket was 50 percent, I invested in a wide variety of limited partnerships that offered substantial write-offs. My work habits were not restricted to any large extent because of the loopholes in the law that allowed me to avoid paying 70 percent or 50 percent of my income to the government. Had the loopholes been eliminated, my work ethic would definitely have been affected in a negative way.

Taxes and Loopholes

Finally, I learned a third lesson. A tax system that combines a graduated income tax with lots of loopholes is an inefficient, wasteful, and unproductive system. As an investment advisor who lived through the 1970s and 1980s, I witnessed billions of dollars poured down the tax-shelter rathole (some of which was my own money) in projects that turned out to be extremely unprofitable. In talking to numerous clients around the country, I have discovered that only a handful of them ever made any money on those limited partnerships. With high taxes, there was little incentive to do real research on the legitimacy of a project, and there was also little incentive for tax-shelter brokers to provide sound economic projects. It was all a game to beat the IRS. A lot of money was exchanged, but little economic progress resulted.

My conclusion is that the higher the tax bracket, the more unproductive the economic system. No doubt the economy is better off with the loopholes than without them, given the high tax rates, but a better solution in terms of social efficiency (what economists call "welfare economics") would be to reduce taxes to as low a rate as possible. Although Samuelson, McConnell, and Baumol and Blinder are afraid to admit it, the lower tax rates instituted during the Reagan administration have been a boon to the U.S. economy.

Optimum economic output is the real economic issue surrounding tax rates, not how much revenue the Treasury can maximize, as the Laffer curve suggests. The Laffer curve, shown in Figure 13-1, suggests a tax rate at which the Treasury can obtain the most revenue, implying that this is the ideal goal. While there is no question that there is a point at which tax rates reach such a high level that federal revenue starts to drop, revenue enhancement through lower taxation should be secondary to the *profit* enhancement that lower taxation can create.

The Laffer curve is not an ideal measurement of market efficiency and social welfare; rather, it is a measurement of government tax capability. But surely economic efficiency and social welfare should be the true report card of public policy, not the maximizing of government revenues. My point is that any increase in tax rates is a move toward market inefficiency and that any decrease in tax rates is beneficial to the overall economy because it better optimizes people's voluntary spend-

FIGURE 13–1
The Laffer Curve

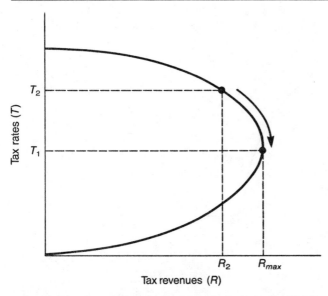

Tax rates (*T*)

T_2

T_1

R_2 R_{max}

Tax revenues (*R*)

Source: From *Economics Today*, 6th Edition by Roger Leroy Miller. Copyright © 1988 by Harper & Row, Publishers, Inc. Reprinted by permission of the publisher.

ing decisions. The diagram I have created in Figure 13–2 is a production-possibility frontier showing maximum economic output at various levels of taxation, in which the highest level of output is at 0 percent tax and the lowest level is at 100 percent tax.

THE PRODUCTION-POSSIBILITY FRONTIER AND INCREASING TAX RATES

There are several points to be made about this production-possibility frontier (p-p frontier). First, the curve is concave. This reflects the belief that a low tax rate on income initially does not restrain economic performance by much. But as tax

FIGURE 13–2

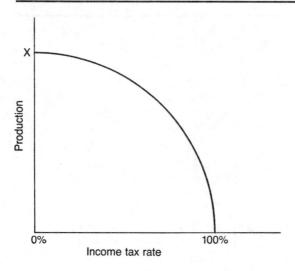

rates reach extremely high levels, say 50 percent or more, economic performance is greatly retarded and will decline much more rapidly until it completely stops at the 100 percent tax rate. In a sense, one may be able to derive a Laffer curve from my p-p curve. At the lowest tax levels, an increase in taxes can occur without hurting productivity very much. In other words, government revenues are probably increasing during this phase. But at the higher tax levels, a further increase in taxes is unlikely to generate more revenue because economic performance is damaged too severely.

Second, note that this curve does not suggest that the government should not exist. While it is true that the curve indicates that optimal national output is achieved at a 0 percent income tax rate, it does not mean that the government is eliminated. It simply means that income taxes are an inefficient way to raise revenues for government operations. There are other methods that could be employed, such as user fees, sales taxes, head taxes, and voluntary contributions.

THE FLAW IN GOVERNMENT FINANCE THEORY

The taxing of income suffers from one serious weakness that makes it inherently inefficient as a means of raising federal revenues: It breaks the vital link between benefits and users. The market process optimizes economic efficiency and output because customers who benefit from a specific good or service are the ones who pay for it. In a competitive marketplace, they are likely to pay a fair price (excluding fraud). But the income tax severs the relationship between benefit and payment. One citizen may send $20,000 to Washington and receive very little in return. Meanwhile, another citizen may pay no taxes yet receive thousands of dollars in welfare, food stamps, or health care. In general, citizens who receive the benefits should pay for them, and citizens who do not receive any benefits should not have to pay unless they choose voluntarily to do so. This market approach encourages the producer to respond to the demands of the customers and to maintain quality at a reasonable price.

Another principle to bear in mind regarding public finance is that the greater the distance between benefit and payment, the less efficient the use of the funds. Hence, local taxation is typically the least inefficient form of taxation, whereas federal taxation is the most inefficient.

THE FALLACY OF THE ABILITY TO PAY

The income tax also violates another valuable market principle. Income taxes are based on the principle that people should be taxed according to their ability to pay. The term *ability to pay* does not necessarily mean a progressive tax structure, in which the marginal tax rate continues to rise. All it means is that individuals who have higher incomes should be able to pay a greater amount in taxes.[1]

The market works entirely differently, however. It is based on the sound principle that you pay for what you receive. If you pay $1 for bread, you get one loaf. If you pay $5, you get five loaves. Under an income tax scheme, you pay according to your financial ability, not according to what you receive.

To demonstrate how devastating the ability-to-pay approach can be in the marketplace, let us consider a hypothetical case. Suppose there is a benevolent king who decrees that from now on goods and services sold in the kingdom will be priced according to the citizens' ability to pay. Each price will be labeled as a percentage of income. For example, an automobile would cost 200 percent of annual income, a television would be priced at 10 percent of income, a turkey would cost 1 percent of annual income, and so forth. What would be the outcome of this benevolent decree? I have frequently presented this question to students, some of whom seem to like the idea a lot, particularly since 200 percent of their student incomes would buy them a nice cheap car. But then they realize the obvious ill effects of such a policy.

First, there would be a tendency to lie about one's income in order to pay a lower price. To deter lying, the king might have to supply income figures from last year's tax returns to the department stores, car dealers, and supermarkets. Second, citizens of the kingdom would stop earning more money. Obviously, there is no longer an incentive to earn more, because prices would simply increase by the same percentage as income. In real terms, the taxpayer makes no gain for working overtime. Third, citizens would finally realize that there is no point in working at all. They could buy a car for nothing because 200 percent of zero is still zero. The stores would be cleaned out, and the whole economy would quickly collapse under the king's benevolent act.

Income taxes only work because the ability-to-pay principle applies to just one creditor—the government. In the marketplace, economists call the ability of sellers to extract a price based on income "price discrimination." For instance, through a more heavy-handed negotiation, a car dealer may be able to get a well-to-do individual to pay a higher price for an automobile than a poor individual would pay. Various forms of price discrimination occur in the economy. Senior citizens get discounts for movies, restaurant meals, and park entrance fees. But for the most part price discrimination does not occur often enough to destroy monetary incentives. Rich people may pay more, but not so much more that they have no incentive to achieve a high income.

APPLYING THE BENEFIT PRINCIPLE

Certainly the ability-to-pay principle is not the fairest basis for taxation. The fairest tax is the user fee, or charge for a government service, because it links the benefit to the payer. Examples include electric and water utilities; garbage collection; bus fares; entry fees into museums, zoos, and parks; tolls on turnpikes; and gasoline taxes. Gasoline taxes are specifically earmarked for maintenance and construction of roads. Those who use the roads pay for them, and those who use the roads more pay more.

The benefit principle could also be applied to public education. Currently, public schools are paid for by local property taxes, which violates the basic principle of linking benefits to users. Homeowners who have no children are required to finance homeowners who do. Homeowners who send their children to a private school have to pay double for their children's education. The worst drawback to this current method of financing public education is that teachers and administrators are paid by the local or state government, not directly by the parents of the students. If the parents paid for the education of their children directly and had the ability to switch schools as they do in the private-school market, the public school system would become much more efficient, cost-effective, and responsive to parents. (Competition is another essential doctrine in the marketplace.) The quality of the public schools would definitely improve. The proposed use of student vouchers to achieve this optimality is definitely a move in the right direction.

ALTERNATIVES TO THE INCOME TAX

Most user fees are established at the local level. How could the benefit principle of taxation be used on the national scale to pay for welfare, social security, veterans' benefits, and national defense? Obviously, it could not be done under the present circumstances. Many government programs, such as welfare and veterans' benefits, are specifically designed so that beneficiaries are not required to pay for the benefits they receive. Perhaps they should, but that is a different question. Certainly, there is no reason why the benefit principle could not be applied to the interstate highway system, however.

Several alternatives to the income tax have been proposed. Some favor the European-style value-added tax (VAT). According to Byrns and Stone, the VAT is probably "more efficient and less inequitable than corporate income taxes, Social Security taxes, or a number of other levies in the government's tool box." But there are two major drawbacks to the VAT: its high bureaucratic cost and its invisibility. Citizens need to see exactly what they are paying to the state so that they will be aware of and resistant to any increase in rates.

A national sales tax would be vastly superior to a VAT. It would be levied only at the final stage of production rather than at all stages, thus lowering the administrative costs significantly. A national sales tax would be a visible tax, noticed every time someone bought an item. It would be difficult to evade yet easy to avoid—simply save instead of spend. It would offer what the textbook economists call "horizontal" and "vertical" equity, meaning that equal taxpayers are treated equally and higher-income taxpayers pay higher taxes since they tend to spend more. A national sales tax would be comparable to a flat tax. If it replaced the income tax (as it must), it would eliminate almost the entire federal tax code as well as the need to file individual tax returns. The flood of paperwork related to tax reporting and filing would end, saving individuals, many businesses, and the government billions of dollars. The national sales tax would terminate the power granted the federal tax agency to audit and invade citizens' financial lives, and thus it would eliminate a serious abuse of personal liberties.

Along with this, the new tax would sharply reduce and, in some cases, eliminate the need for accountants, tax lawyers, and income tax preparers. This in itself would greatly increase the productivity of the nation. The national sales tax would not eliminate the IRS entirely—it would still need to enforce the sales tax rules on individual retail firms and discourage barter and other forms of evasion. But the IRS would no longer audit personal returns. Given the current size of government, studies estimate that the rate of the national sales tax would reach 12 to 15 percent if it took the place of personal and corporate income taxes.

The only major criticism of the national sales tax is that it is a regressive tax, meaning that high-income individuals would tend to pay a lower rate as a percentage of income because they would tend to save more. The national sales tax would not be imposed on savings or investment. But after 50 years of overtaxing savings and investment and subsidizing consumption, isn't it time we reversed this Keynesian trend and encouraged capital formation and productivity? Moreover, perhaps a consumption tax would encourage low-income earners to begin saving a little, the only true path to financial independence.

Although I am not suggesting that a national sales tax would be an ideal tax—there is no such thing as an ideal, neutral, or fair tax—it certainly would be an improvement over the current hodgepodge of taxing methods.

COMPARING TAX RATES AMONG COUNTRIES

To get the right perspective on taxes, it is worthwhile to compare how various countries tax their citizens. There is a surprising variety of tax methods among nations. Needless to say, the top 10 textbooks do not do enough comparison, and the comparison that they do can often be misleading.

Samuelson's chart, shown in Table 13–1, indicates that of the eight major countries listed, Japan has the highest marginal tax rate, whereas the United States has the lowest rate

TABLE 13–1
Top Tax Rates in Major Countries

Country	Top Marginal Tax Rate*
Japan	75%
France	65
Britain	60
Germany	56
Sweden	44
Denmark	40
Canada	34
United States	28

*The additional amount of taxes per dollar of additional taxable income by taxpayers with the highest incomes.

Source: Paul A. Samuelson and William D. Nordhaus, *Economics,* 13th ed. (New York: McGraw-Hill, 1989), p. 790.

and the broadest base. Baumol and Blinder report that, by international standards, Americans are "among the most lightly taxed people in the industrialized world." By implication, the authors believe that the tax burden need not be reduced. Figure 13–3 illustrates the tax burden among selected countries.

Unfortunately, these economists draw the wrong conclusions from such charts. It is important to disaggregate the tax structure in each country and not to rely on a simple look at marginal tax rates or the total tax revenue divided by national income. A different tax structure can greatly alter economic performance. For example, many countries have a high income tax rate but have a wide variety of loopholes and exemptions.

In addition, many do not have any capital gains tax. Table 13–2 indicates the wide variety in capital gains tax rates.

According to Table 13–2, the United States has the highest rate of taxation on capital gains of any major country. Moreover, if you look at McConnell's chart of economic growth (reproduced in Chapter 5), you'll note that the countries with the highest growth rates (e.g., Japan, Netherlands, Italy, West Germany) exempt all or most capital gains from taxation, whereas the countries with the lowest rates of economic growth (e.g.,

FIGURE 13–3
The Burden of Taxation in Selected Countries, 1984

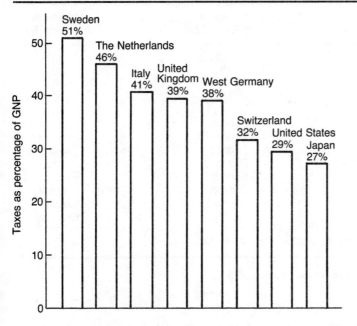

Source: William J. Baumol and Alan S. Blinder, *Economics: Principles and Policy,* 4th ed. (New York: Harcourt Brace Jovanovich, 1988, p. 717.

the United States, Great Britain, Canada) have the highest capital gains tax rates. This kind of comparison is extremely relevant when the United States debates whether to raise or lower the capital gains tax. If the United States, Canada, and Great Britain want to equal the economic performance of countries in the Far East, one method they should consider is to reduce their capital gains rate sharply.

JAPAN AND THE PACIFIC BASIN

Samuelson notes that Japan has the highest marginal tax rate of any advanced country. But wealthy Japanese, because of various loopholes and exemptions, don't pay 75 percent of their earnings to the government. Japan's overall tax level is ac-

TABLE 13–2
Capital Gains Tax Rates

Selected Countries	Maximum Long-Term Rate	Maximum Short-Term Rate
United States	33%	33%
United Kingdom	30	30
Sweden	18	45
France	16	16
West Germany	Exempt	56
Belgium	Exempt	Exempt
Italy	Exempt	Exempt
Japan	Exempt	Exempt
Netherlands	Exempt	Exempt
Hong Kong	Exempt	Exempt
Singapore	Exempt	Exempt
South Korea	Exempt	Exempt
Taiwan	Exempt	Exempt

Note: Japan recently imposed a small capital gains tax.

Source: *The Wall Street Journal,* March 8, 1988.

tually small (27 percent of GNP). Furthermore, Japan, like other Pacific Basin countries, taxes investments and capital at very low rates. Until recently, there was virtually no tax on savings accounts or capital gains in Japan. Is it any wonder that the average Japanese citizen has $70,000 in a postal savings account? This huge savings rate, the highest of any industrialized country, has provided the capital base for Japan's explosive growth in the past 40 years and is one of the main reasons behind the explosive rise in the Tokyo stock market in the 1980s.

ARE TAXES TOO HIGH?

The standard writers in economics never address the all-important question "Are taxes too high?" Perhaps one reason is their Keynesian bias—the belief that the government needs to be large in order to have a stabilizing influence over the economy. But Figure 13–4, from Samuelson, indicates the incredible growth of government during the 20th century.

The discussion of the Laffer curve surrounds the issue of optimizing government revenues and the question of whether tax cuts will increase or reduce revenues. Several writers suggest that the Reagan tax cuts were responsible for the large federal deficit, but there are definitely factors at work besides tax cuts that brought about the mammoth $200 billion deficit. The 1981–82 recession sharply reduced revenues more than any tax cut did. (In fact, only marginal tax rates were reduced during this period; average rates went up.) The reduction in the marginal tax rates did not really take full effect until the late 1980s. The real problem causing the deficit is a spendthrift Congress.

Critics of supply-side economics argue that taxes need to be raised to reduce the deficit, a popular myth. The fact is that tax increases do not reduce the deficit; they simply allow the government to spend more. Economists who have spent time in the nation's capital know that this is the case. The first issue

FIGURE 13–4
Government Spending and Taxes, 1900–1988

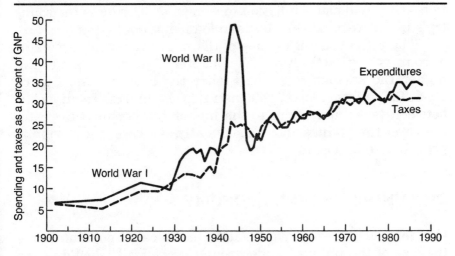

Source: Paul A. Samuelson and William D. Nordhaus, *Economics*, 13th ed. (New York: McGraw-Hill, 1989), p. 757.

in the congressional budget process is determining how much revenue the Treasury will receive in the fiscal year. After estimating revenue, members of Congress determine how much they can spend. There is a built-in deficit limit that Congress seeks. This was evident recently when *The Wall Street Journal* reported, "A budget plan for the fiscal year [which] projects a deficit of between $170 billion and $179 billion and calls for a $12 billion tax boost was approved by the Senate and House budget negotiators. The agreement calls for $14 billion more in domestic spending than the president originally requested." The message is clear. Without a lawful restraint on Congress (most states require a balanced budget by law), the representatives of the people will continue to spend as much as they can get away with. In reality, a reduction, not an increase, in revenues should be the goal of the tax cuts. Such a reduction would put more pressure on Congress to reduce spending, the real culprit. A tax increase would do just the opposite, encouraging members of Congress to spend their newfound gains in at least seven different ways.

Keynesians usually support tax increases as a way of reducing inflationary pressure. For example, during the Vietnam War boom in the mid-1960s, they favored a surtax. But higher taxes will in fact have the opposite effect to reducing inflation—they will cause inflation to worsen as it reduces the country's incentives and thus leads to lower national output.

The rate of savings is one of the most important factors in a country's growth rate. As Chapter 5 demonstrated, the higher the savings rate, the higher the growth rate. Figure 13–5, taken from Dolan, demonstrates the inverse relationship between taxes and savings—the higher the personal tax rate, the lower the savings and, consequently, the lower the economic growth rate in a country.

THE UNDERGROUND ECONOMY

One measure of excessive taxation and bloated government is the size of the untaxed underground economy. It should be estimated regularly to determine to what extent taxes are too

FIGURE 13–5
Inverse Relationship between Taxes and Savings

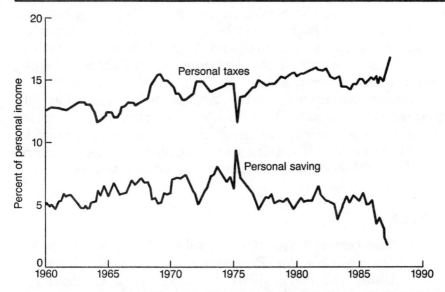

Source: Perspective 11.1 from *Economics,* Fifth Edition, by Edwin G. Dolan and David E. Lindsey, copyright © 1988 by The Dryden Press, a division of Holt, Rinehart and Winston, Inc., reproduced by permission of the publisher.

high in industrial nations. One of the major mistakes of the U.S. government in the 1980s was to sharply increase compliance in the tax code by increasing the penalties and the number of federal agents employed to catch tax evaders. The tremendous growth in the underground economy, reported by a wide variety of studies, should have sent a signal to the nation's capital that the tax burden is too heavy and that taxes should be reduced sharply, not just for the wealthy but for all citizens. Increasing compliance is not the answer—it is a symptom of the problem. In fact, contrary to public opinion, forcing tax evaders to pay their fair share will do nothing to eliminate the deficit; it will simply allow Congress to spend more. More important, it will also give more power to the IRS to terrorize honest citizens. As economist Dan Bawly, who did an extensive study of the underground economy in the early 1980s, states, "If the IRS were to make every effort to collect every cent due to it, America would be much closer to being a police state."[2] After surveying the tax nightmare in major countries around the world, Bawly makes three conclusions: (1) Taxes are too high everywhere, in virtually every nation; (2) tax law is too complicated; and (3) governments everywhere waste huge amounts of their citizens' wealth on boondoggles and unethical activities.

Bawly recommends in the preface to his book that "the free society substantially reduce and simplify taxation rates, as well as cut government involvement in national economies by half or more."[3] If nations do not reduce the size of government, the subterranean economy will continue to grow.

NOTES

1. The best critique of the graduated income tax is *The Uneasy Case for Progressive Taxation,* by Walter J. Blum and Harry Kalven, Jr. (Chicago University of Chicago Press, 1953).
2. Dan Bawly, *The Subterranean Economy* (New York: McGraw-Hill, 1982), p. 135.
3. Bawley, *Subterranean,* p. xii.

RECOMMENDED READING

Lee, Dwight R., ed. *Taxation and the Deficit Economy.* San Francisco: Pacific Research Institute, 1986. This is the best collection of essays I've seen on the ill effects of taxes on capital formation and economic growth. Contributors include Paul Craig Roberts, James Buchanan, Israel Kirzner, and Michael J. Boskin.

CHAPTER 14

THE NATIONAL DEBT

It is difficult to conceive of governmental bankruptcy when government has the power to create new money by running the printing presses!
—Campbell R. McConnell and Stanley L. Brue
Economics (1990)

How serious is deficit financing and the resulting national debt? The top 10 textbooks offer a number of reasons why most economists do not regard the national debt as a serious threat to the economy. In fact, many consider it a blessing. The reasons include the following:

1. The national debt and annual deficits are not as bad as people think they are.
2. Deficit financing is essential during a recession or war.
3. The national debt is not a serious problem because "we owe it to ourselves."
4. Deficit spending may actually stimulate private savings and capital formation.
5. The federal government can never go bankrupt as long as it has the power to tax and print money.

Let's consider each one of these arguments.

THE NATIONAL DEBT AS A NONPROBLEM

Several textbooks show charts and cite studies indicating that the federal deficit and national debt are not a problem. They suggest that in absolute terms the debt level is monstrous, but as a percentage of GNP the debt level is not serious. Figure 14–1 is used by Lipsey and Steiner to illustrate the relative importance of the national debt.

FIGURE 14–1
The Relative Importance of the National Debt

(A) National debt as proportion of GNP

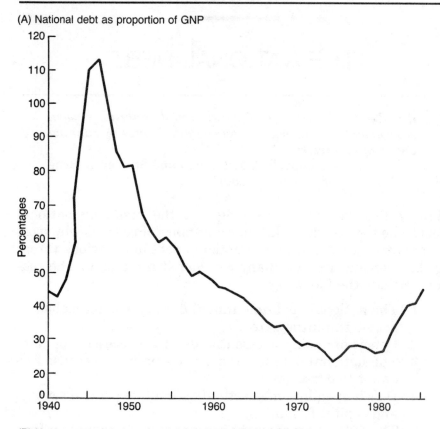

(B) Net interest paid on national debt as proportion of GNP

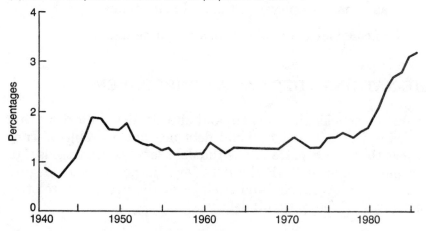

THE CASE FOR A LARGE FEDERAL DEBT

According to several surveys, the majority of economists oppose balanced budgets because balancing the budget or running a surplus would supposedly make matters worse during a
recession or depression. According to Byrns and Stone, the conventional wisdom is, "Annually balancing the budget could
prove disastrous during recessionary periods."

The traditional Keynesian solution to a recession is to cut
taxes and increase federal spending or, in other words, to deliberately run a deficit. This time the Keynesians are half right—
they believe in cutting taxes. However, the other half of the
prescription, increasing federal spending, may well make matters worse. We noted in Chapter 9 that the cause of a recession
is an imbalance between consumption and investment. Previous inflation by the government creates an artificial boom,
particularly in the capital-goods industries. A recession is
characterized by a collapse in the capital-goods industries. Deficit financing does not revitalize the investment sector when
new federal funds are spent on social programs, which stimulate consumption more than investment, creating an even
greater imbalance. Even attempts by the federal government
to stimulate investment by building roads, dams, monuments,
and buildings may offset private investment in other areas.
Businesses may switch from high-risk projects in the private
sector to more secure projects in the government sector. Economists must not ignore the unseen harm that deficit financing
may cause.

Monetarists and Deficit Spending

My defense of balanced budgets may seem antediluvian compared to the Keynesian orthodoxy, but monetarists who regard
fiscal policy as relatively impotent should exhibit some sympa-
thy. According to the monetarists, the government could cut
spending sharply during a recession and the economy could
still recover if the central bank adopts an expansionary
monetary policy. To them, deficit financing is, therefore, a non
sequitur. However, Milton Friedman has recently argued that

the large deficit during the Reagan administration produced the beneficial side effect of keeping federal spending at a less expansionary level than it might otherwise have been. On the other hand, if Washington had run large surpluses during the 1980s, wouldn't running in the black have put greater pressure on Congress to reduce taxes further?

SKYROCKETING NATIONAL DEBT

Nevertheless, government policy in most Western nations remains highly Keynesian. During the Reagan era, for example, marginal tax rates were cut during the 1981–82 recession, while total federal spending continued to grow at a high rate. The national debt is now around $3 trillion, and the interest on that debt is now the largest item in the federal budget.

Is this a burden? The majority of top 10 textbook writers don't think so. Many condone deficit financing, even to the point of arguing that the national debt helps the economy and capital formation, and stimulates private savings. The idea that a huge deficit promotes private savings is a classic example of muddled ivory-tower thinking. Surely the man on the street isn't that dumb. After having witnessed the effects of a ballooning national debt over the past 50 years, he knows that the debt is never paid off but simply refinanced with more debt. Furthermore, there is another effect far more deleterious to private savings, namely, depreciation of the currency. High deficit spending forces the central banks to monetize the debt through currency depreciation. The resulting price inflation destroys the advantages of saving and encourages consumption. Moreover, whoever heard of someone consciously saving money in order to pay debts incurred by someone else? Somehow the academic economist has missed this practical response to government financing.

The views of Robert Eisner, former president of the American Economic Association, have been well-publicized among economists. He contends that the national debt is not real because (1) much of the debt goes toward capital investments (roads, buildings, etc.) that have substantial long-term value, and (2) the debt should be adjusted for inflation. These arguments are answered elsewhere but, in short, the capital investments selected by government are often malinvestments or investments that could have been done less expensively by private enterprise, and one of the reasons the interest rates on government debt have gradually increased is precisely because of government-induced inflation.

"We Owe It to Ourselves"

Many economists reject the notion that the national debt is a burden because, as McConnell claims, "we owe it to ourselves." The public (through the government) borrows money from the public (through individual bondholders). Thus the public debt is a public credit, except when foreigners, such as the Japanese or the British, may own domestic bonds. This is a concern, but most economists don't dwell on it because foreign-owned domestic bonds remain a small percentage of the national debt.

But the idea that we owe it to ourselves is a fallacy of composition. The question that must be asked is, "Who are the *we* and who are the *ourselves?*" They are not the same people. Individual taxpayers are not necessarily the holders of government bonds. Bondholders are often wealthy individuals, whereas taxpayers are largely middle-class. There is clearly a transfer of wealth going on here; whereas the decision to buy bonds is voluntary, the decision to issue the bonds by taxpayers is not voluntary.

The phrase "we owe it to ourselves" is a dangerous misconception. We could carry this reasoning to all kinds of dangerous conclusions. For instance, we could conclude that the level of taxation does not matter because we pay it to ourselves. Why not double Social Security levies? For after all, this would only mean transferring funds from one group of Americans to another. Or, to take it to a more explicit extreme, we could say that the Jews in Germany committed suicide because they did it to themselves.

Some economists really believe that the growing interest obligation on the national debt is not a problem. Although taxpayers foot the bill for higher interest payments, it is not a burden. According to Miller, "After all, the taxes are paid by some Americans; the interest is received by others. In principle this is merely a redistribution that cannot properly be called a burden on *all* of society."

But this is wishful thinking. One could argue in the same vein that high interest rates are not bad for the economy in general. For example, during the early 1980s, when Treasury bills (T bills) were paying 14 percent and money market funds were paying as high as 18 percent, one could say that some people were hurt by high interest rates (banks and businesses), while others benefited (cash investors). But could we really say that, on balance, the economic effect of high interest rates is neutral? No. In reality, the net effect was negative for the economy. The negative effect on business and consumers far outweighed the additional purchasing power the cash investors got from putting their money in T bills and money market funds.

The interest costs of the national debt are a serious burden on society. If they are paid through increased taxes, economic efficiency is hurt as money is coercively transferred from one sector to another. If the interest costs are rolled over by issuing additional Treasury securities, the compounding effect makes the interest burden grow even more rapidly and crowds out private investment even more.

CAN THE GOVERNMENT GO BANKRUPT?

Many textbook writers ridicule the conservatives' fear that the national debt can grow so large that it will bankrupt the government. According to Baumol and Blinder, "The U.S. government need never fear defaulting on its debt." The government always has the power to tax, and it can use the printing press as a last resort to escape financial ruin.

Granted, many conservatives have seriously misjudged the ability of the government to run deficits year after year without causing panic or imminent bankruptcy. The textbook writers are quick to point out that the deficit and the national debt remain relatively small in relation to the size of the economy, as is shown in Figure 14–1. Others have noted that in some countries, such as Japan and Belgium, the national debt is higher as a percentage of GNP. Thus, there is no current crisis, and we have a long way to go before bankruptcy.

Nevertheless, the Treasury could run into trouble in a severe recession or depression, which would result in a dramatic rise in the size of the debt even as a percentage of GNP. The fact that many countries—such as Germany in the 1920s, China in the 1940s, and Argentina in the 1970s—have indeed declared bankruptcy on a national scale should be food for thought. Anytime a country has to devalue its currency sharply, repudiate its debt, or engage in runaway inflation, it amounts to partial or complete bankruptcy. Byrns and Stone state, "Debt can be floated almost perpetually, however, as long as the government of a country is reasonably stable and maintains its credit." Those are big ifs. Although at the present time it is highly unlikely that the U.S. government would place a moratorium on any of its debt securities, it is conceivable that at some time in the future the United States would suffer from such high rates of inflation that the national debt could become so unmanageable that the world would lose faith in the U.S. government's ability to govern. The U.S. bond market could collapse ("no bid"), or become extremely illiquid. Dolan is one of the few textbook writers to draw comparisons between the United States and other countries that have depreciated their currencies as a stopgap to cover the deficit: "Is this scenario too farfetched to be a real threat? Not at all. Creating new money to cover the government deficit is the source of the runaway inflation, at rates of hundreds or even thousands of percent per year, that devastated such countries as Bolivia, Argentina, Brazil, and Israel in the early 1980s." It should be noted, also, that none of these countries has a long-term debt market. Their markets collapsed long ago as a result of these countries' inability to control their financial affairs. Businesspeople in these countries seldom make long-term plans.

BUYING T BILLS: THE IRONY OF THE CONSERVATIVES

One of the reasons why the U.S. government has had relatively little trouble marketing its national debt is, ironically, due to the support of conservative investors. The staunchest critics of deficit spending are often the biggest buyers of T bills and securities. Even goldbugs, who constantly complain about taxes, waste, and bureaucracy in government, help finance the very government they oppose. They buy government-only money market funds and T bills right along with their purchases of gold and silver coins because they regard government securities as risk-free investments. But such investments are not risk-free, considering the possibility, however remote, of debt repudiation sometime in the future, as well as the more reliable possibility of losses due to inflation and taxation.

SAMUELSON'S SURPRISE

It is surprising that, of all economists, Samuelson—the man who introduced the legitimacy of deficit financing into America—is now outspoken in raising doubts about the national debt. Although he rules out the possibility of national bankruptcy, he lists three serious consequences of excessive debt creation:

1. External debt (bonds owned by foreigners).
2. Efficiency losses from taxes ("distorting effects on incentives that are inescapably present in the case of any taxes").
3. Displacement of private capital, which he regards as serious.

Samuelson is absolutely right. The crowding-out effect—that Treasury financing becomes a substitute for private investment—is obvious and egregious to Wall Street financiers. The corporate and municipal bond markets are relatively small and illiquid compared to the gigantic government bond sector, by far the largest bond market in the United States (and the world). It is also substantially larger than the entire stock market. Corporate bond issuers typically have to pay two to three percentage points more than Treasury bonds pay to raise funds. The ability of the government to run large deficits through borrowing or money creation has allowed the state to grow fat and wasteful.

SOLUTIONS TO THE DEBT PROBLEM

There are many possible solutions to the national debt problem. One is to outlaw future deficits in an amendment to the Constitution. This solution does little to reduce the size of government, however. After all, under a Constitutional amendment, the legislature could increase both spending and taxes and still have a balanced budget. An amendment would also not necessarily reduce the current national debt. An amendment calling for the reduction in government spending itself might be a better solution, thus allowing the Treasury to gradually pay off the debt through surpluses. Another possibility is a moratorium of some kind on interest payments or some other form of refinancing. This would have the added advantage of creating suspicion among private investors about government securities. No longer would they be treated as risk-free investments. Of course, the government would never risk such a moratorium unless it were desperately against the wall. It is interesting, however, to note that Albert Malabre, news editor of the establishment publication *The Wall Street Journal,* has raised this possibility as a serious alternative in his recent book, *Beyond Our Means.*

PRIVATE VERSUS PUBLIC DEBT

McConnell concludes his chapter on the national debt and federal deficit by suggesting that debt, both public and private, plays a positive role in our society. In fact, according to McConnell, savings mean debt creation because when savings are put in the bank, they are lent to businesses and consumer borrowers: "The process by which savings is transferred to spenders is debt creation." But McConnell is only partly right. Not all savings take the form of a debtor–creditor relationship. A large part of savings is directly invested in business through the stock market. Investors buy securities, which represent ownership of the company, as opposed to buying bonds—equity ownership instead of debt ownership. Or they may invest in business through a limited partnership or other venture capital arrangement. Admittedly, the debt market, which includes both the bond market and savings accounts, is substantially larger than the securities market. But my point is that the debt market is not the only alternative for savings. In fact, a whole society could theoretically be built around various forms of business ownership and partnership rather than debt. Nevertheless, private debt does play a useful role in society, although it can be dangerously misused by businesses and individuals.

Public debt is another matter. It allows the government to be less disciplined, causes taxes to rise, crowds out private investment, raises interest rates, and puts pressure on the central banks to depreciate the currency with the long-term potential of causing runaway inflation and national insolvency.

RECOMMENDED READING

Browne, Harry. *The Economic Time Bomb*. New York: St. Martin's Press, 1989. How growing federal deficits, a bank crisis, or a boom–bust monetary policy could create a national crisis and possible depression.

Malabre, Alfred. *Beyond Our Means*. New York: Random House, 1987. How America's long years of debt, deficits and reckless borrowing now threaten to overwhelm us.

CHAPTER 15

THE INEQUALITY OF INCOME

The most efficient economy in the world may produce a distribution of wages and property that would offend even the staunchest defender of free markets.
            —Paul A. Samuelson and William D. Nordhaus
            Economics (1989)

According to the modern textbooks, the purpose of all economic societies is to solve three fundamental problems: *what* goods should be made, *how* they should be produced, and *to whom* they should be distributed. In a market economy, according to most economists, the first two questions are answered positively and efficiently. The *what* problem is solved by supply and demand, and the *how* question is answered by the theory of production and marginal productivity.

But many egalitarian economists doubt seriously whether the market can distribute income and wealth fairly and equitably. "Competitive markets are particularly adept at solving the *what* and *how* problems," says Samuelson, "but markets have no particular talent for finding the best solution to the *for whom* question." Baumol and Blinder adamantly insist that there is a trade-off between socially desirable income equality and market efficiency: "The market is generous to those who are successful in operating efficient enterprises that are responsive to consumer demands, and it is ruthless in penalizing those who are unable or unwilling to satisfy consumer demands efficiently."

THE LORENZ CURVE AS A FAVORITE MEASURING ROD

All of the top 10 textbooks rely on an obscure configuration called the Lorenz curve as a way to measure income and wealth inequality in the United States, and to make comparisons between countries.

What is the Lorenz curve? Figure 15–1 reproduces the Lorenz curve for the United States for 1986. Essentially, the Lorenz curve measures the percentage of a nation's total income as earned by various income classes. Typically, the Lorenz curve is divided into five income groups. In 1986, for instance, the lowest fifth (the lowest-income earners) received 4.6 percent of the nation's income, while the highest fifth (the highest-income earners) received 43.7 percent of the nation's income. The Lorenz curve would be perfectly straight if each fifth earned exactly 20 percent of the nation's income. But because they do not, the Lorenz curve is always bowed out, indicating inequality of income distribution.

FIGURE 15–1
A Lorenz Curve for the United States

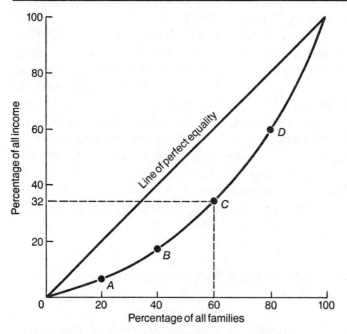

Source: William J. Baumol and Alan S. Blinder, *Economics: Principles and Policy,* 4th ed. (New York: Harcourt Brace Jovanovich, 1988), p. 828.

THE REALITY OF EQUAL DISTRIBUTION OF INCOME

Such inequality sounds unfair. The purpose of the Lorenz curve is to demonstrate how far a country is removed from the line of perfect equality, the straight line noted in Figure 15–1. However, the chief problem with the Lorenz curve is that it establishes an unfair and misleading guide for measuring social well-being. By using value-laden terms, it implies that the ideal Lorenz curve is one that achieves perfect equality. Who can be against equality? It sounds like the only egalitarian choice. The Lorenz curve is reminiscent of another inappropriate term in economics, *perfect competition* (see Chapter 18). Who can oppose the ideal of perfect competition?

Unfortunately, mainstream economists only confuse readers by describing the straight-line Lorenz curve as absolute equality in the distribution of income. Not a single top 10 textbook tells the reader in simple language what perfect income distribution really means: Everyone earns the same amount of income! If a nation's distribution of income lies along the 45-degree line on the Lorenz curve, it means that the teacher, the lawyer, the miner, the manufacturer, the plumber, the farm laborer, and the administrator each earn the exact same wage or salary. It means that the lowest income group earns 20 percent of the nation's income, and the highest income group earns only 20 percent. But this can only mean that there is no bottom or top group—they all earn the same. In short, perfect equality on the Lorenz curve means pure socialism!

WHY INEQUALITY OF INCOME IS ESSENTIAL

Is this the ideal that real people want to achieve? Not at all. The only just distribution of income is the one that pays individuals a legitimate amount equal to the fruits of their labors. Inequality of income is an essential, necessary feature of life if anything is to be accomplished at all. All of the textbook writers point to justified reasons why income differs among individuals—innate abilities, education, experience, hard work, and luck, among others.

Baumol and Blinder themselves include the following question and answer:

> What would happen if we tried to achieve perfect equality by putting a 100 percent income tax on all workers and then divide the receipts equally among the population? No one would have any incentive to work, to invest, to take risks, or to do anything else to earn money, because the rewards for all such activities would disappear.[1]

Even John Maynard Keynes once wrote, "In fact, it was precisely the *inequality* of the distribution of wealth which made possible those vast accumulations of fixed wealth and of capital improvements which distinguished that age [the 19th century] from all others."[2]

Yet, despite such disclaimers, the textbook economists continue to use the Lorenz curve. After establishing the line of perfect equality as the ideal, many economics professors use the Lorenz curve to suggest that a move toward this ideal straight line is socially desirable. A majority of the texts show how progressive taxation and subsidies reduce income equality and push the Lorenz curve toward perfect equality (see Figure 15–2).

In fact, many economists are deeply distressed by income inequality in the United States. On one occasion, Samuelson calls income inequality in the United States a cancer that ought to be eliminated, adding that he personally deplores the fact that income distribution has remained relatively stable since the end of World War II.[3]

Most economics writers also make international comparisons, again implying that social well-being is improved when income inequality is reduced (see Figure 15–3). They note that Sweden and Great Britain, two countries whose governments emphasize welfare-state policies, have less inequality of income than does the United States.

But are Swedish and British citizens generally economically better off than Americans? Income distribution does not give the answer. In fact, one might argue that an *increase* in

FIGURE 15–2
The Distribution of Income before and after Taxes and Benefits

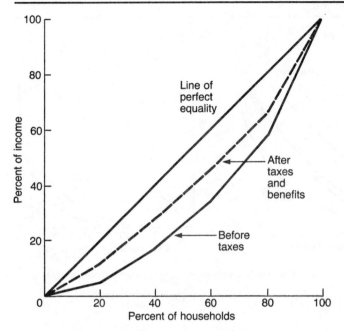

Source: From *Principles of Economics*, 3/e, by Roy J. Ruffin and Paul R. Gregory, p. 833. Copyright © 1988 by Scott, Foresman and Company. Reprinted by permission.

income inequality might be socially and economically beneficial if a socialist nation frees up its resources and labor to act more productively. Granted, the extreme inequality of wealth observed in many Latin American countries (such as that in Brazil, demonstrated in the Lorenz curve in Figure 15–3) is far from ideal. But it is the cause of the inequality, not the inequality itself, that lends to economic disharmony. The lack of a democratic market economy and a political structure that discriminates in favor of the wealthy, aristocratic class by granting monopolies, subsidies, and special concessions are the real problems in Latin America.

My point is this: The shape of the Lorenz curve does not prove anything on its own. In one country extreme income inequality might be a sign of economic success, while in another

FIGURE 15–3
How Inequality Differs in Different Societies and Is Greater for Wealth than for Income

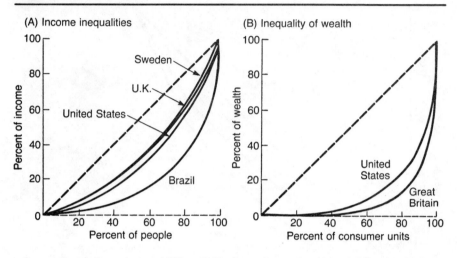

Source: Paul A. Samuelson and William D. Nordhaus, *Economics*, 13th ed. (New York: McGraw-Hill, 1989), p. 647.

country it might be a sign of failure. One cannot tell how a nation can improve its economic condition by looking solely at income distribution. What is really important is not income distribution but to what extent the market process works within a country. A move toward a noninflationary market economy would most likely reduce income inequality as more citizens participate in the economic recovery.

In addition, the Lorenz curve is often unable to show an increase in a country's standard of living over time. Several textbook writers note that the distribution of income has not changed materially in the past 40 years in the United States; the Lorenz curve has not moved. Yet there is clear evidence according to other measures (per capita real income, variety of goods and services, stock prices, vacation time, etc.) that the quality of life for almost all Americans has increased substantially during this period.

The one exception may be the quality of life of America's poor. Artificial methods of reducing income inequality and shifting the Lorenz curve toward the perfect equality line may have actually reduced the lowest income group's standard of living. Charles Murray, in his innovative work, *Losing Ground*, cites evidence that the War on Poverty has significantly reduced the quality of life of the poor since 1965. For example, aptitude test scores have fallen and the number of illegitimate children has risen spectacularly, while the number of the poor has actually grown despite billions of dollars in aid.[4] While spending billions of dollars to avoid a national depression, the government has, in effect, created a permanent depression for millions of America's poor.

A BETTER ALTERNATIVE

What alternatives might be substituted for the Lorenz curve as a way to determine the social well-being of a nation? The distribution of income can be shown in a more practical manner using Figure 15–4, in which we break down the income level by household numbers. For example, in 1987, 2 million households earned less than $2,500; five million earned between $12,500 and $15,000; and another 5 million earned between $45,000 and $50,000; and so on. The median family income in 1987 was $26,000. We can see from Figure 15–4 that income levels are spread out fairly evenly in the United States, although the income line rises rather sharply at first and then tapers off gradually. Samuelson argues that the graph in Figure 15–4 should be more like a bell-shaped curve, but there is no reason why it should be.

Let me also suggest that statistics showing *absolute* increases or decreases in per capital real income would be far more relevant to the economist than income distribution. Statistics that indicate increases in per capita real income do indicate economic progress. Thus, in Figure 15–4, if the whole curve shifted to the right, so that the number of poor households fell sharply and the number of middle-class and wealthy households increased accordingly, the country would be far better off as a whole, regardless of the relative changes among income groups. Gradual movements in the Lorenz curve, on

FIGURE 15–4
Distribution of Household Income: United States, 1987

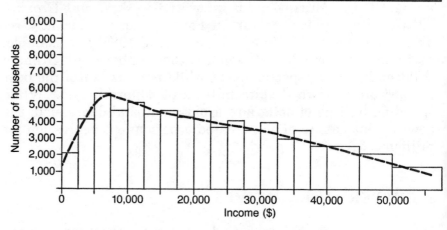

Source: U.S. Bureau of the Census, *Current Population Reports*, 1987.

the other hand, do not accurately reflect economic progress because the curve is only a measure of *relative* income differentials.

It is interesting in this regard that John Kenneth Galbraith appears to support my thesis. In *The Affluent Society* he states, "It is the increase in output in recent decades, not the redistribution of income, which has brought the great material increase, the well-being of the average man."[5]

Samuelson's is one of the few textbooks that measures economic progress in terms of per capita real income (although Samuelson also highlights the Lorenz curve). Regarding Figure 15–5, Samuelson comments, "With advancing technology and improved capital goods, American workers enjoy higher wages while working shorter hours."

Two countries can have a similar distribution of income, yet one can be poor and the other rich. For instance, according to Miller, the United States and Spain have similar Lorenz curves, yet the standard of living is substantially higher in the United States. What really counts is the real income of individuals, not how well one person or country is doing compared to another.

FIGURE 15–5
Economic Progress, 1890–1988

Source: Paul A. Samuelson and William D. Nordhaus, *Economics*, 13th ed. (New York: McGraw-Hill, 1989), p. 641.

It is improvement in absolute wage levels, not changes in relative wage levels, that really concerns the low-income and middle-income earners. If *everyone* in society achieves a high level of economic well-being—so that each person, not just the wealthy, enjoys the necessities and pleasures of life—then it is unlikely that economic class warfare will develop. Social unrest is not likely to occur if no one is poor; there are few rich people who complain about the super rich. Free-market economies, unrestrained by state control and inflation, have come a long way in achieving this goal of improved absolute wage levels.

It is often said that one of the most insidious effects of a high rate of inflation is that it makes the distribution of income more unequal. This effect is indeed the case, but the Lorenz curve is not the best way to illustrate it. Inflation, in effect, destroys the middle-income and low-income classes, while making the high-income class richer. But it is the destruction of the lower classes of workers—always the majority in a nation—that is the real evil of runaway inflation, not the growing inequality of income.

IS THERE REALLY A THEORY OF DISTRIBUTION?

Ultimately, the entire theory of income distribution should be reexamined. In the free market, there is no theory of distribution separate from the theory of production. Income is not distributed, it is produced! The *for whom* question in economics cannot be distinguished from the *what* and *how* questions. Those who sell their goods and services receive the fruits of their labor in accordance with the discounted marginal value of such labor.

A separate theory of distribution can only arise in an economy in which the government intervenes in the marketplace and reduces or increases an individual's income by force through the political process. Only the government, through taxation, takes away wealth from the producers and distributes it, through subsidies, to the consumers. In the free market, wealth may be donated to help the poor and the less fortunate or to promote a charitable cause, but such actions by their very nature increase social utility for all concerned; political welfarism, however, increases the utility of some at the expense of others.

NOTES

1. William J. Baumol and Alan S. Blinder, *Economics: Principles and Policy,* 4th ed. (New York: Harcourt Brace Jovanovich, 1988), p. 835.

2. John Maynard Keynes, *The Economic Consequences of the Peace* (New York: Harper & Row, 1920), p. 19.
3. Paul A. Samuelson, "Liberalism at Bay," in *Collected Scientific Papers of Paul A. Samuelson* vol. 4 (Cambridge: MIT Press, 1986), pp. 872–73. This was a speech Samuelson gave at the New School for Social Research in 1971.
4. Charles Murray, *Losing Ground: America's Social Policy, 1950–1980* (New York: Basic Books, 1984).
5. John Kenneth Galbraith, *The Affluent Society* (Boston: Houghton Mifflin, 1958), p. 96.

CHAPTER 16

JAPAN AND THE FOUR TIGERS

By the year 2000 Japan may well be enjoying the highest standard of living of any industrialized country in the world.

—Richard G. Lipsey, Peter O. Steiner,
and Douglas D. Purvis
Economics (1987)

The above quotation is the final sentence of a half-page article in Lipsey and Steiner's textbook. Imagine devoting only half a page to the most dramatic story in economics and finance in the past 50 years. Miller's forecast is the same—"Japan could become the richest country within the next 30 years"—and Miller devotes only one paragraph to it. The underplaying of the most important economic events often plagues modern textbooks. Although they are updated every two to three years, the textbooks often miss out on some of the most significant occurrences in economic history. As an investment and economic analyst, I have recognized the importance of studying Japan and other countries in the Far East, since they seem to be taking over the financial world. I do not pretend to be an expert on the Far East, but I have traveled to Japan, Hong Kong, and China several times and have observed the remarkable transformations occurring in each country.

The lack of international coverage of the Pacific Basin in the textbooks is surprising, given the desire of writers to internationalize their course material. Samuelson states, "No complete understanding of modern economics is possible without a thorough grounding in the world economy." Yet for most economists, international economics still seems highly theoretical.

Students and professors could learn a great deal about the economics of growth, taxes, and government by studying Japan and the four tigers (Taiwan, Hong Kong, Singapore, and South

Korea), but 5 of the top 10 textbooks say virtually nothing about Japan, or they discuss it only as it relates to the car import quota issue. Meanwhile, all of the textbooks devote at least an entire chapter to the dismal economies of the Soviet Union and China. Not a single textbook has a chapter exclusively devoted to the two economic miracles of the postwar period, Japan and West Germany.

The economic miracle of Japan and its neighbors deserves better. Therefore, I've decided to spend a chapter on these countries. Much can be gained by studying their amazing achievements since World War II.

THE SECRET OF THE ORIENTAL BOOM

The economic miracle of Japan and the four tigers is historically unparalleled in modern industrial society. In one generation, these developing nations have literally gone from rags to riches. Specialists in development economics have had to create a new category for the four tigers, calling them "newly industrialized countries" (NICs). They have far outdistanced other developing countries of modest growth such as Mexico and Greece.

Japan and the NICs have much in common: hard work, high rates of saving and investment, heavy dependence on export markets, and small but strong governments. It would be fundamentally wrong to credit the insights of the Keynesian revolution for Japan's rapid expansion, as Samuelson does, or to credit central planning, as Bronfenbrenner suggests. In fact, the remarkable success of the Pacific Basin countries is precisely due to their rejection of crude Keynesianism and excessive central planning. These countries have done just the opposite of the Western nations by taxing consumption at high rates through VATs and taxing savings at low rates. They have encouraged investment and capital formation by exempting most investment from taxation, while discouraging consumption.[1] In fact, credit cards and consumer loans are not in vogue in many parts of the Far East.

The belief that the newly industrialized economies are largely state-directed is a misinterpretation of history. The size of the government in each NIC remains relatively low compared to other industrialized nations, and the federal budget is usually balanced. Except for Hong Kong, they have all engaged in some form of industrial policy, but such activities have been more in the form of incentives than outright ownership and control, which has proven so disastrous in socialist countries. They all restructured their fiscal and monetary affairs, which provided a stable environment for economic growth and marketing, but final decision-making as to which investment areas to pursue was largely left to individual entrepreneurs.

Let us look at each country more closely.

JAPAN

Japan is smaller than the state of California, yet it has a population of 125 million. It lacks natural resources, importing all of its petroleum. Yet Japan has gone from being a poverty-stricken, war-torn island following World War II to having the second largest economy in the free world. Since the war, Japan's real per capita income has increased over tenfold and is now larger than U.S. per capita income. The Toyko stock market is the biggest in the world, and one of its listed stocks is worth more than the entire West German and Hong Kong stock markets combined. In 1970, both the Dow Industrials and the Nikkei Index were close to 1,000—by the end of the 1980s, the Dow was around 2,800 and the Nikkei was over 30,000. The total savings deposits of the Japanese are six times as large as deposits held by Citibank. Japan is the world's biggest credit holder.

One of the primary reasons for strong Japanese growth rates has been Japan's tax policy. Gwartney and Stroup's textbook is one of the few to highlight this fact. Japan's tax structure has encouraged savings, stock market investing, capital formation, and export markets. As noted in Chapter 13, there was virtually no capital gains tax on stock profits or tax on interest for many decades. Only recently did Japan impose a

20 percent withholding tax on savings accounts and a small capital gains tax.

The Japanese savings rate is the highest in the industrial world—17.5 percent of disposable personal income, compared to 5 percent in the United States—undoubtedly due to favorable tax breaks for savings and the absence of a social security system. But the Japanese also make effective use of their savings. Too much of the Western world's savings ends up in government securities and other unproductive assets. Instead, the Japanese put their savings into productive assets—new machines, tools, and education, all of which are used to make high-quality consumer and capital goods that are demanded around the world. Only a small percentage of savings are invested in government securities, including U.S. Treasuries.

The Japanese have also adopted the Confucian virtues of hard work, thrift, and maintaining employee morale through strong business management techniques. The average worker puts in 60 hours a week, and takes only three days of vacation time a year. As one observer reflected, the Japanese attitude is, "Perfection on the production line; staying late at the office; never taking vacation time; obeying rules without question."

The government has definitely played a significant role in the economy through the powerful Ministry of International Trade and Industry (MITI) and the Ministry of Finance, but it would be an exaggeration to suggest that Tokyo engaged in full-scale central planning. Japan rationed credit in the 1950s and 1960s, and allocated capital to key industrial targets. But the Japanese government lost its monopolistic power to control credit and the flow of capital in the 1970s. In fact, some of Japan's major disappointments, such as shipbuilding and the aerospace industry, received much government encouragement and funding. On the other hand, its two most successful industries, automobile and consumer electronics manufacturing, were opposed by MITI. Other hugely successful markets in cement, paper, glass, and motorcycles received little assistance from MITI.

Inflation has been a serious problem in the past in Japan. The yen was fixed equal to the U.S. dollar in the 1870s. Because of massive inflation during the 20th century, today the exchange rate is around 150 yen to the dollar. Fortunately, for the past 15 years, Japan has learned to stabilize its currency.

In short, Japan's success story is not due to industrial policy but is based on high savings rates, productive investment, a strong work ethic, superior management skills, low taxes, and a small but stable government that recognizes its limitations.

HONG KONG

Imagine a small country of 400 square miles that has no natural resources, imports all of its oil and most of its food and water, is literally thousands of miles from its principal trading partners, receives no foreign aid, and has the greatest population concentration anywhere on earth. No doubt most economists would not give this country much chance of survival.

Nevertheless, the small British colony of Hong Kong has broken the vicious cycle of poverty to become the second most prosperous country in the Pacific Basin. Hong Kong's per capita income rose from $180 in 1950 to $8,000 today. Despite a tripling of the population during this time, its unemployment rate declined and remains below 3 percent. Hong Kong is the largest exporter in the world of garments and toys, and the third largest gold and diamond trade center. It has the third largest port in the world, behind New York and Antwerp, and exports more than Brazil or Mexico. And in per capita terms it is the world's largest purchaser of American goods.

The economic miracle of Hong Kong defies all naive theories of economic growth. The simplistic wisdom is that a country needs natural resources to become wealthy; that it requires foreign aid to get started; that it demands a strong central government; that it needs to protect its infant industries from competition; and that an overpopulated, uneducated citizenry is destined to live a vicious cycle of poverty. (Most of the textbooks review these theories.) Hong Kong meets none of these criteria: Its government policy is laissez-faire, and its people are among the best dressed and most refined in the world. Hong Kong is the envy of its neighbors.

Why has Hong Kong been successful? First, it has internal and social stability. As a colony of Great Britain, it was provided with much-needed political stability and the rule of law. But the British Crown also adopted a hands-off policy toward economic development. Authorities call it "positive noninterventionism." There is little central planning, although the government is involved in subsidized housing and education. The 6 million Chinese in Hong Kong decide for themselves what they will produce, sell, and export. There are no antitrust laws, there is no minimum wage, and the government budget is usually in surplus. Even the country's currency is printed by two quasi-private banks. Hong Kong is one of the very few duty-free ports in the world. Only liquor, tobacco, and oil are charged an import duty. Private companies provide electricity, gas, telephone services, bus service, ferry service, and even the underground tunnel between Hong Kong and Kowloon.

Hong Kong has a system of low taxation and balanced budgets. The maximum tax rate is 18 percent on corporations and 16.5 percent on personal income. There is no tax on interest, dividends, capital gains, or foreign earnings.

Hong Kong can teach us an important lesson: Economic achievement does not depend on having a lot of money or natural resources. People are an asset, not a liability. The government should provide political stability, a legal framework, and broad economic freedom. Hopefully, the Chinese government will have learned this important lesson when it takes over in 1997.

TAIWAN, SINGAPORE, AND SOUTH KOREA

The success stories of Taiwan, Singapore, and South Korea have much in common with that of Hong Kong. Taiwan is densely populated, has few natural resources, and imports most of its industrial raw materials. In 1949, when Generalissimo Chiang Kai-shek took over what was then called the island of Formosa, it was just another poor, underdeveloped island in the Pacific. It was not until Taiwan reduced its dependence on U.S. aid that the country took off economically.

After studying the postwar incentive programs in West Germany and Japan, officials legislated the Statute for Encouragement of Investment in 1960. This new statute encouraged savings, capital formation, and export markets. It included five-year tax holidays for export-oriented enterprises, the duty-free import of capital goods, and accelerated deductions for new machinery and equipment. Dividends and capital gains were free of tax, as was up to $10,000 in interest income. Taiwan also imposed a 5 percent business VAT and worked closely with trade union leaders.

The results were remarkable. Per capita income rose from $70 at the end of World War II to nearly $5,000 today. Millions of new jobs were created, real wages rose spectacularly, and unemployment remains extremely low. Taiwan has the most equitable distribution of income in the developing world.

Singapore, also mainly populated by Chinese, is a trade-oriented principality with few natural resources. It has prospered as a free port. The government has instituted a wide variety of investment incentives and tax exemptions to promote trade and foreign investment. Interest income and capital gains are exempt from tax. As a result, Singapore has had an average growth rate of 9.3 percent since 1960. Over $1 billion in foreign investment comes into Singapore each year. Gross capital investment as a percentage of GNP is 40 percent, one of the highest investment percentages in the world.

Some economists argue that Singapore is an example of state capitalism, not the free market, because of the extensive participation by the state in trading, airlines, shipping, shipbuilding, radio and television, electronics, steel and petrochemicals. Singapore also has an annual wage policy, and controls immigration closely. "The state intervenes in almost everything," Nigel Harris says, "from the long-term and the strategic, the regulation of currency and the shaping of a future industrial structure, to the reproductive habits of Singaporeans and the quality of the goods that tourists can buy, and even the dropping of litter and the length of hair permitted to tourists."[2] However, Harris ignores the fact that Singapore does not usually maintain complete control and ownership of businesses, but is only a part owner through stock ownership. Thus, Singapore has been careful not to eliminate the profit incentive in its enterprises. Singapore also is, like Hong Kong, a strong advocate of free trade.

Finally, there is South Korea. The country is small and densely populated and, like the others, has limited natural resources. After the Korean war, the nation was flat on its back. Most of its industrial facilities had been destroyed, 10 million people were homeless, it depended mainly on U.S. financial aid, and per capita income did not rise above $100 until the mid-1960s. Finally, starting in 1961, the government brought fundamental changes to the financial system. Taxes were sharply reduced to encourage export growth and business development. The new program included tax incentives, five-year tax holidays, and various exemptions. No tax was imposed on stock market profits and a 10 percent flat rate was set on interest and dividends. In 1976, the government imposed a VAT on consumption. Meanwhile, government spending was kept under control, representing no more than one fourth of GNP. The new tax changes paid off. Today, South Korea's per capita income exceeds $3,000 a year and South Korea, like Japan and its other Pacific neighbors, enjoys a massive trade surplus. Unemployment remains below 4 percent.

Although South Korea has had more serious social problems than the other Pacific Basin countries, it has made tremendous economic progress. The government has been more involved as a central planner and participant than the governments of other NICs. For example, the size of the government is larger in South Korea than in Taiwan, and the savings rate is lower. Interestingly, Taiwan has 50 percent higher income than South Korea.

SUMMARY

This chapter emphasizes many of the similarities between Japan and the four tigers. No doubt cultural and political factors have played a significant role in their rapid development. In addition, each of these countries has adopted a predominantly private-enterprise, competitive market economy that, along with highly favorable tax policies, has had a dramatic impact on business and foreign trade. While Western nations have overconsumed and underinvested on a massive scale, Japan and the four tigers have underconsumed and overinvested on a massive scale. While the West developed tax policies aimed at redistributing wealth, the Far East endorsed tax policies aimed at expanding output. While the West increased the size of government, the Pacific Basin kept state interference to a reasonable level. The results are now in. The West has suffered relatively low rates of economic growth, while the Pacific Basin countries have exploded in economic output and are now threatening to take over the financial markets and the world economy. Japan and the four tigers deserve careful monitoring, and perhaps even imitation, over the coming decade.

NOTES

1. The Keynesian prescription for economic growth is stated by Minsky: "the policy emphasis should shift from the encouragement of growth through investment to the achievement of full employment through consumption production." See Hyman Minsky, *Can "It" Happen Again? Essays on Instability and Finance* (Armonk, N.Y.: M. E. Sharpe Inc., 1982), p. 113. Clearly Japan and the Pacific Basin nations of Hong Kong, Singapore, Taiwan and South Korea have rejected this Keynesian theory of growth.

2. Nigel Harris, *The End of the Third World: Newly Industrialized Countries and the Decline of an Ideology* (London: Penguin, 1986), pp. 60–61. Interestingly, Harris points to Brazil and Mexico as the two best examples of NICs in Latin America, rather than Chile, which has adopted a strong free-market policy and has, not coincidentally, achieved the highest growth rate among Latin American countries in the 1980s.

RECOMMENDED READING

Bauer, P. T. *Equality, the Third World and Economic Delusion*. London: Weidenfeld and Nicolson, 1981. The foremost growth economist critiques development aid, the vicious circle of poverty thesis, and modern economic growth theories. It includes the classic article "The Lesson of Hong Kong."

Morishima, Michio. *Why Has Japan 'Succeeded'?* Cambridge: Cambridge University Press, 1982. A fascinating account of Japan's economic miracles since the 19th century by one of Japan's most famous economists.

Rabushka, Alvin. *Hong Kong: A Study in Economic Freedom*. University of Chicago, 1979. A revealing look into the world's most laissez-faire economy.

CHAPTER 17

THE POVERTY OF SOCIALISM

The Soviet economy is proof that, contrary to what many skeptics had earlier believed, a socialist command economy can function and even thrive.
—Paul A. Samuelson and William D. Nordhaus
Economics (1989)

The final chapter in every economics textbook addresses comparative economic systems. Free-market capitalism is compared to various kinds of socialism. The pros and cons of Marxism and central planning are debated. Countries with various levels of socialistic command economies are highlighted, especially the Soviet Union, China, Yugoslavia, and Sweden.

WAS MARX A GENIUS?

Several of the top 10 textbooks are surprisingly sympathetic toward Karl Marx, the ideological founder of modern socialism. Samuelson calls Marx a great albeit controversial economist, who was sometimes wrong in his predictions. Baumol and Blinder are conspicuous apologists. In their chapter entitled "The Economics of Karl Marx," they conclude:

> The writings of Marx are stamped by brilliance and originality. Parts of the writings are long-winded and dull (in fact, Marx told Engels he did this deliberately to make his work "weightier"), but they contain many sparkling and powerful passages. Many of Marx's ideas are still highly illuminating, even to non-Marxists, and in areas such as business-cycle analysis, almost all modern thinking stems from his, either directly or indirectly.

In short, he contributed enormously to current thought within the discipline of economics as well as in politics throughout the world.[1]

Some economics writers also contend that Marx cannot be held responsible for the problems in the Soviet Union and other communist countries because Marx devoted almost all his attention to the *capitalist* economy. Only a small percentage of Marx's voluminous writings deals with the nature of socialism. Nevertheless, apologists for Marxist economics are too quick to forget that Marx defended the basics of any socialist regime—confiscation of private property, abolition of capitalist profit, common ownership of production, and central planning from high-level government technocrats (the dictatorship of the proletariat). Marx may have focused on the weaknesses of capitalism, but all his criticisms were made in an effort to destroy the capitalist structure and replace it with totalitarian socialism. When it came to instituting socialism, he was a communist who "support[ed] every revolutionary movement against existing social conditions."[2]

Marx (along with Engels) outlined his 10-point revolutionary program in *The Communist Manifesto*. Many of his techniques were used by communist leaders when they took over a country. Some recommendations, such as free education and a graduated income tax, have already been adopted by Western nations. The 10-point plan is as follows:

1. Abolition of property in land and application of all rents of land to public purposes.
2. A heavy progressive or graduated income tax.
3. Abolition of all right of inheritance.
4. Confiscation of property of all emigrants and rebels.
5. Centralization of credit in the hands of the State, by means of a national bank with State capital and an exclusive monopoly.
6. Centralization of the means of communication and transport in the hands of the State.
7. Extension of factories and instruments of production owned by the State; the bringing into cultivation of

waste lands, and the improvement of the soil generally in accordance with a common plan.

8. Equal liability of all to labor. Establishment of industrial armies, especially for agriculture.

9. Combination of agriculture with manufacturing industries; gradual abolition of the distinction between town and country, by a more equitable distribution of the population over the country.

10. Free education for all children in public schools. Abolition of children's factory labor in its present form. Combination of education with industrial production, etc., etc.[3]

None of the top 10 textbooks reprints the 10-point plan of Marx and Engels—perhaps because *The Communist Manifesto* is polemical in style—but it should not be ignored.

It seems improbable that economists could defend Marx on purely economic grounds. His labor theory of value, which states that the value of a good or service is determined by the hours and materials used to produce it, was borrowed from the classical economists David Ricardo and Adam Smith. It has proved to be a grave distortion of economic reality. As the Austrian economist Carl Menger proved a generation later, value is ultimately determined by subjective demand, not the costs of production.

Marx also argued that capitalists accumulate more capital and get richer while wages remain at subsistence levels so that workers cannot participate in the growing prosperity. According to Marx, as capitalism progresses, there is "a corresponding increase in the mass of poverty, oppression, enslavement, degeneration and exploitation."[4] But the evidence is overwhelming that the opposite is true. As profits increase, so do wages. Workers' wages have increased dramatically during the ongoing industrial revolution; the workers' subsistence wage never materialized. The fact that workers do not usually earn as much as the business owners is not due to exploitation of the working class, but due to two factors: (1) The businessperson, as the owner of the means of production, takes greater risks in order to achieve greater rewards, and (2) workers receive wages before the final product is sold and before the business owner is paid. Thus workers are paid their *discounted* marginal value so that they do not have to wait.

Certainly the rate of profit in capitalist countries has not declined, as Marx predicted. Nor does socialism appear inevitable in an age of privatization and deregulation. Free-market capitalism is flourishing in more countries than ever before, even in those under communist control. Moreover, according to Marxist doctrine, fully developed capitalist countries would be the first to adopt communism; instead, communism has had its least influence in the more advanced societies.

Marx is, in fact, one of the few economists who is wrong from the first page of his massive economics treatise. Volume 1 of *Capital* begins by declaring that an exchange of a commodity means that there is an equality between the economic values of the buyer and seller.[5] In reality, just the opposite is true. Exchange takes place because the buyer and seller value the product unequally—the buyer wants the commodity more than the money, and the seller wants the money more than the commodity. If this psychological law of exchange were not so, exchange would not take place.

To his followers, Marx's primary attraction is in his forceful doctrines on alienation, class warfare, exploitation, and other social and historical characteristics of capitalist nations. The whole descriptive approach of the economy by Marx is antagonistic rather than cooperative. His method, however, can hardly be described as scientific. He only highlighted the worst cases of exploitation and ignored studies that indicated an improved standard of living in Western industrialized nations. He apparently made no attempt to investigate firsthand the alleged plight of the workers nor any attempt to interview capitalists. Historian Paul Johnson concludes that "so far as we know, Marx never set foot in a mill, factory, mine or other industrial workplace in the whole of his life."[6] The deskbound critic was completely hostile to revolutionary workers who had practical work experience.

WAS MARX A GOOD FAMILY MAN?

Sympathetic writers talk of Marx's passionate empathy toward the working class, his demands for a decent wage and improved working conditions, and his great feeling for his family's welfare. In this respect, Marx is an enigma. In the classroom's most popular book on the history of economics, Robert L. Heilbroner writes that, despite his reputation as a contentious and vengeful man who feuded constantly with his contemporaries, Marx was a devoted husband and father.[7] In a sympathetic biography, Saul K. Padover notes, "Marx, the harsh critic and angry radical in his public life and writings, was a different man in private. In his personal life, he was extraordinarily kind and generous and, when not tormented by illnesses, gay. . . . [As a] self-assured male, Marx had a genuine affection and esteem for women. . . . [And] Jenny was the only woman in his life."[8]

Apologists for Marx are almost always blind to the darker side of the creator of communism. They write of his devotion to his family and his love letters to his wife but ignore or condone his illicit affair with the family's household servant, Lenchen, which produced an illegitimate son whom Marx would have nothing to do with. Interestingly, Marx also never paid this servant a penny for her housework.

Karl and Jenny Marx were poverty-stricken but not for want of money. They received large sums over the years from Engels, other supporters, and from Marx's writings. One estimate is that Marx was poor only 15 years of his 65-year career, and that his income placed him in the top 5 percent of London residents in the 1860s.[9] But the Marxes were financially incompetent and could not control their spending habits. Marx entertained lavishly, speculated on the stock market, and spent large sums on liquor, books, travel, and other consumer goods until he had to beg for more or borrow from pawnshops at usury rates. Such irresponsible spending habits often left his family starving, destitute, and in ill health. Marx's family life was often a nightmare, resulting in the early death or eventual suicide of most of his children. Historian Robert Payne, in his biography of Marx, concludes, "He exploited everyone around him—his wife, his children, his mistress and his friends—with a ruthlessness which was all the more terrible because it was deliberate and calculating."[10]

Despite his colorful and forceful language, Marx's diatribe against capitalism and his endorsement of the violent overthrow of constitutional republics have produced more alienation, greater inequality and class distinction, and more poverty and death than ever before in the history of the world. Millions of innocent people have been murdered and sent to prisons and concentration camps in the Soviet Union, China, Vietnam, Korea, Cambodia, Cuba, and Nicaragua, all in the name of Marxism–Leninism. The estimates of politically related deaths in the Soviet Union alone amount to an unbelievable 50 million. Some economics writers have the courage to say so. Lipsey and Steiner refer to the Kremlin as a monstrous tyranny. But most of the top 10 textbooks are silent about the terrible human tragedy that communism has wrought during the 20th century.

HOW REAL IS SOVIET ECONOMIC GROWTH?

Most of the top 10 textbook writers accept the conventional view that the Soviet Union and other countries with command economies have achieved a highly developed stage based on accepted GNP statistics. According to these figures, compiled by the Central Intelligence Agency and other government sources, economic growth in the Soviet Union since the 1930s has been dramatic, even twice as rapid as that in the United States. Ruffin and Gregory make the startling claim that the Soviet Union has grown "more rapidly in the long run than any major capitalist country with the exception of Japan."

How GNP Figures Lie

Based on such dramatic growth rates, one might expect the standard of living in the Soviet Union to equal or surpass Western standards of living, but even most economists recognize the deep gulf between the Soviet Union and the industrialized West and Japan.

Yet the apologists persist in extolling the virtues of Soviet central planning. Lipsey and Steiner boldly declare, "The Soviet citizens' standard of living is so much higher than it was even a decade ago, and is rising so rapidly, that it probably seems comfortable to them." Certainly there are shortages and black markets, Lipsey and Steiner admit, but the citizens of the Soviet Union now enjoy better chess, better gymnastics, better soccer, and free education, medical help, and dental care. There is no economic instability or unemployment.

Surely this is misreading the data. GNP must not be equated with a country's standard of living. Much of the Soviet GNP is misallocated and wasteful, especially when it is directed toward military spending, which represents a significant percentage of Soviet national production. Baumol and Blinder, as well as McConnell, have made the point that the Soviet leaders have deliberately restricted consumption to boost investment in steel, petroleum, chemicals, and machine tools. In seeking to imitate the market's formula for material progress through forced savings, the Soviet Union expected to achieve real economic growth. Most of the top 10 textbook writers seem to think that this strategy worked, as Samuelson indicates (see quote at the beginning of this chapter). In reality, it achieved misallocated and stilted growth, if it can be called growth at all. As Soviet expert Marshall Goldman states, "This system keeps producing steel and basic machine tools, when what is wanted is food, consumer goods, and more modern technology."[11] Moreover, any legitimate growth achieved by the Soviet Union is due in part to borrowing advanced technology from the West.

The Soviet Failure

If one measures a country's standard of living by the quality and output of final consumer goods, the Soviet experiment in central planning has been an unmitigated disaster. Basic food items are in chronic short supply. Meat, butter, and sugar are routinely rationed. In 1917, the Communists came to power promising Bread, Land and Peace. But the Soviet economist Aleksandr S. Zaychenko stated recently, "Russians today eat worse than did Russians in 1913 under the czars."[12] Considering the harsh economic conditions in czarist Russia, this statement is amazing. The distribution and storage facilities in the Soviet Union are so wasteful that one third of all produce rots before reaching the market. The Soviet Union has 4 million non-producing farm bureaucrats—more than the entire farm population in the United States.

In a nation once proud of its zero unemployment, the country now suffers from vagrancy, unemployment, homelessness, alcoholism, child labor, disease, and high suicide rates. The Soviet Union is now below most third-world countries in every health category. Death rates in all age groups have been rising at an alarming rate in the Soviet Union. A boy born in the Soviet Union today has a shorter life expectancy than one born in Mexico. Housing for most Soviets is extremely inadequate. The Soviet publication *Izvestia* reported recently that the average unskilled laborer's family of four lives for more than eight years in a single 8-by-8-foot room. Only one third of Soviet households have hot running water and another one third do not even have cold running water. The number of telephones, private automobiles, and other basic necessities is surprisingly small. It is a shocking statistic that in South Africa blacks own more cars per capita than do citizens in the Soviet Union. Official Soviet statistics recently released indicate that approximately 40 percent of the Soviet population and 79 percent of the country's elderly live in poverty.[13]

LEARNING THROUGH FOREIGN TRAVEL

Sometimes I wonder if any of the textbook writers who are impressed with the advancement of socialist regimes have actually been to the Soviet Union, China, Cuba, or other countries with command economies. They are armchair economists who rely too heavily on official statistics to determine a country's standard of living.

I have traveled extensively, including traveling to the Soviet Union and China, and have always found myself revamping my views of a country after visiting it. But my traveling experiences are few compared to those of economist Lawrence W. Reed, who has been to 25 countries in the past three years. His conclusion: "Actually being there adds whole new dimensions to the subject, explodes one stereotype after another, and often leaves the traveler wondering how the textbook author could have written what he did."[14] Reed has been to the Soviet Union, China, Poland, East Germany, Nicaragua, and Bolivia, to name just a few countries.

Reed has been to the Soviet Union many times, and his assessment is similar to that of journalists who have been there recently. The Soviet Union is, in many ways, a third-world country, if not a medieval one. The buildings are old and dilapidated, the stores are full of goods nobody wants, meat and other basic consumer items are in short supply, and free services are seldom up to quality. Soviet dentists seldom use a painkiller to pull a tooth. Medical care is free but is of extremely low quality. Urban hospitals are overcrowded and poorly run, while rural hospitals are underutilized. Sanitation is often very poor. The water in Leningrad is yellow and undrinkable. "Phenomena that we take for granted—such as disposable dishes, needles, and paper products—are simply not available in the Soviet Union," says Kate Schecter, whose family returned recently to visit the Soviet Union, where they used to work.[15] Even the toilet paper in the Soviet Union is so rough and in such short supply that tourists are asked to bring their own.

The pervasive black market is the only flourishing alternative in the Soviet economy. Despite the constant fear of getting caught, black-market entrepreneurs are relentless in their efforts to make a deal. Reed reports, "The network of illegal transactions is a major component of whatever the Soviet GNP is, but you would not know that by reading textbooks."[16]

In the appendix to his penetrating work *The Grand Failure*, Zbigniew Brzezinski contrasts the standards of living in the free world and communist countries in terms of motor vehicles, telephones, infant mortality, trade, and income on a per capita basis during the period 1960 to 1985. Brzezinski's charts ought to be reproduced in every textbook. (Gwartney and Stroup have added a similar chart in the latest edition.)

They demonstrate a shocking difference—the communist world loses on every count by a large margin. People in the free world have more automobiles and telephones, lower infant mortality rates, and higher incomes than their communist counterparts. Brzezinski concludes:

> Comparisons of Communist and non-Communist countries at similar stages of socioeconomic development—such as East Germany and Czechoslovakia with West Germany, Poland with Spain, Hungary and Yugoslavia with Austria and Italy, and China with India—indicate that virtually no Communist regime improved its standing vis-à-vis its comparable rival, in terms of GNP, trade in competitive world markets, or domestic standard of living.[17]

THE REAL LESSON ABOUT CENTRAL PLANNING

Does central planning work, as some economists maintain? Ruffin and Gregory boldly state, "But the Soviet economy—despite the dire predictions of Hayek and Mises—has survived as a centrally planned economy for more than 60 years." Are they right? The fact is that the Soviet government, like all other socialist regimes, has had to free up its economy and political structure in order to survive. That is the meaning of *perestroika* and *glasnost,* and the opening of the Berlin Wall. Central planning does not work!

Both the Soviet Union and China have had to allow small plots of land to be privately owned and developed in order to survive agriculturally. Miller points out that 1 to 3 percent of the Soviet farmlands (privately owned) produce 20 to 33 percent of the agricultural output. Gosplan, the Soviet Union's state planning commission, has had to look the other way when local entrepreneurs engaged in illegal black (free) market transactions. The state has had to sell its raw products and hard currency (gold) to the free world in order to obtain the much-needed supplies that the Soviets could not produce themselves. They have had to rely on Western technology to advance economically.

Some countries have freed their economies more than others and have prospered as a result. The Eastern bloc countries of Yugoslavia and Hungary are examples. To the extent that they have adopted free-enterprise techniques and opened their doors to world markets, they have enhanced their standards of living. But they still face serious problems in areas where their leaders continue to interfere with the market process. As Brzezinski states, echoing Ludwig von Mises, "Ultimately no halfway house exists between centralized communism and a decentralized and self-managing society."[18] Fortunately, a few textbooks are starting to recognize this fact. In regard to the new edition of his textbook, Professor James Gwartney, for example, stated recently, "We stress that prosperity is associated with free markets, and that socialism leads to stagnation and poverty."[19]

RICH AND POOR NATIONS

During the 20th century, many poor countries have become rich, but many rich countries have become poor. Czechoslovakia used to be one of the wealthiest nations in Europe. Cuba used to be one of the richest islands in the Caribbean. Argentina was considered an industrial nation in the 1920s. Each of these countries has adopted socialist measures and has suffered the consequences.

One of the most rewarding exercises in an economics class could be to compare cities or countries close in proximity but different in terms of government control. There are numerous examples of extremely rich and extremely poor countries separated only by an artificial border: Taiwan and China, South Korea and North Korea, West Germany and East Germany, Chile and Argentina, or even the United States and Mexico. In each case, the difference can largely be explained in terms of free versus controlled markets.

Why India Has Remained Poor

Countries such as India that have had a long-standing policy of interference in the economy have yet to prosper. Mutual fund magnate John Templeton tells an interesting story in this regard. When he was a young man in 1936, he took a round-the-world tour and was struck by the poverty he saw in both India and Hong Kong. When he returned 40 years later, he noted a sharp contrast:

> The standard of living in Hong Kong had multiplied more than tenfold in forty years, while the standard of living in Calcutta had improved hardly at all. The major difference is the difference between free enterprise and socialism. The government of India regulates nearly everything, so there's very little progress; whereas in Hong Kong the government keeps its hands off.[20]

Only recently has India started to open up its markets.

The Tragedy and Hope of Ghana

Many countries that used to flourish have suffered as a result of their attempts at state central planning. Ghana is just one example. Known previously as the Gold Coast, Ghana has been the world's leading producer of cocoa and a major exporter of gold. Then, in the early 1960s, it became the first self-governed democracy in Africa. Ghana's first president, an avowed Marxist, imposed national socialism, which, he asserted, would encourage rapid industrialization and an extensive welfare system. The state nationalized the cocoa market, pegged exchange rates, and imposed price controls.

The results were predictable: Exports fell, black markets flourished, government revenues dropped sharply, and the standard of living declined. As economist Sven Rydenfelt concludes, "Ghana is a textbook case of a country in which the government, through price controls and a state purchasing monopoly, has demonstrated an ability to destroy the entrepreneurial environment rapidly. The consequences—for exports, imports, the standard of living, and economic growth—have been fatal. . . . Seldom, if ever, has a rich country been transformed into a poor one as rapidly and unequivocally as has Ghana."[21] Fortunately, Ghana has recently turned away from its bankrupt policies toward free markets.

A Better Path for Latin America

Latin America serves as an experimental microcosm of third-world mercantilism and state socialism. Most of the poverty-stricken countries in Latin America have never known a democratic market economy. Instead, the Latin American governments have served the special interests of the wealthy aristocratic class, a small elite group constantly seeking state-controlled monopolies and concessions. Their bureaucratic agencies have been so gigantic, complex, and paternalistic that ordinary citizens have turned to the black market, called the "informal market" by Latin American economists, to survive. Without this informal free market, the social and economic conditions of the Latin Americans would be infinitely worse, despite the fact that the informal economy, like all black markets, is vulnerable to fraud, extortion, and frequent crises. According to Peruvian economist Hernando de Soto, 60 percent of Peru's economy consists of "informals." For example, 95 percent of the public transportation system is owned and operated by private companies that have not been properly licensed by the state. Most real estate is built without building permits or licenses because it would take over a year to comply with the myriad of regulations issued every day.

Mercantilism, overregulation, and state monopolistic control are some of the reasons Peru and other Latin American countries remain poor. Runaway inflation, wasteful government spending, excessive labor power, and high taxes are other serious problems. Latin American countries also suffer from an excessively nationalistic spirit, nurtured over the past three centuries, which has resulted in laws inhibiting foreign capital and expertise from being used locally. "Mexico only for the Mexicans," "Brazil only for the Brazilians," and so forth are common slogans that prevent these countries from advancing. It is not surprising that, according to the World Bank, most Latin American nations have suffered from extremely low or negative growth rates, falling standards of living, and a collapse in road building, public utilities, and basic infrastructure.

What do Latin American countries need to do to imitate the success of Japan and the four tigers? First, they need to establish political and legal stability. Second, they need to stop inflation and reduce the size of government. Third, they need to sharply reduce taxes, privatize nationalized industries, and eliminate state-owned monopolies and cartels. Fourth, they need to abolish the vast array of laws and price regulations controlling local businesses. And fifth, they ought to encourage foreign capital by allowing foreigners to own and operate local businesses. Once these measures are adopted, capital and talent will stop leaving the area, and Latin America will finally achieve the revolution it has been seeking. De Soto reflects this vision when he states, "I want a free and prosperous society in which people's intelligence and energies are used for productive purposes and to bring about beneficial political changes. . . . I refuse to accept a society in which effort is wasted on obtaining legal privileges and in which an arbitrary state fiercely punishes us for our hopes. These are the obstacles that block the path to liberation."[22]

Latin Americans could learn a great deal from Chile, which has recovered dramatically from its chaotic conditions under the Marxist Allende regime. The Chilean economic miracle is ignored by the top 10 textbooks, perhaps because Chile has until recently been run by a sometimes repressive dictatorship. Nevertheless, as a result of liberalization and stabilization policies designed by free-market economists ("the Chicago boys"), the material progress made by Chileans since 1973 has been impressive. Price controls have been lifted, tariffs have been cut sharply, banks have been privatized, social security has been radically changed to a private pension system, and fiscal discipline has been established. Consequently, Chile has the highest growth rate of any Latin American country. The inflation has fallen dramatically to reasonable levels, and foreign debt has been reduced. Unemployment has declined and real wages have risen.

The Postwar German Economic Miracle

Command economies can also learn a lot from West Germany's experience following World War II. This provides another classic example of the tremendous commercial boom that can occur when the government frees the economy after years of strict central planning and control. Unfortunately, only one of the top 10 textbook writers (Samuelson) tells this dramatic story.

Following World War II, the new Allied-controlled regime in Germany maintained strict central planning with price controls, rationing, and a nightmare of industrial regulations. As a result, by 1948—three years after the war—Germany was paralyzed. Production of coal, food, and other basic commodities hit an all-time low. Barter became the chief means of transacting business. The money was worthless and black markets flourished. War-torn Germany remained unbuilt. Meanwhile, thousands of refugees were pouring into Berlin and West Germany.

Then, in June of 1948, economic minister Ludwig Erhard suddenly made a dramatic, controversial decision to end virtually all price controls, rationing, and onerous regulations of business, while at the same time establishing a sound currency reform. Erhard was under enormous pressure from the socialists and central planners to engage in piecemeal reform, but instead he took the bold move of ending state control at once. Erhard's courageous maneuver paid off; Germany changed overnight. As one observer, Jacques Rueff, put it:

> The black market suddenly disappeared. Shop windows were full of goods; factory chimneys were smoking; and the streets swarmed with lorries. Everywhere the noise of new buildings going up replaced the deathly silence of the ruins. If the state of recovery was a surprise, its swiftness was even more so. In all sectors of economic life it began as the clocks struck on the day of currency reform. . . . One day apathy was mirrored on their

faces while on the next a whole nation looked hopefully into the future.[23]

The German economic miracle began in 1948. By the next decade, the war-torn nation had been completely rebuilt, workers' real wages had increased dramatically, and West Germany was on its way to achieving the highest standard of living in Europe. It was all because of Erhard's brave experiment in *Marktwirtschaft*.

Does Central Planning Work in Sweden?

Sweden is often used as a prime example of a centrally planned welfare state that works. Sweden has free child care, free medical care, free education, and sometimes free housing and transportation. Baumol and Blinder contend that Sweden's social programs have accomplished their goals—there are no signs of poverty in Sweden, they say, and the full employment policy seems to have borne fruit. Sweden has been characterized as having steady low unemployment and one of the highest standards of living in the world. Many leaders of the newly elected democracies in Eastern Europe look toward Sweden as the model economy of free enterprise and social justice.

But Sweden has its dark side. The government may guarantee everyone a job, but it can't legislate away the problems of wasteful underemployment and absenteeism, both serious problems in Sweden. Medical care may indeed be free, but there are often long waiting periods for routine operations. A couple may have to wait three years to get an apartment and then months more to get a telephone. Crime has reached epidemic proportions in Stockholm and other large cities. Drug addiction and juvenile delinquency are on the rise. Suicide is second only to traffic accidents as a cause of death. The government in Stockholm has imposed severe foreign exchange controls and prohibits its citizens from buying foreign stocks. There are sectors that do not work well in Sweden—specifically, the government-controlled businesses. What does work in Sweden? It is the private sector, which represents 90 percent of the businesses, and a huge underground economy that flourishes in the face of 70 percent marginal tax rates. Recently, Sweden has considered privatizing some public services and reducing marginal tax rates, which should reverse the growing malaise in this northern country. In short, to the extent that Sweden has prospered, it is in spite of central planning and the welfare state, not because of it.

THE CHOICE BETWEEN SYSTEMS

The textbooks state that there is a wide variety of economic systems to choose from, each of which decides the *what, how,* and *for whom* of every economy. The people can choose a system of private enterprise or public enterprise, of which there are many categories. Lipsey and Steiner say that 1.25 billion people on earth explicitly reject the free market; they are referring to China and the Soviet Union, even though the citizens of both countries have had little chance to express their preference. Lipsey and Steiner must have had a rude awakening when over 1 million Chinese demonstrated in Beijing in support of economic and political democracy in early 1989 and then were assaulted by the "representative" government.

In reality, the choice between economic systems is a false dichotomy. True enough, all socialistic regimes have systems—e.g., syndicalism, utopian socialism, Fabian socialism, Christian socialism, and communism. But these all have one characteristic in common: They are systems of coercion. They interfere with the freedom of the people to act on their own behalf. In the free market, people make choices for themselves. Under government systems, governments make decisions for them.

In a very real sense, the free market is not a system at all; it is the absence of a system. No one is coerced into producing a particular product or paying a specific price. Individuals can decide for themselves what they want to produce, what they want to buy, and how to cooperate voluntarily with others to achieve their goals. Under a free market, distribution cannot be logically separate from production. Those who produce the goods receive the income, and those who want the products buy them. Only in the alternative system of collectivism can there be a distinction between the theory of distribution and the theory of production.

Critics may respond, "But surely capitalism is a system, based on a certain type of government." Certainly, *capitalism* as a term is often used in a historical context, which one might call "corporate capitalism," with all its defects. Corporate capitalism is a political system that involves businesses, banks, and other large corporations that seek special favors, rights, subsidies, monopolistic powers, and protectionist measures from the legislature. But such corporate welfarism is not what I describe as the free market, which means the absence of political influence.

Most systems are characterized by state-imposed programs that tell individuals to do things differently from the way they would choose to do them on their own. It is simply not true, as Lipsey and Steiner maintain, that 1.25 billion people in the Soviet Union and China have rejected the free market. The communist system has been imposed on them from the top. If the communist leaders gave up their power and let the people of the Soviet Union and China decide for themselves what, how, and for whom to produce, they would do things quite differently and become more successful at raising their standard of living. There would be no more central planning by government, but there would be decentralized planning by individuals, businesses, and organizations. As Thomas Sowell states, central planning means the "forcible superseding of other people's plans by government officials."[24]

WHY STATE CENTRAL PLANNING
DOES NOT WORK

Why does state central planning not work? What are the inherent flaws in the Marxist–Leninist concept of a state monopoly in which the economy is run from the top downward as one giant company? Why do socialist countries eventually turn to the free market for solutions to shortages and gross mismanagement?

There are four basic reasons why forced collectivism is an inherently weak system: (1) State planning separates costs from the users of a good or service, (2) state monopolies lack competitive bidding, (3) the economy is too complex and interrelated to be controlled by central planners, and (4) state-controlled industries lack the ability to innovate and discover new products and services. Let us consider each point.

First, economic efficiency can only be maintained when the cost of a good or service is paid for by the beneficiary or user. For example, when medical care is paid for by general tax revenues and is thus "free" to all citizens, the demand for medical care becomes wastefully excessive and the supply decreases in quality as it increases in price. The critical nexus between cost and benefit has been severed, and the real cost to society rises dramatically.

Second, state-controlled businesses undermine the benefits of competition. Businesses cannot operate efficiently in a complex economy without competitive bidding for resources. Competitive bidding establishes the proper prices for specific goods and services. Without competition between firms, pricing products would simply be a matter of guesswork, resulting in shortages and surpluses. The firm can more easily determine what price to charge for its product by knowing what competitors are charging, as well as what it costs to produce the product. Without outside competition from similar goods and factors of production, the producer would be at a complete loss to determine his true costs. He would be unable to decide either the price of his product or the amount he should produce.

The problem with central planning is that the government tries to function as a single large company with no competition. This is its downfall. Even a totally free economy could not function properly if there were one big monopoly running everything. There always need to be at least several companies competing in each industry so that there may be some point of comparison. Businesspeople are always comparing companies' costs and prices. The central planners have admitted the basic fact that a state monopoly that produces everything could not calculate profits or prices efficiently. In the case of nationalized industries such as the steel or airline industries, bureaucrats have indicated that they used world market prices to estimate their own prices and costs. Otherwise, they would have failed miserably.

Third, the time factor is also a major reason state central planning does not work. Armchair socialists often forget that the economy is highly interlinked, that one stage of production depends on another, and that it takes time for goods and services to be produced. The stages-of-production model outlined in Chapter 3 is useful in explaining this critical problem. Suppose that the government sets too low a price for the production of cowhide, causing inventories to decrease and shortages to arise. Cattle ranchers fail to build up their herds for future slaughter. The state realizes its mistake and raises the price. This will alleviate the problem eventually, but it takes time for cattle producers to rebuild their herds. Meanwhile, the current shortage of cowhide causes a shortage in leather making, which in turn causes a shortage at the shoe manufacturing stage. At the various production stages, machines lay idle because of the shortage. It is important to note that in the production process, it only takes one complementary factor to create a shortage. The shoe manufacturer may have plenty of glue, nails, shoelaces, and laborers to manufacture shoes, but if the plant does not have enough leather the manufacturer will not be able to meet the government's quota.

Given the length and complexity of the production process from raw commodities to final consumer goods, it would be almost impossible for a central planner to coordinate everything along the supply line without creating massive shortages somewhere else along the line.

The free market minimizes these shortages and delays. Prices change almost instantly when a shortage or surplus arises. Because of competition, there are always other suppliers if a firm needs a particular input that is in short supply. Furthermore, the market process encourages the holding of extensive inventories in all areas in order to respond to varied consumer needs and occasional short-term shortages at various stages of production.

The Debate over Socialistic Calculation

The impossibility of economic calculation under socialism was originally demonstrated by the Austrian economists Ludwig von Mises and Friedrich Hayek in the 1920s and 1930s. They said that market prices provided critical information to everyone in the marketplace in determining what needs to be produced, in what quantities, and by what means. Price is an information coordinator for consumers and producers. Mises and Hayek said that accurate decision making in prices and production could not be achieved in a pure socialist economy.[25] Several textbooks comment on the Mises–Hayek critique of socialism. Oscar Lange, Fred Taylor, and A. P. Lerner responded to it. Lange and other defenders of socialism argued that prices could be estimated and adjusted by the state planners according to supply and demand.[26] But in a sense, this was an admission that socialism had to imitate the free market in order to work—and it is a poor imitator at best. When market socialists allow competition, but only one or two producers in each area, the price mechanism does not operate efficiently.

Fourth, one of the gravest shortcomings of socialism is its apparent inability to innovate or to discover new processes. There is always an incentive in the free market to seek out new products and services as well as ways to reduce costs, but under socialism the state planners must rely on past formulas and production methods rather than future improvements. In short, there is no mechanism for innovation and discovery. It is not surprising that new products almost always come from the free world and that communist countries, which contain one third of the world's population, account for only 3 percent of technological innovations.

Baumol and Blinder acknowledge the grave difficulties in central planning decision making in a chapter entitled "The Price System and the Case for Laissez Faire." In a discussion of input–output analysis, which shows the complex variety of inputs necessary to produce an economy's outputs, they recognize the near impossibility of central planning. They conclude with a surprisingly strong case for the free market:

A full, rigorous central-planning solution to the production problem is a tremendous task, requiring an overwhelming quantity of information and some incredibly difficult calculations. Yet this very difficult job is carried out automatically and unobtrusively by the price mechanism in a free-market economy.[27]

In one of the most revealing admissions by a socialist, Robert Heilbroner, author of the best-selling book *The Worldly Philosophers,* announced recently that the long-standing debate between capitalism and socialism is over: Capitalism has won, Mises and Hayek have finally been vindicated. Heilbroner goes on to state, "The Soviet Union, China, and Eastern Europe have given us the clearest possible proof that capitalism organizes the material affairs of humankind more satisfactorily than socialism: that however inequitably or irresponsibly the marketplace may distribute goods, it does so better than the queues of a planned economy; however mindless the culture of commercialism, it is more attractive than state moralism; and however deceptive the ideology of a business civilization, it is more believable than that of a socialist one."[28] And so ends a critical chapter in the history of economics.

HUNT AND SHERMAN: THE SOCIALIST CRITIQUE

The most popular textbook on radical economics is written by E. K. Hunt and Howard Sherman.[29] Their introductory course is indeed very different from the traditional elementary economics textbook. It is explicitly biased toward socialist thought and is a radical critique of neoclassical economics. The standard textbook analyses of microeconomics and macroeconomics are presented but only so that they may be attacked by radical economists. By radical, Hunt and Sherman do not mean the radical views of free-market economists such as Mises and Rothbard, but rather socialists such as Marx and Veblen.

The structure of Hunt and Sherman's textbook is in many ways more interesting than that of the standard textbooks,

which the authors claim are often dull and mechanical. Like
Marx, they are more interested in discussing the more exciting
present social and political issues, such as poverty, racism, sexual discrimination, monopolistic power, unequal education opportunities, tax loopholes, pollution, population, war spending,
and imperialism. Some of the following chapter headings illustrate this difference:

1. Market Allocation of Resources: Efficiency versus
   Fairness.
2. Government: Welfare or Warfare?
3. Economic Underdevelopment: Natural Causes or
   Imperialism?

Unlike any other text, Hunt and Sherman's begins with an
evolutionary history of political economy and the history of
economic thought. The writers discuss slavery, feudalism,
mercantilism, capitalism and the industrial revolution, insti-
tutionalism, revolutionary socialism, and imperialism. They
devote two chapters to Marx, another to Veblen, and one to
Keynes.

Hunt and Sherman debate the modern capitalist system
from both points of view, as both defenders and critics. They
emphasize many problems in economic life and debunk several
popular myths, such as the idea that inflation is good and the
idea that high population density is necessarily a cause of
underdevelopment. But generally they have little good to say
about the capitalist system, which they seem to think is responsible for practically all of the ills in the world (pollution,
discrimination, war, inequality of wealth, poverty, etc.). As rad-
icals they contend that "total alienation pervades and dominates contemporary American capitalism," and argue that the
impersonal giant corporations leave workers full of emptiness,
apathy, boredom, and despair.

Unfortunately, Hunt and Sherman make no mention of the
emptiness, apathy, boredom, and despair workers face on a
much greater scale in socialist countries. They say nothing
about the pollution, discrimination, poverty, and war among
collectivist nations. They make only a cursory reference to the

shortages and long lines for many goods in the Soviet Union, due to repressed inflation and overplanning.

Hunt and Sherman are pessimists on virtually every page. On income distribution they summarize, "Income is very unequally distributed in the United States. . . . In the radical view, capitalists are extremely wealthy parasites." On labor they state, "Workers are not forced to work by physical coercion, as are slaves and serfs, but are 'free' to work for a capitalist or not to work and hence to starve." Workers apparently cannot save, start their own businesses, or climb out of a vicious circle of poverty and exploitation. According to Hunt and Sherman, the Horatio Alger rags-to-riches story is a myth.

But most of this exhibits sheer ignorance. There are hundreds of thousands of examples of people who have started at the bottom and worked themselves to the top. Millions of workers do save enough to buy their own homes, start their own businesses, or retire on excellent company or individual pension plans. And many enjoy the challenge and variety of working for a major corporation.

Hunt and Sherman contend that only "a few people receive the overwhelming bulk of all profits generated by the economy." This is patently false. Millions of workers are the beneficiaries of higher profits through increased employment, higher wages, and greater fringe benefits, including profit-sharing plans. Over 50 million Americans own stocks of publicly trading companies, thus participating directly in the profitability of capitalism.

The Henry Ford story of the $5-a-day wage is a classic example of how increased profits help people throughout the entire economy, not just the wealthy. Sales at Ford grew dramatically from $42 million in 1912 to $89 million in 1913. Out of this mammoth increase in net assets, Henry Ford decided to more than double the income of his employees, from $2 a day to $5 a day. As a result, there was a tremendous surge in productivity and skyrocketing morale among Ford workers. Needless to say, the famous $5-a-day story is conspicuously absent from Hunt and Sherman, as well as from the top 10 textbooks. (But you can find the story told in detail in

John Chamberlain's *The Roots of Capitalism,* Robert Sobel's
The Entrepreneurs, and Jonathan Hughes's *The Vital Few.*)

Hunt and Sherman make outrageous claims, such as, "Private enterprise economy emphasizes production primarily for
the wealthy [producing] trinkets, useless gadgets, and other
trivia [for the rich instead of] necessities of life [for the poor]."
How wrong can they be? The free market does indeed offer
merchandise at Bloomingdale's, Saks Fifth Avenue, Harrod's,
and other swank department stores, but it also offers merchandise at Sears, J. C. Penney, and K mart. It does make Cadillacs
and BMWs, but it also makes Chevys and Toyotas. It does produce Hilton and Hyatt hotels, but it also produces Holiday Inns
and Motel 6s. It does offer food at high-priced restaurants like
Maxim's and 21, but it also offers food at McDonald's and
Burger King. It does build houses in Beverly Hills and Scarsdale, but it also builds houses in Levittown. And the free market offers all of these goods and services at a profit.

On the issue of central planning, Hunt and Sherman state,
"Both theory and historical evidence indicate that public ownership with planning can eliminate both unemployment and
inflation (except for externally caused inflation)." But if shoddy
goods are produced, or none at all, is this not inflation? If workers and managers are misplaced in the economic system, is not
this another form of unemployment that economists call "underemployment"? I wonder how Hunt and Sherman will react
to the new openness in Eastern Europe.

Hunt and Sherman's book suffers from many of the defects
I've associated with the standard textbooks. It includes virtually nothing on the gold standard; the ill effects of a minimum wage law; or the economic miracles of West Germany,
Japan, and the four tigers. While extolling the Soviet Union's
remarkably rapid economic growth rate since 1928, which allowed it to achieve its status as a developed country by 1938,
they argue that socialist state ownership is an essential instrument to overcome backwardness in third-world countries.
Meanwhile, Hunt and Sherman ignore the disastrous results of
Marxist regimes in third-world countries that have tried expropriation, nationalization, and taxing the rich—Ghana, Cuba,
Nicaragua, Tanzania, Poland, and Romania, to name just a few.

In the theoretical debate over economic calculation under socialism, the authors cite Lange and Taylor but make no reference to Mises and Hayek, who raised the issue in the first place.

The Strengths and Weaknesses of the Market

Radical socialist economists—including Marx, Veblen, Galbraith, and Harrington—have traditionally focused on serious economic problems that need addressing. Hunt and Sherman point out the redistributive ill effects of inflation, which usually benefit the rich and hurt the poor. They note how the legislature and federal government are controlled largely by wealthy individuals and big corporations that seek protectionist legislation and special privileges. They stress how low-income citizens are often taxed at higher rates than the wealthy, whose special loopholes offset the graduated income tax. They emphasize how big business supports and benefits from a large military budget, which Hunt and Sherman label wasteful.

The Darker Side of Corporate Capitalism

The accusations made by Hunt and Sherman are serious and cannot be ignored. They represent the dark side of corporate capitalism. It is unfortunate that many free-market advocates fail to emphasize the fraudulent activities engaged in by market participants—dishonest salesmen; stock fraud promoters; and businesses that take advantage of consumers, engage in predatory pricing, and profit from political influence.

Fortunately, some free-market advocates—including Milton Friedman, Thomas Sowell, and Murray Rothbard—have condemned the special privileges and monopolistic practices of corporate bureaucracy. A recent example is *The Suicide Corporation: How Big Business Fails America,* written by Paul H. Weaver, a former Ford executive. Weaver discusses in great detail how major corporations have sought the protection of the welfare state through "tariffs, subsidies, official monopolies, tax breaks, immunity from certain tort actions, government-supported research and development, free manpower training programs, countercyclical economic management, defense spending, wage controls, and so on through the long list of the welfare state's indulgences and beneficences."[30]

Unfortunately, the radical socialists have chosen the wrong direction for eliminating these abuses and special benefits to the wealthy business class. The solution is not to engage in wholesale nationalization and central planning, but to eliminate the special privileges and unfair advantages and force the large corporations to compete on an equal basis with small business and foreign companies. Tariffs, subsidies, and monopolies should be abolished. Such action will not necessarily eliminate large firms, but it will put them on a more equal footing with other businesses.

SUMMARY

In summary, socialism does not work because it limits the freedom of people to do what they want and what they think is best for themselves. Intelligent people, those responsible for the management and creation of the production processes, do not like the government telling them what they can and cannot do. When the government tries to intervene, the results are counterproductive—lower productivity, underground activity, and emigration.

Miller suggests that the Marxist slogan "From each according to his ability, to each according to his needs" appeals to many social reformers, including Christians, as a high-minded ethical standard. Such attractive slogans have made revolutionary socialism popular in areas of the world that suffer from severe poverty, social unrest, and strong-armed dictators. But high-sounding moral phrases can be misleading and sometimes dangerous. The Marxist slogan just mentioned implies a forced, not a voluntary, organization. There is a serious difference between saying "All that I have is yours" and "All that you have is mine." Moreover, the Marxist slogan also implies that any income earned beyond one's needs should be turned over to the central government and distributed to those who earned less than their needs. In short, this amounts to a 100 percent marginal tax rate. Once the Marxist slogan is seen for what it really is, one can understand why pure socialism imposes huge disincentives to work, which causes an eventual collapse.

NOTES

1. William J. Baumol and Alan S. Blinder, *Economics: Principles and Policy,* 4th ed. (New York: Harcourt Brace Jovanovich, 1988), p. 884.
2. Karl Marx and Friedrich Engels, "The Communist Manifesto," in *Karl Marx, Selected Writings* (Oxford: Oxford University Press, 1977), p. 246.
3. Ibid.
4. Ibid.
5. Karl Marx, *Capital,* Vol. 1 (New York: Viking Penguin, 1976), p. 127. The first chapter, entitled "The Commodity," states, "The valid exchange-values of a particular commodity express something equal."
6. Paul Johnson, *Intellectuals* (New York: Harper & Row, 1989), p. 60.
7. Robert L. Heilbroner, *The Worldly Philosophers* (New York: Simon & Schuster, 1953), p. 124.
8. Saul K. Padover, *Karl Marx: An Intimate Biography* (New York: McGraw Hill, 1978), pp. 461, 468, 471.
9. Gary North, "The Myth of Marx's Poverty," in *Marx's Religion of Revolution* (Tyler, Tex.: Institute for Christian Economics, 1989), pp. 251–54.
10. Robert Payne, *Marx* (New York: Simon & Schuster, 1968), p. 12.
11. Marshall I. Goldman, *USSR in Crisis: The Failure of an Economic System* (New York: W. W. Norton & Co., 1983), p. 2.
12. *The New York Times,* January 1, 1989, p. 1.
13. Zbigniew Brzezinski, *The Grand Failure* (New York: Scribners, 1989), pp. 236–42.
14. Lawrence W. Reed, "Comparative Economic Systems:

Teaching Through Overseas Travel," in *Economic Education in the PreCollege Setting* (Santa Monica, CA: Reason Foundation, 1988), p. 112.

15. Kate Schecter, "Soviet Medicine," in *Back in the USSR,* ed. Kate Schecter et al. (New York: Scribner's Sons, 1989), p. 301.
16. Reed, "Comparative Economic Systems," p. 112.
17. Brzezinski, *The Grand Failure,* pp. 236–37.
18. Ibid., p. 250.
19. Quoted in Tom Bethell, "Socialism by the Textbook," *National Review* (October 13, 1989), p. 38.
20. John Templeton, *The Templeton Prizes* (Garden City, N. Y.: Doubleday, 1983), p. 72.
21. Sven Rydenfelt, *A Pattern for Failure: Socialist Economies in Crisis* (San Diego: Harcourt Brace Jovanovich, 1984), pp. 113–15.
22. Hernando de Soto, *The Other Path* (New York: Harper & Row, 1989), p. xxvii.
23. Quoted in Ludwig Erhard, *Prosperity Through Competition: The Economics of the German Miracle* (New York: Praeger, 1958), p. 13. This is Erhard's fascinating account of his critical role as economic minister.
24. Thomas Sowell, *Knowledge and Decisions* (New York: Basic Books, 1980), p. 214.
25. Friedrich A. Hayek, ed., *Collectivist Economic Planning* (New York: Augustus M. Kelley, 1975 [1933]). For an update on this debate, see Don Lavoie, *Rivalry and Central Planning: The Socialist Calculation Debate Reconsidered* (Cambridge: Cambridge University Press, 1985).
26. See Oskar Lange and Fred M. Taylor, *On the Economic Theory of Socialism* (New York: McGraw-Hill, 1964).
27. Baumol and Blinder, *Economics,* p. 586.
28. Robert Heilbroner, "The Triumph of Capitalism," *The New Yorker* (January 23, 1989), p. 98.
29. E. K. Hunt and Howard Sherman, *Economics: An Introduction to Traditional and Radical Views,* 5th ed. (New York: Harper & Row, 1986).

30. Paul H. Weaver, *The Suicide Corporation* (New York: Simon & Schuster, 1988), p. 18.

RECOMMENDED READING

Brzezinski, Zbigniew. *The Grand Failure: The Birth and Death of Communism in the Twentieth Century.* New York: Scribners, 1989. The former national security advisor under President Jimmy Carter says that communism is "the most extravagant and wasteful experiment in social engineering ever attempted." (p. 240) According to Brzezinski, it is only a matter of time before the Soviet Union becomes a "disunion" and communism in general is abandoned.

Goldman, Marshall I. *USSR in Crisis: The Failure of an Economic System.* New York: W. W. Norton, 1983.

Rydenfelt, Sven. *A Pattern of Failure: Socialist Economies in Crisis.* San Diego: Harcourt Brace Jovanovich, 1984. Reviews the recent economic performance of socialist countries, such as Ghana, Cuba, Poland, and India.

de Soto, Hernando. *The Other Path.* New York: Harper & Row, 1989. Through the eyes of Peru, one sees why Latin America remains poor despite its great people and abundant natural resources.

CHAPTER 18

THE STRANGE CASE OF PERFECT COMPETITION

Market economies do have their own weaknesses. When firms possess market power, output is restricted below the social optimum.
— Roy J. Ruffin and Paul R. Gregory
Principles of Economics (1988)

Free-market supporters usually state that the problem in the economics profession is not in the field of microeconomics, which involves the theory of supply and demand for individual markets, but almost exclusively in the field of macroeconomics, which justifies massive government intervention. The previous chapters have attempted to respond to the major weaknesses in macroeconomic analysis.

But there are also some fundamental defects in the way microeconomics is taught in the classroom. One example is the concept of perfect competition, which is set up as an ideal in the marketplace. Any shift away from this ideal is viewed as a tendency toward monopoly, resulting in an alleged reduction in output, an increase in prices at less than optimum conditions, and therefore a justification for antitrust action by the government to make the economy more competitive.

WHAT IS PERFECT COMPETITION?

Perfect competition is described as a set of conditions in the market structure that favor optimum output. Most of the textbooks list four standard characteristics of perfect competition:

1. A large number of independent buyers and sellers are present; no one of these is large enough to have any influence on price.
2. The product is homogeneous; buyers choose a good that they regard as the same, no matter which seller they buy it from.
3. There is perfect knowledge—complete information about prices, qualities, etc.
4. There are no barriers to entry or exit; any firm can move in or out of the industry without difficulty or cost.

Economists frequently point to most agricultural markets as perfectly competitive. Stock markets and commodity markets are also perfectly competitive, they say, and international competition has forced many previously monopolistic markets (such as automobile and steel production markets) to approximate the conditions of perfect competition. Neoclassical economists often regard the perfect competition model as ideal because, they claim, it maximizes output at the lowest long-term cost of production. Miller illustrates the point of long-term equilibrium under perfect competition in Figure 18–1.

THE CASE OF IMPERFECT COMPETITION

After developing the purely competitive model, mainstream economists contrast it with the "imperfect competition model," based on the work of Joan Robinson and Edward Chamberlin in the 1930s. The textbooks refer to three basic categories of imperfect competition—monopoly, oligopoly, and monopolistic competition. The characteristics of the imperfect competition model are, in general, as follows:

1. Few buyers or sellers exist in the marketplace, so that one firm can be large enough to influence the price it charges for its products or the costs of production.
2. Products are heterogeneous—they differ in quality, design, and price. The monopolistic supplier uses brand names, advertises, and engages in price discrimination, charging some buyers less and others more.

FIGURE 18–1
Long-Run Equilibrium

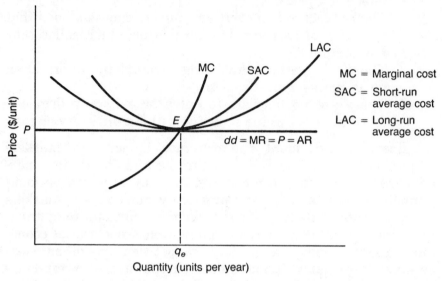

Quantity (units per year)

Source: From *Economics Today*, 6th Edition by Roger Leroy Miller, p. 539. Copyright © 1988 by Harper & Row, Publishers, Inc. Reprinted by permission of the publisher.

3. Information is imperfect, creating profitable opportunities for insiders.
4. There are barriers to entry and exit; it may require substantial capital to enter a monopolistic market.

Examples of goods produced under imperfect competition include automobiles, aircraft, steel, ships, newspapers, drugs, petroleum, household appliances, and computers. According to the above definition, almost all industries have some elements of monopolistic power in them.

According to proponents of perfect competition, imperfect competition is less than ideal because it restricts output and raises prices, depending on its monopolistic power. Production is carried forward to a point less than the firm's long-term marginal cost. Figure 18–2, taken from Baumol and Blinder, demonstrates the economic loss resulting from a move away from ideal competition.

FIGURE 18–2
Long-Run Equilibrium of the Firm under Monopolistic Competition

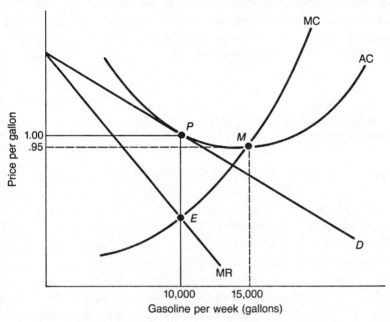

Source: Figure 28–2 from *Economics: Principles and Policy,* Fourth Edition, by William J. Baumol and Alan S. Blinder, p. 615, copyright © 1988 by Harcourt Brace Jovanovich, Inc., reprinted by permission of the publisher.

Baumol and Blinder use the example of a gas station to compare monopolistic competition and perfect competition. In Figure 18–2, we note that the point of long-term equilibrium for the purely competitive gas station is M, so that the station sells 15,000 gallons of gasoline per week, at 95 cents per gallon. On the other hand, the point of long-term equilibrium for the monopolistic gas station is P, so that the firm sells 10,000 gallons per week at $1.00 per gallon.

The message is clear: Any type of imperfect competition is economically bad for the country. The monopolistic gas station sells less gasoline at a higher price than does the purely competitive station. The model implies that forcing the gas station to reduce its price from $1.00 to 95 cents would increase gasoline sales substantially, thus reducing the profit per gallon without hurting the company's net profits. In general, the model implies that some form of price-control legislation (especially on natural monopolies, such as public utilities) or antitrust legislation (such as the breaking up of the gas station monopoly by the major gasoline companies) could lower prices, increase production, and enhance the nation's standard of living.

WHAT'S WRONG WITH THIS MODEL OF COMPETITION?

The dichotomy between perfect and imperfect competition in the neoclassical model is a wrong-headed, inaccurate, and artificial description of real competition in the marketplace. There are several reasons why the perfect competition model is neither perfect nor ideal as a description of what firms ought to be doing to maximize economic well-being.

First, the terms of definition create a negative image for business. Since most companies do not qualify under the strict meaning of pure competition, they are labeled imperfect and monopolistic. Such pejorative terms do not belong in a supposedly objective presentation of theoretical economics, even if such terms have a long tradition in the literature.

Second, it is not appropriate for all industries to involve a large number of sellers. Many sectors of the economy—including mining, manufacturing, and department-store retailing—necessitate huge capital requirements to enter a certain business, thereby discouraging small firms from getting started. Moreover, it is usually necessary to have big firms in order to achieve large economies of scale and to be able to purchase resources in bulk at a discount. The discounting of large orders tremendously reduces per-item costs and ultimately benefits consumers as retail prices also decline.

In short, imposing a perfect competition model on an industry by breaking it up into many smaller firms would be costly. It would reduce, not increase, the general welfare. To break up several large firms into a large number of smaller firms would actually raise prices, reduce output, and lower a nation's standard of living. If General Motors, Ford, Toyota, and other major automobile manufacturers were forced to break up into 100 different firms, the price of cars would undoubtedly increase substantially.

Certainly, an observer can see that some industries are characterized by a large number of firms, whereas others are characterized by only a few. What is the optimum number? This is impossible to predict. As long as businesses and individuals are not restricted artificially by law, the market process (through the actions of entrepreneurs) will determine the optimum number of firms in each industry at any point in time, as well as the size of each firm. Cost cutting will usually encourage largeness, but excessive bureaucracy will tend to encourage smallness.

Monopolistic power is, in large measure, granted by the state, not the free market. National and local governments create monopolistic conditions by imposing licensing restrictions (on professions, television and radio stations, etc.), passing zoning regulations, or granting exclusive privileges (e.g., first class mail to the U.S. postal service). If the definition of a monopoly is, as according to Miller, "a single supplier that constitutes the entire industry," then certainly such a condition would hardly ever occur naturally in the free market over the long run; it would have to be state-imposed.

Market Concentration Does Not Signify Monopoly Power

It is also important to point out that the existence of only a few firms does not necessarily mean that a competitive environment does not exist nor that optimum pricing and output cannot be met. Even if there are only a few firms in an industry whose product is considered a necessity, one firm cannot automatically raise prices and capture monopolistic profits. The firm would quickly lose business to its competitors (which include foreign producers, not just domestic producers). Collusion between the firms would be essential to maintaining a high level of profits. Yet, as most textbooks indicate, cartel arrangements are difficult to enforce. The market encourages a breakdown of such cartels because, quite simply, cheating is profitable and excessive prices encourage the increase of output outside the cartel. Even the state-controlled Organization of Petroleum Exporting Countries (OPEC) has had great difficulty controlling the price of oil and has only managed to maintain its power longer than a market cartel partly because it is state-controlled.

Third, customers usually desire product differentiation and brand names. Sometimes individuals and businesses want low-priced, homogeneous products, but most of the time they demand a wide variety in quality and price. Processers may not demand more than one kind of wheat, but store buyers want to choose from among 30 types of bread, as anyone can see by visiting a major grocery store. If the government were to suppress consumer demands and to impose only one generic style of consumer products, the standard of living would definitely decline. It is improper to call the demand for homogeneous generic goods perfect and the demand for heterogeneous brand names imperfect.

Fourth, information is never perfect. To assume perfect knowledge is to deny a basic axiom of human activity. The future is always uncertain; market conditions are always changing. The idea of profit and loss implies imperfect knowledge. A theory based on perfect knowledge and absolute certainty of the future cannot serve as a basis of market behavior.

AN IMPERFECT MODEL, EVEN FOR AGRICULTURE

The worst thing about the perfect competition model is that it essentially denies real competition. (Strangely, the perfect competition model imitates a purely monopolistic cartel model in that all participants end up charging the same price.) No one appears to influence price or costs; these are given in the model. Participants in the market are price takers, not price makers. There is little if any rivalry and there are no entrepreneurs making judgments about the future. Producers merely imitate other producers rather than trying to reduce costs, improve products and services, or create new ones.

In this sense, even agriculture does not fit the perfect competition model. There is considerable rivalry and entrepreneurship among farmers even though there are millions of them. Farmers are constantly making decisions about what to grow or raise. Many keep up-to-date on new farming methods, new technologies and equipment, use of computers, and so forth. Farmers choose from among a wide variety of agricultural products—wheat, corn, soybeans, cattle, hogs, chickens, etc. The price for each product may be determined by a huge market outside the influence of a single farmer, but the individual farmer does decide the combination of products that he will produce. Moreover, the costs of raising crops or animals, and of running a farm in general, are not fixed by any means. Farmers may be price takers, but they are not cost takers. The costs of agricultural land, equipment, and other factors of production vary considerably from farmer to farmer. During the 1980s, most U.S. farmers faced low prices for grains, but although some farmers went bankrupt, others survived and even prospered by keeping their costs below normal.

COMPETITION: A SITUATION OR A PROCESS?

One of the most devastating critiques of the neoclassical model of competition is presented by Israel Kirzner (who, disappointingly, is cited very briefly in only 2 of the top 10 textbooks). In his penetrating work, *Competition and Entrepreneurship,* Kirzner criticizes both the perfect and imperfect competition models for describing competition as a situation rather than a process. Both of the competition models are what Kirzner calls "equilibrium models." As Richard Ebeling put it, the neoclassical model makes competition passive, like a noun, rather than active, like a verb. Kirzner asserts that the Robinson–Chamberlin monopolistic competition model did nothing to destroy the inaccuracy of the perfect competition model: "On the contrary, its attack on the relevance of the theory of perfect competition tended to strengthen use of the perfectly competitive economy as a norm from which to judge the efficiency of the real world."[1]

D. T. Armentano, in his in-depth work entitled *The Myths of Antitrust,* is even more blunt in condemning the perfect competition model: "Businessmen and consumers would hardly describe selling markets with no direct price competition, no product differentiation, no brand names, no selling costs, no location advantages, no advertising, no economies of scale, and no innovation as 'purely competitive'!"[2] In fact, they would regard such characteristics as the essence of competition, not a movement away from it.

In conclusion, the perfect competition model is a false description of what really happens in the economy. As such, it should be rejected. As Joseph Schumpeter concludes, "Perfect competition is not only impossible but inferior, and has no title to being set up as a model of ideal efficiency."[3]

THE CENTRAL ROLE OF THE ENTREPRENEUR

The fundamental flaw of the neoclassical competition model is that it denies the role of the entrepreneur, the central figure in the whole economic process. By *entrepreneur,* economists mean the business owner and producer who assumes the risk, uncertainty, and responsibility of running an enterprise. He invests capital, including his own, hoping to make a profit and to avoid losses. But since no profit or loss exists in the perfect competition model in the long run, the entrepreneur theoretically plays no role. Dolan is one of the few textbook writers who attempt to incorporate entrepreneurship into the neoclassical model, but such an attempt is like mixing water with oil. Even Dolan admits, "There is no way to capture entrepreneurial behavior precisely in terms of equations or graphs, because the notion of entrepreneurship is itself one of change, uncertainty, and innovation." In addition, the entrepreneur is missing from the standard monopoly model as well, since by definition there is no rivalry.

Used originally by J. B. Say, *entrepreneur* is a French word meaning one who undertakes a business venture and assumes the risk in order to make a profit. As such, it is the entrepreneur as business owner and risk taker who supplies what consumers demand. Without the decision maker, economic performance and living standards could not be advanced. Who are the entrepreneurs? Historian Robert Sobel says they are "men and women of vision and energy [who] have seen possibilities where others saw none, seized opportunities when others hesitated, persevered when others gave up."[4] Entrepreneurs are innovators who reshape patterns of production and distribution, develop new products and processes, open new markets and sources of supply, devise new forms of organization, and improve existing companies (for which they are sometimes called "intrapreneurs"). They are also speculators who seek a profit in the stock, commodity, and foreign currency markets, or who take advantage of discrepancies between markets for the same good (an act known as "arbitrage"). They may try to take over existing companies considered to be undervalued or poorly managed. They are opportunists and visionary organizers who bring together capitalists, landlords, workers, and specialized knowledge to create goods and services that they hope consumers will demand. Kirzner describes entrepreneurs as individuals who are alert to opportunities and new ways of accomplishing tasks. Entrepreneurship is also a discovery process. Many times individuals are surprised by the outcome of new processes and decisions in the marketplace.

Risk and uncertainty are often high but so is the potential reward. Successful entrepreneurs have often been the object of envy because they command large incomes. But their wealth is justified if they have earned it honestly by offering unique skills and taking risks others would not take. Everyone is a risk taker and decision maker, including wage earners and consumers, but business owners are willing to take much greater risks and therefore should be compensated accordingly.

Since entrepreneurship does not fit into the neoclassical model of competition and monopoly, the textbook writers do not dwell on it as a concept. "It is a scandal," notes Mark

Blaug, "that nowadays students of economics spend years in the study of the subject before hearing the term *entrepreneur*."[5] With a few exceptions, economics writers do not make much use of it.

ECONOMISTS' RESPONSE TO CRITICISM

Mainstream economists have gradually recognized the unrealistic and inaccurate nature of their models of competition, even while continuing to use them. One of the most refreshing improvements in the textbook discussion of competition is found in Dolan's fifth edition, coauthored with David Lindsey. After presenting the traditional market structures of competition and monopoly, Dolan includes a chapter entitled "Entrepreneurship and the Market Process," which points out the severe limitations of the neoclassical model. Dolan states:

> Neoclassical models are not adept at dealing with those aspects of entrepreneurship that, through innovations in organization and technology, seek to shift cost curves. Nor are they well suited to aspects of entrepreneurship that seek to shift demand curves or to create new products for which demand curves previously did not exist at all.[6]

Dolan emphasizes the positive, crucial role that entrepreneurs play in marketing, advertising, arbitrage, and other forms of economic activity. According to Dolan, marketing is ignored entirely in the neoclassical model of pure competition. He notes that neoclassical models "assume, for the most part, that the problem of marketing has been solved before the analysis begins."

Efforts have been made to accommodate these criticisms, but the basic models of competition and monopoly have survived in the textbooks and are still used extensively because they lend themselves easily to mathematical and graphic description and, according to their proponents, fit many real-world situations.

Price Takers versus Price Searchers

Others have adopted a method originally developed by Armen A. Alchian and William R. Allen in their innovative textbook, *University Economics* (which went through three editions, but unfortunately has not been updated for years). Instead of dividing firms into perfect and imperfect markets, Alchian and Allen divide industries into "price takers" and "price searchers."[7]

Paul Heyne advances the concept of Alchian and Allen in his unorthodox and creative work, *The Economic Way of Thinking,* now in its fifth edition. It is probably the best up-to-date textbook on how the economy really works on a microeconomic scale. (Sadly, it falls way below the top 10 textbooks in annual sales.) Heyne rejects the monopolistic–competitive dichotomy, which he says is misleading and "erroneously implies that price searchers face no competition."[8]

THE UNIVERSAL MODEL OF PROFIT SEEKING

But although the model of price taking and price searching is a step in the right direction, I believe we should go a step further and establish one model of competition for all firms in the free market. The ultimate goal of every firm in the marketplace is not to be a price taker or price searcher, but to be a "profit seeker." By emphasizing profit, our model can include other important factors in the market, such as product quality, variety, customer services, new products and services, price changes, and cost cutting. By using the term *profit seeker,* I am not suggesting that firms are only short-term profit maximizers. They may have other goals that will enhance the company over the long run. In short, by emphasizing the long-term profit motive, we can include in our model the wide variety of economic activities that we witness in the market, whether these are price taking, price searching, shifting demand curves, shifting cost curves, or creating entire new markets.

How can we picture long-term equilibrium for all firms or industries seeking a profit? Figure 18–3 illustrates the long-term situation. Figure 18–3 is quite different from the standard textbook description of the long-term equilibrium of a firm. First, note that the average cost curve is flat for a period of output. Standard textbooks usually show only one point where the average cost curve is at a minimum. But most businesspeople know that once economies of scale are reached, average costs can remain stable at various points of output.

Second, long-term equilibrium is achieved when the profit rate equals the interest rate on investments throughout the economy. According to the standard textbook analysis of the competitive case, firms expand output to the point at which marginal revenue equals marginal cost as well as average cost. But in Figure 18–3, we show that the firm expands output to the point at which the profit margin equals the average interest return on all investments. In the evenly rotating economy, the firm earns a natural interest rate of return, equal to society's time preference.[9]

FIGURE 18–3
Firm's Long-Run Equilibrium Profit Level

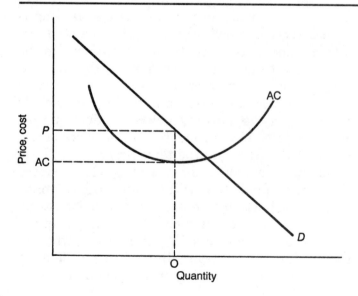

Figure 18–3 applies to all market participants and makes no distinction between firms on the basis of size, market share, or alleged market power. Maximum output is achieved at the lowest cost, whether the demand curve is flat or downward-sloping (in economist's jargon, highly elastic or inelastic).

In the textbook case, only the perfect competition model shows the marginal revenue curve tangent to the point of lowest long-term cost, thus achieving maximum output at the lowest cost. But in the generalized model, all firms on the free market can achieve maximum production at the least expensive cost.

In short, only through government restrictions and special privileges can output be permanently reduced and prices artificially raised. The free market—if it is truly free and without fraud—provides for maximum social efficiency, optimum output, and the lowest prices while fulfilling consumer demand. In Figure 18–3, we see that there is no persistent misallocation of resources in the free market; costs are minimized and output is maximized whether the demand for a good is elastic or inelastic.

It is also important to realize that achieving equilibrium in the marketplace, where the profit margin is equal to the average interest return on other investments, does not signify a resting place where entrepreneurial decision making ends and businesspeople stop searching for ways to improve their positions. Prices for a firm's products and services may be stable where supply equals demand, but the business owner remains alert to possible methods to cut costs, improve quality, build a new and more attractive infrastructure, introduce new products, and so forth. Economic observers have noted over the years the gradual improvement in the quality and variety of goods, services, and infrastructure in many areas of the world brought about by companies whose products have supposedly reached a stable profit level. In sum, equilibrium economics does not mean static conditions—change can and does continue to take place.

DOES COST DETERMINE PRICE?

Before leaving the world of microeconomics, let us discuss one other major error that many textbooks commit, namely, the idea that in the long run price is determined by the cost of production. Referring to his perfect competition diagram (reproduced in Figure 18–1), Miller states, "Thus, perfectly competitive firms always sell their goods at a price that just equals marginal costs." The neoclassical orthodoxy teaches that prices of goods and services are objectively determined by their costs of production in the long run, a concept standardized by the British economist Alfred Marshall.

In reality, costs—like all prices—are subjective in nature and ultimately are determined by demand. Of course, in a static equilibrium condition, a company must be able to charge a high enough price to cover its costs, or it will eventually go out of business. It is also true that many businesspeople attempt to price their products according to a cost-plus-markup theory. But, in reality, this markup approach to pricing is simply a practical method of estimating higher demand for products. Businesspeople know that prices can be adjusted sometimes by more than the cost increase and sometimes by less.

Businesspeople also know that their costs are not as fixed or given as most economists would have us believe. In a dynamic setting, the costs of production are actually quite flexible. Mainstream economists believe that fixed costs can vary only in the long run, but actually they can become unfixed very quickly when economic conditions change. Costs are really nothing more than prices of goods and services in an earlier stage of production, and therefore costs are subject to change according to supply and demand conditions as well.

Let us examine the case of the oil industry during the 1970s and 1980s. The price of oil and oil-related products skyrocketed in the 1970s as a result of the OPEC cartel and inflationary demand. In response to rising prices, entrepreneurs stepped up their rate of oil exploration and development. Marginal oil wells suddenly became viable sources of new oil. As a result, the demand for oil rigs, equipment, labor, tankers, and refineries increased dramatically during the 1970s. In short, the costs of petroleum production rose. They were in no way fixed or given.

By the 1980s, entrepreneurs had been so successful in finding new supplies and bringing new oil to market that the energy crisis of the 1970s turned into the oil glut of the 1980s. The new supplies depressed the price of oil and oil-related products. Consequently, the demand for oil-related equipment and labor declined sharply in many parts of the world. Overall, the price of oil rigs and other related inputs declined during the oil glut. Oil rigs bought at previously high price levels often had to sell for less. Oil companies facing bankruptcy or a sharp cutback sold equipment and supplies at below cost. Eventually the oil industry stabilized at a new point of equilibrium, with both prices and costs at lower levels, and a profit margin was reestablished.

Changes in the oil industry provide just one of the innumerable examples of how consumers, producers, and resource owners work together through the market process. Prices and costs are constantly shifting throughout the structure of the economy in accordance with changing patterns of supply and demand. Neither prices nor costs are fixed when there is a shift in supply or demand. As the economy approaches long-term equilibrium, both prices and costs adjust systematically to achieve a profit level equal to the natural rate of interest. Thus we see that all economic activity forms a time-consuming market process that involves consumers, entrepreneurs, and resource owners.

NOTES

1. Israel Kirzner, *Competition and Entrepreneurship* (Chicago: University of Chicago Press, 1973), p. 92.
2. D. T. Armentano, *The Myths of Antitrust* (New Rochelle, N.Y.: Arlington House, 1972), p. 31. See also his updated work, *Antitrust Policy: Anatomy of a Policy Failure* (New York: John Wiley & Sons, 1982), for an excellent critique of antitrust policy in theory and prac-

tice. Armentano concludes that various antitrust and antimerger measures (The Sherman Act, the Clayton Act, the Robinson–Patman Act, etc.) are detrimental to the American economy.

3. Joseph Schumpeter, *Capitalism, Socialism and Democracy* (New York: Harper & Row, 1962), p. 106.
4. Robert Sobel and David B. Sicilia, *The Entrepreneurs: An American Adventure* (Boston: Houghton Mifflin, 1986), flyleaf.
5. Mark Blaug, *Economic History and the History of Economics* (New York: New York University Press, 1986), p. 229.
6. Edwin G. Dolan and David E. Lindsey, *Economics,* 5th ed. (Hinsdale, Ill.: Dryden Press, 1988), p. 676.
7. Armen A. Alchian and William R. Allen, *University Economics,* 3rd ed. (Belmont, CA: Wadsworth Publishing, 1972), pp. 111–28.
8. Paul Heyne, *The Economic Way of Thinking,* 5th ed. (Chicago: Science Research Assoc., 1987), p. 166.
9. Murray Rothbard, *Man, Economy and State* (Los Angeles: Nash Publishing, 1962), pp. 644–45. I acknowledge Rothbard for making this point so succinctly.

RECOMMENDED READING

Armentano, D. T. *Antitrust Policy: Anatomy of a Policy Failure.* New York: John Wiley & Sons, 1982. An updated version of Armentano's classic work, *The Myths of Antitrust.*

Gilder, George. *The Spirit of Enterprise.* New York: Simon & Schuster, 1984. This whole book is about entrepreneurs and their great contributions to society. The story of how the Cubans revitalized Miami is a classic chapter.

Kirzner, Israel. *Competition and Entrepreneurship.* Chicago: University of Chicago Press, 1973. The classic introduction to the real meaning of competition.

Sobel, Robert, and David B. Sicilia, *The Entrepreneurs: An American Adventure.* Boston: Houghton Mifflin, 1986. A delightful history of inventors, financiers and businessmen who changed the world for the better. Well-researched and illustrated accounts of the men behind oil, automobiles, soap, razors, elevators, etc

CHAPTER 19

THE ECONOMIST AS
INVESTMENT ADVISOR

Economics cannot teach you how to get rich.
—Roy J. Ruffin and Paul R. Gregory
Principles of Economics (1988)

Economists frequently underestimate the power their theories can have in everyday use. Ruffin and Gregory warn students that economics does not supply magic formulas that tell them how to choose a winning stock, or which way interest rates or the dollar are headed; economics is unable to predict the IBM of tomorrow.

The top 10 textbooks are remarkably silent regarding the investment markets, despite the critical role investments play in the economy. (Only one text, Baumol and Blinder's, has a chapter devoted to stocks and bonds.) Many academicians do not believe that the financial markets are very important; they may actually be disruptive. Economists draw a sharp distinction between the money economy, represented by the financial markets, and the real economy, the actual production of goods and services. What's important, they believe, are capital goods, not capital. Stock market fluctuations have very little to do with the real economy, they reason. Thus, Hyman Minsky has rightly criticized the neoclassical model as "the economics of capitalism without capitalists, capital assets, and financial markets."[1] The purpose of this chapter is to dispel this orthodox notion and to demonstrate why the investment markets are far more important than economists realize.

It is unfortunate that textbooks do not spend more time on the investment markets. The world of high finance provides an excellent laboratory in which to test economic theories. Prices of stocks, bonds, gold, and currencies vary every day in response to changing supply and demand; new information; economic crises; and the attitudes of millions of businesspeople, investors, and speculators. The opportunity is always present to make considerable profits and suffer losses. Economic analysis is also very useful in choosing which investment theories make sense and which don't—fundamental, technical, cyclical, contrarian, etc.

When I became the editor of a financial publication in the early 1970s, I felt woefully inadequate in my knowledge of the financial world. Economics is a cousin to finance, but I found that the academic world makes it a distant cousin. Even though I had majored in economics in college and received a master's degree and a doctorate in economics and banking, I knew very little about price-earnings ratios, margin buying, selling short, futures, and options. My academic teachers never spent much time explaining the basics of high finance, probably because they did not know much about high finance themselves. I had to learn everything on my own. I took intensive courses and workshops, read books and magazines, studied manuals, and passed commodity and stock market examinations.

ECONOMISTS AND FINANCIAL ADVICE

The Armchair Economist

There are two problems with economists when it comes to financial advice. First, economists are all too often uninterested in applying economics to specific investment decisions, and therefore they downplay the value of such application. They are seekers of knowledge, not mundane materialists. Ludwig von Mises once told his fiancée, "If you want a rich man, don't marry me. I am not interested in earning money. I am *writing* about money, but will never have much of my own."[2] Jenny

Marx once complained about her husband, "I wish Karl would accumulate capital instead of just writing about it."[3] Financial economist Burton G. Malkiel summarizes the academic disdain for monetary success: "A professor may inherit lots of money, he may marry lots of money, and he may spend lots of money, but he is never, never supposed to earn lots of money; it's unacademic."[4] Generally, the economists who have made a lot of money have done so through book royalties and speeches, not through shrewd investing in the futures markets. Friedman, Samuelson, and other wealthy economists are adamant about not rendering specific short-term investment advice.

Can Traders Beat the Market?

Second, many economists do not believe that you can beat the market. That is, they believe that investors cannot consistently make big money in stocks, commodities, or any other financial market. I heard this peculiar view when I was an undergraduate, and it is still very much in vogue among academic theorists. It's called the "efficient-market theory," and it remains the dominant theory in finance schools. Samuelson and Baumol and Blinder discuss it favorably, and proponents of rational expectations often support it. It is the notion that markets are extremely efficient in the sense that in them all new information is quickly discounted. Therefore, no one can capture consistent profits by trading stocks, commodities, or options. As Samuelson summarizes, "You can't outguess the market." I call the efficient-market theory the perfect competition model of the financial world.

Efficient-market theory proponents point to numerous studies indicating that most professional money managers, stockbrokers, and investment advisors are unable to beat the averages (as measured by the Dow Jones Industrial Average or the S&P 500) or to perform better than a randomly selected portfolio of stocks. Nor can they accurately predict earnings by major corporations over a one-year or five-year period.

THE RANDOM WALK METHOD
OF INVESTING

The best alternative, says the armchair theorist, is to select stocks on a random basis. This is called the "random walk method" of investing. The most popular book on this subject is *A Random Walk Down Wall Street* (now in its fourth edition), by Burton G. Malkiel, dean of management at Yale University. Malkiel defines *random walk* as follows:

> A random walk . . . means that short-run changes in stock prices cannot be predicted. Investment advisory services, earnings predictions, and complicated chart patterns are useless. . . . Taken to its logical extreme, it means that a blindfolded monkey throwing darts at a newspaper's financial pages could select a portfolio that would do just as well as one carefully selected by the experts.[5]

While Wall Street analysts often dismiss the random walk method as academic nonsense, mainstream economists are enamored by it. Paul Samuelson likes Malkiel's book so much that he says he has given each of his children a copy. On the cover of Malkiel's first edition, Samuelson is quoted as saying, "There is no sure way to investment affluence, but Malkiel has outlined some of the booby traps and improved the odds in the reader's favor."

Baumol and Blinder also subscribe to the random walk idea, believing that forecasting individual stock prices is virtually impossible: "There is a mass of statistical evidence that the behavior of stock prices is in fact unpredictable."

The random walk method does not mean people should not invest in the stock market. Rather, proponents recommend that investors adopt a "buy-and-hold" strategy because stocks as a whole have an upward trend. Studies indicate that over the past 60 years, the U.S. stock market in general (as measured by the S&P 500 or its equivalent) rose at an average compounded rate of 10 percent.[6] Proponents of the random walk method usually oppose any form of trading the market because one cannot consistently predict the direction of the market in the short term, and because commissions and taxes will reduce the overall return. It is understandable that major brokerage firms do not usually subscribe to this approach; it would significantly reduce their role in the marketplace.

WHAT'S WRONG WITH THE EFFICIENT-MARKET THEORY?

In reality, there are several major objections to the efficient-market theory and the random walk method to investing. First, a minority of investment counselors and money managers have had superior market performance over the long run. Famous examples include the mutual fund magnate John Templeton; the investment advisor and founder of the Value Line Investment Survey, Arnold Bernhard; and the fundamental analyst Warren Buffett, to name a few. According to *Forbes'* annual survey of mutual funds, a number of money managers have outperformed the market over a long period of time and are regularly featured in the magazine's honor roll. Peter Lynch, former manager for the Magellan Fund, is an example. Recent studies indicate that the stock selections by the Value Line Investment Survey have consistently outperformed the market averages, and that its earnings forecasts have been more accurate than sophisticated methods based on past performance. One of the efficient-market theory's proponents, Fischer Black, a former professor at MIT who is currently with Goldman Sachs, concludes, "Value Line rankings . . . are certainly one of the exceptions to my rule that active portfolio management is generally worthless."[7]

  In response, critics contend that it is always possible, even in random betting, that a small minority of investment experts will outperform the market. A person flipping coins could possibly get heads 10 times in a row, for example. But consistent market performers do not engage in randomly flipping coins or blindly choosing stocks, and their record has been consistent for 30 years or more. Moreover, making superior returns year after year typically involves making hundreds of investment decisions each year.

Second, certain groups of investors tend to beat the market—for example, corporate insiders and specialists on the New York Stock Exchange. Richard Band, editor of *Personal Finance* and a certified financial analyst, studied the stock trading habits of officers and directors of publicly traded companies and concluded that "the insiders certainly do much better than the public at trading shares of their own companies."[8] Insiders apparently take advantage of knowledge not generally available to other investors.

Third, certain methods of investing consistently outperform the averages. Efficient-market theory proponents argue that professional traders will eliminate such anomalies over time, but this has not happened. One example is the January effect, the fact that stocks rise in January more consistently than any other month. (Why haven't investors recognized this well-advertised situation and started buying in December?) Another example is the method of buying stocks based on low price-earnings ratios. Financial analyst David Dreman has used this approach to make consistently higher profits. He recommends buying a diversified portfolio of low price-earnings (P/E) stocks and holding them for varying periods, in some cases up to nine years. Comparing his method to other investment techniques, he discovered, "Low P/E stocks not only gave you better performance, but were marginally safer."[9]

Fourth, although the efficient-market theory states that markets have incorporated nearly perfect knowledge, it is hard to imagine that the markets reflect current knowledge of corporate earnings and other financial data on the eve of a financial crisis or stock market crash. The October 1987 stock market debacle shook the foundations of the efficient-market theory because it became clear that prior to the crash the market did not contain all the vital information. The public is clearly wrong when trends suddenly and dramatically change.

THE KEY TO UNDERSTANDING
MARKET ACTION

In my studies of investment analysis, I have found that econo-mists and followers of the markets fall into three basic catego-ries. Each group fits somewhere along a continuum of market philosophy. The following spectrum illustrates the different types of investment philosophy.

Perfect	**Imperfect**	**No**
knowledge ⟵——	knowledge ——⟶	knowledge
of future	of future	of future

Those investors who fall into the "perfect knowledge of fu-ture" category are often technical traders who believe that the markets are totally rational, predictable, and mechanically precise. They feel that recent trends, volume, momentum, and other investment data reveal the future of asset prices, espe-cially in the short run. They may also rely on previous cycles or wave analysis to determine the future direction of prices. Some may even go so far as to predict exact dates for financial or economic events (such as the next depression) and specific targets for prices of investments. They strongly believe that there is a direct correlation between past events and future events. This category also includes econometricians who be-lieve that there is a strong direct correlation between markets and movements in interest rates, the money supply, elasticities, and other stringent relationships. This would include strict monetarists, who accept the crude quantity theory of money, i.e., that if the government doubles the money supply, prices will exactly double in the long run—although monetar-ists usually argue that economic activity is unpredictable in the short run.

Interestingly, I have found that the academic background of many technical traders is in the physical sciences. Such trad-ers often majored in engineering, physics, mathematics, or other pure sciences. Consequently, they search for mechanistic formulas in the stock market and the economy.

At the other extreme, there are those investors who believe that the markets are totally irrational and unpredictable in both the long run and short run. They fit into the "no knowledge of future" category. They believe that the market knows and instantly discounts everything, but the individual analyst knows nothing. Where will the market go next week, next month, or next year? "I don't know" is their most common response. "No one can predict the future" is another familiar phrase. The random walk and efficient-market theory followers are usually in this group.

The no-knowledge group includes some market traders who depend on moving averages to decide whether to invest in stocks or mutual funds, or to be on the sidelines. They believe they can beat the market by following the trends, switching into the market when the trend is upward and switching out of the market when the trend is downward. To determine a stock's moving average, analysts add up the stock's price for a certain number of weeks, divide by that number to find the average price, and then compare it to the current price. If the current price rises above its moving average, you buy; if it falls below its moving average, you sell. Switchers argue over which moving average is best (17 weeks, 39 weeks, 200 days, etc.), but they claim they can beat the averages even though they suffer occasional whipsaws (losses caused by short-term switches when the market is nearly trendless).

Keynesian economists often fit into the no-knowledge group. John Maynard Keynes, who was an avid speculator, believed that our knowledge of the future was virtually unpredictable. He likened the stock market to a casino or game of chance. In *The General Theory*, he opined, "For it is, so to speak, a game of Snap, of Old Maid, of Musical Chairs—a pastime in which he is victor who says *Snap* neither too soon nor too late, who passes the Old Maid to his neighbour before the game is over, who secures a chair for himself when the music stops."[10] A year later he wrote, "The fact that our knowledge of the future is fluctuating, vague and uncertain, renders wealth a peculiarly unsuitable subject for the methods of the classical economic theory." Regarding the future of events, he wrote, "there is no scientific basis on which to form any calculable probability whatever. We simply do not know."[11]

THE MIDDLE GROUND: KNOWLEDGE
IS IMPERFECT

I believe the truth lies somewhere in the middle ground between the two extremes of perfect knowledge and no knowledge. Our knowledge of the markets and the future is not perfect, but neither is it totally imperfect. Economic events and investment prices are not always predictable, but sometimes they are quite predictable. Markets are not totally efficient, but neither are they completely inefficient. This middle-ground position is similar to Hayek's view of money in the economy— not as a "tight joint" nor as a "broken joint," but as a "loose joint" (see Chapter 20).

In making investment decisions, we must always remember that economic activity and the financial markets in particular are based on the social science of human action. People are not like machines; we have free will. We learn from our mistakes and can alter our outlook. The social sciences are quite distinct from the physical sciences. Sir Isaac Newton once said, "I can calculate the motions of heavenly bodies, but not the madness of crowds."

There is some truth in the old refrain "History repeats itself." Past trends do repeat themselves *sometimes*. That is the partial truth underlying technical chart analysis, which sometimes reflects the repeatable psychology of investors. Financial history is replete with stories of speculative manias and manmade crises. Markets tend to go through cycles of optimism and pessimism, euphoria and depression, speculative bubbles and fantastic bargains. Psychologically, the public vacillates between greed and fear. Smart investors who act quickly, before the crowd acts, should be able to profit from overvalued and undervalued situations.

But investors must never forget that people are not totally predictable. History does repeat itself, but never in the same fashion and never according to the old timetable. Chartists usually discover this fact after a few years of experience in the markets—the cycles or waves shorten or lengthen unexpectedly. Chartists often remark that there is nothing wrong with the charts, only the chartist. Speculative bubbles and fantastic bargains will continue, but they will not always follow the same time pattern, nor in the same investment arena. People's visions of the future change and so do investment fads. One year the hot investment may be diamonds, another year high technology stocks, and the next year Parisian real estate.

THE SPECULATOR AS ENTREPRENEUR

The speculator/entrepreneur plays a key role in forecasting changes in the economy and the financial markets. The efficient-market theory, like the model of perfect competition, basically denies the analytical ability of the speculator/ entrepreneur by concluding that the individual investor cannot outwit the market. According to a strict interpretation of the efficient-market theory, profit-seeking activity by traders is virtually irrational because investors are penalized by taxes when they sell and transaction costs when they trade.

But the truth is that markets are not always efficient and all-knowing, nor do they all offer the same reward. Uncertainty exists in all investment markets, although some markets are less uncertain or less efficient than others. The stock market is certainly more efficient than the rare coin, diamond, or real estate markets. Some markets can be severely overvalued or undervalued for weeks, months, or years. Accurate information is often costly and sometimes unavailable. Insiders may know something that the average investor does not. As such, it pays to be a specialist—to be more alert and more knowledgeable than other investors or the public in general. The public is sometimes wrong about its decision to buy or sell stocks; markets are not perfectly coordinated. Hence, there is a wide scope of potentially profitable opportunities for speculators willing to do their own research and take a risk. All actions involve the potential for both profit and loss.

The speculator plays a vital role in moving the uncoordinated and imperfect market toward equilibrium, just as the speculator/entrepreneur is vital in providing goods and services that customers desire. Contrary to the provincial views of Marxists and some Keynesians, the speculator does play a beneficial role in society. Baumol and Blinder make this point explicitly, noting that speculators make it possible for producers and consumers to hedge and thus help smooth out price fluctuations. Speculating in stocks and commodities is not a zero-sum game, nor is it simply a gamble.

Successful speculators are rewarded through profits, whereas unsuccessful speculators lose money. Competition is keen in the financial markets, making it more challenging (but not impossible) for speculators to make superior returns. They must always be alert to changes in market conditions or new investment opportunities. Investors who seek to repeat profitable adventures of the past may be disappointed. Moreover, when speculators look at an overvalued situation, they must decide whether the market is temporarily undervalued or permanently undervalued.

Yet the end result is the same as that in the production process. Through trial and error, the market is a weeding-out process, rewarding those who have the capacity to make good judgments about people and their needs while discouraging those who make bad judgments.

ECONOMICS AS A SUBJECTIVE SCIENCE

Economics is, of necessity, a qualitative science. Even though the financial pages give the impression that investing is a numbers game based on averages, yields, cash flows, and ratios, it should be realized that the market is a human arena and therefore subjective. Events in the economy and in the financial markets are often based on the emotions and attitudes of people, not the physical nature of things, and therefore cannot be precisely measured. Economists cannot predict the exact timing of an event nor the magnitude of price and quantity changes. They may be able to predict the direction of interest rates, the exchange rate of the dollar, or the value of the stock market, but they cannot say definitively when something is going to change or by how much. If a worldwide famine hits, economists and commodity traders can predict that the price of wheat is going to skyrocket, but they cannot be sure how high the price will go. Investors should be wary of any financial advisor who predicts that the stock market is going to go to 1,000 by July 4. Yet it is amazing how often this kind of "voodoo investing" is attempted. Many economists have tried in vain to adapt the scientific method to analyze economic events and financial markets. Like the classical economists who sought an objective, intrinsic theory of value, such economists are bound to be disappointed.

THE THEORY OF CONTRARY INVESTING

Timing is critical in the fast-moving marketplace. Not everyone can get out at the top or buy at the bottom. Why? Because prices of all assets are determined by marginal buyers and sellers. For every buyer there is a seller. Hence, if everyone tried to get out at the top in expectation of a crash, prices would collapse immediately and no one could get out in time. Or if everyone tried to buy at the bottom, prices would rise so rapidly that no one would get a bargain. This is the core of truth in the theory of contrary investing.

Therefore, because of the very nature of markets, only a small minority of speculators can sell at the top or buy at the bottom in any particular case. A contrarian must be a loner. He practices an art, not a science. Although there are technical benchmarks to help determine the top or bottom of a market, there is no scientific formula to prove either to be the case. Risk and uncertainty always exist, although they can be minimized through research and superior thinking. It is a self-contradiction to suggest that everyone should be a contrarian; the crowd cannot go against the crowd.

However, this fact does not mean that most people must lose in the financial market. I have found that the vast majority of investors are conservative by nature and seek to buy and hold individual stocks and bonds for the long run. If the economy is sound and continues to grow over the long run, the stock market will rise. Prices of stocks may not be predictable on a short-term basis, but over the long run, prices will tend to rise as earnings expand in a growing economy. In the long run, earnings determine the value of securities. This is the nugget of truth in fundamental analysis, and it is the reason securities analysts like Benjamin Graham were successful investors—they took the long view.

In addition, although only a minority of people may make a killing in a market by buying low and selling high, it is possible that a much larger number of individuals, perhaps even a majority, could make extremely high profits in other markets that come along. There are literally hundreds of undervalued or overvalued opportunities that occur every year around the world. Large numbers of investors can go bargain hunting as long as they look in many places and at more than one industry, investment market, or foreign country. As the old Wall Street adage goes, there's more than one way to climb a mountain. Moreover, individuals may be so successful with only a few trades that they could place their profits in bonds or money-market funds and live off the proceeds. If they are successful enough at first, they need not continue trading and risk losing what they have already gained.

HOW USEFUL IS ECONOMICS?

Clearly, economics can be valuable in the world of business and high finance. Businesspeople and investors who apply the principles of economics correctly can achieve financial success. Economics cannot provide all the answers, but it can lay the foundation for prosperity.

As an investment newsletter writer and financial analyst, I have found my background in economics to be extremely beneficial. For example, knowledge of central bank policies regarding interest rates, open market operations, and the money supply is valuable in making investment recommendations. Market behavior is being more and more influenced by negative government policies—monetary inflation, excessive government spending, nationalization, wage–price controls, foreign exchange restrictions, and war. On the positive side, such government actions as deregulation, privatization, and anti-inflation policies also influence market behavior. Understanding the basics of the business cycle can be extremely useful for a businessperson or an investor, and so can the economist's view of the structure of production outlined in Chapter 3. An economist who understands subjective value can also help distinguish between good and bad financial theories.

HOW GOVERNMENT POLICY AFFECTS INVESTMENT DECISIONS

Businesspeople and entrepreneurs recognize that government policy, good or bad, has a dramatic impact on the economy and on financial markets. John Templeton, whose mutual funds are invested around the world, learned early in his career that the most profitable opportunities are found in countries that provide political and economic stability and a free-enterprise attitude: "Avoid investing in those countries with a high level of socialism or government regulation of business. Business growth depends on a strong free-enterprise system. . . . Governments should stop interfering with what people want to do."[12] (Templeton, by the way, earned a degree in economics at Yale University before Keynesianism took over.)

Over the years, Templeton has invested in such countries as Japan, West Germany, and the United States, all of which have encouraged free enterprise. He was one of the first to invest in Japan after World War II. Japan and the four tigers (highlighted in Chapter 16) have been stellar performers both economically and financially because they offer low tax rates on investment, a small but stable government, and a strong belief in hard work and savings. Meanwhile, Templeton has avoided highly socialized countries such as Israel, Sweden, and Mexico.

The intelligent investor should also be on the lookout for changes in government policies that might affect the stock market and exchange rates. A generous tax exemption for stock purchases sharply boosted the French market. Privatization and elimination of the foreign exchange controls lifted Britain out of its malaise. High real interest rates in Australia brought about a recovery in the Australian dollar. On the other hand, the political victory of the socialists in France caused the French stock market and the franc to decline initially. Runaway inflation in Brazil created havoc in the financial markets and in the value of the cruzado. A general strike in the Chilean copper mines caused a sharp increase in copper prices.

The business cycle is largely a government-induced phenomenon. An unanticipated monetary inflation by central banks may cause a temporary investment boom that businesspeople and speculators can profit from. But as the Austrian economists have taught us, to depreciate the nation's currency is to destabilize the economy. Runaway inflation can be disastrous, causing rising prices and falling real output. A boom must eventually end in a bust if it creates an imbalance between capital-goods industries and consumer-goods industries. Falling interest rates become rising interest rates, cutting the boom short. Over the years, the fiat money standard has created a series of boom–bust cycles and economic crises and will continue to do so. The battle lines are drawn between the government forces of inflation and the free-market forces of deflation. The nimble speculator will attempt to profit from these countervailing forces, whereas the conservative investor often becomes the victim. Businesspeople and investors all hope to protect themselves from an economic and financial downturn, but it is impossible for everyone to do so; there are bound to be casualties. The problem is often one of timing and liquidity. Some businesses cannot sell out quickly enough when the boom ends.

The worldwide increase in the demand for gold and silver coins responds directly to the fickle, unstable government policies that create inflation, recession, and crises. Gold and silver are bought by conservative investors as an insurance hedge against such troubled times.

THE PRINCIPLES OF FINANCIAL SUCCESS

Economics explains why some businesses succeed and others fail. What are the principles of success? They are best summed up by Rosenberg and Birdzell, the authors of *How the West Grew Rich*. Rosenberg and Birdzell list four basic concepts:

1. The ability to accumulate large amounts of capital.
2. The need for innovation, discovery, and entrepreneurship.
3. A stable political government.
4. The encouragement of open markets and competition.

Individuals will be financially successful—and a nation as a whole will increase its standard of living—if they save and invest wisely in the competitive business world, either directly through their own entrepreneurship or indirectly through investing and speculating in the financial markets. In any case, a stable government and a competitive, open environment are absolutely essential in order for individuals and businesses to flourish.

Unfortunately, economics textbooks are often schizophrenic when it comes to the value of saving and investing. In their sections on economic growth, writers readily admit the need to postpone current consumption in order to achieve greater consumption in the future, but in the macroeconomic section they are overly influenced by the Keynesian anti-savings mentality, arguing that new savings can hurt the economy (see Chapter 5). In an economic downturn, savings are supposed to be bad whereas consumption and consumer debt are supposed to be good. Such an attitude, if taken to an extreme, could lead to individual and national bankruptcy.

John Templeton has the right approach. He is opposed to the consumerist, big-spending attitude that is at the root of Keynesian thinking. Templeton is a strong advocate of thrift, especially during hard times. During the Great Depression, he ignored the advice of economists John Maynard Keynes and Frank Taussig, who irresponsibly encouraged people to go out on a spending spree to stimulate the economy. Instead, he pledged to set aside 50 percent of his income for his personal investment portfolio.

And after the crash of 1929 and the advent of the Great Depression, the importance of thrift became even more apparent.

There was ample evidence on the streets of the 1930s to reinforce the notion that saving as much of your money as possible and investing it wisely are essential to security and success. Quite simply, those who practiced thrift received great rewards, and those who didn't suffered much more from financial setbacks and economic uncertainties.[13]

Templeton knew that money spent is money lost. Money should be set aside so that it can be put to work to make more money. This is a basic principle of financial responsibility that should be taught in today's classrooms.

SUMMARY

Investors as entrepreneurs can make money and can even beat the market if they are nimble enough. They represent only a select class of individuals, however. It is not irrational to seek a better return, but neither is it easy. Just because only a few actors become celebrities does not mean that a struggling actor should quit trying. The principles outlined in this chapter should help you become wealthy if that is what you seek.

NOTES

1. Hyman Minsky, *Stabilizing an Unstable Economy* (New Haven: Yale University Press, 1982), p. 120.
2. Margit von Mises, *My Years with Ludwig von Mises,* 2nd ed. (Cedar Falls, Iowa: Center for Futures Education, 1984), p. 24.
3. Quoted in Paul Johnson, *Intellectuals* (New York: Harper & Row, 1989), p. 74.
4. Burton G. Malkiel, *A Random Walk Down Wall Street,* 4th ed. (New York: W. W. Norton, 1985), p. 17.
5. Ibid., p. 16.
6. Charles P. Jones, *Investments: Analysis and Management* (New York: John Wiley & Sons, 1987), p. 242.
7. Fischer Black, "Yes, Virginia, There Is Hope: Tests of the Value Line Ranking System," paper presented at

the Center for Research in Security Prices (Chicago: University of Chicago, Graduate School of Business, 1971). See also Lawrence Brown and Michael Rozeff, *Journal of Finance*, March 1978. These articles are summarized in Arnold Bernhard, *How to Use the Value Line Investment Survey* (New York: Value Line, 1988). Since these studies, Value Line has, except for a few years, outperformed the S&P 500.

8. Richard E. Band, *Contrary Investing* (New York: McGraw-Hill, 1985), p. 66.

9. David Dreman, *The New Contrarian Investment Strategy* (New York: Random House, 1982), p. 149.

10. John Maynard Keynes, *The General Theory of Employment, Interest and Money* (London: Macmillan, 1936), pp. 155–56, 159.

11. John Maynard Keynes, "The General Theory of Employment," *Quarterly Journal of Economics* (February 1937), and *The Collected Writings of John Maynard Keynes,* vol. XIV, p. 114. Contrary to current belief, Keynes was not a completely successful investor. He did have an uncanny ability to buy stocks near their bottom and hold for the long run. Consequently, his net assets increased dramatically from £16,000 to over £400,000 by the time he died in 1946. (Does this mean, "In the long run, we are all wealthy"?) On the other hand, he was unable to predict the 1929 crash or 1937 recession and was completely helpless in getting out at the top. As a result, he lost three fourths of his wealth in 1929 and two thirds in 1937! See Donald E. Moggridge, "Keynes as an Investor," in *The Collected Writings of John Maynard Keynes* (London: Macmillan, 1983), vol. 12.

12. Quoted in William Proctor, *The Templeton Prizes* (Garden City, N.Y.: Doubleday, 1983), p. 71.

13. Ibid., p. 50.

RECOMMENDED READING

Browne, Harry. *Why the Best-Laid Investment Plans Usually Go Wrong*. New York: William Morrow, 1987. A critical analysis of financial theories. Browne makes the case for a permanent portfolio consisting of stocks, bonds, gold, and cash.

Clason, George. *The Richest Man in Babylon*. New York: E. P. Dutton, 1955. The most important financial book ever written.

Dreman, David. *The New Contrarian Investment Strategy*. New York: Random House, 1982. A stimulating review of the major investment theories, and why his form of contrarian advice works.

Malkiel, Burton G. *A Random Walk Down Wall Street*, 4th ed. New York: W. W. Norton, 1985. Fortunately, Malkiel's book is not just ivory tower thinking—he is a veteran of Wall Street and has been a successful investor over the long term. Even though I reject many aspects of the random walk thesis, I highly recommend Malkiel's book. He himself admits, "I have never claimed I was a 100% random walker. I am a random walker with a crutch." (*Forbes,-* June 26, 1989.)

CHAPTER 20

THE NEXT ECONOMICS

In recent years, there has been a resurgence of interest in the Austrian school among U.S. economists. A common theme in the new Austrian literature is the need to understand that markets are more than curves crossing on a graph.
—Edwin G. Dolan and David E. Lindsey
Economics (1988)

In the early 1980s, the managerial philosopher Peter F. Drucker wrote a penetrating article entitled "Toward the Next Economics" for a symposium on the crisis in economic theory. The article criticizes Keynesianism for its inability "to tackle the central policy problems of the developing economies—productivity and capital formation." None of the alternatives, including monetarism, rational expectations, or Marxism, could respond to the most severe problem in today's world, namely, the decline in capital formation. In sum, Drucker concluded, it was time for a new economic theory.

> That there is both a productivity crisis and a capital-formation crisis makes certain that the Next Economics will have to be again micro-economic and centered on supply. Both productivity and capital formation are events of the micro-economy. Both also deal with the factors of *production* rather than being functions of demand.[1]

Drucker did not specify which school of thought in economics could qualify for his version of the next economics, but I believe that the modern Austrian school—led by Murray Rothbard, Israel Kirzner, Roger Garrison, and others—is the best choice. It stresses the central role of entrepreneurship, savings, and risk taking on a microeconomic level. It does not depend on government spending programs to artificially stimulate the economy, although it does encourage the state to provide a stable, beneficial atmosphere in which business can flourish through deregulation, privatization, and tax reductions across the board. Unlike the Keynesian and monetarist schools, the Austrian school is production (supply) oriented, not consumption (demand) oriented. The key to economic growth and an increase in the standard of living, according to the Austrians, is for government to get out of the way and allow individuals and businesses to save, invest, and spend as they see fit with minimal taxes and interference.

There may indeed be a growing interest in the Austrian school of economics among U.S. economists, as Dolan suggests, but unfortunately you would never know it by reading the textbooks and the establishment publications. Most students can go through an entire year of economics courses without hearing the names Ludwig von Mises or Friedrich Hayek, let alone the names of the new Austrians mentioned above. Only a handful of textbooks offer biographical essays on Ludwig von Mises or Friedrich Hayek, the founders of modern Austrian economics. Most have something to say about Joseph Schumpeter, but the coverage is not extensive. The Austrians have influenced several other schools of thought, including the supply-side school and the rational expectations school, although such schools disagree with certain aspects of the Austrians' theories. A review of name indexes in the backs of the top 10 textbooks reveals how little interest there is in Mises, Hayek, Schumpeter, and the modern Austrians compared to Keynes and those in other more popular schools of thought.

It is clear from Table 20–1 that Keynesian economics still dominates the profession, particularly in the sections on macroeconomic theory. No doubt monetarism, rational expectations, and other rival theories have gained popularity over the past 20 years, but the Keynesian theory has yet to be dislodged. The Austrian school is seldom mentioned at all, despite its ready application to today's economic problems. The only reason the Austrian school has more citations than Galbraith does is because it includes references to Joseph A. Schumpeter, who emphasized the importance of entrepreneurship and technological change and therefore is mentioned several times. Hayek is mentioned only half a dozen times, and

TABLE 20–1
References to Economics Schools of Thought in Top 10 Textbooks

School	Index Frequency
Keynes and Keynesianism	442
Friedman and Monetarism	252
Marx and Marxism	131
Rational Expectations	119
Laffer and Supply Side	95
Austrianism	67
Galbraith and Institutionalism	53

Note: This is an estimate of economists' influence in the textbooks, based on the combined references to specific theories and their leaders in the name and subject indexes.

Mises, the founder of the modern Austrian school, is mentioned even less often. In Samuelson's "Family Tree of Economics," published on the back flyleaf of his textbook, the Austrians are not even listed as a separate school, despite the fact that they do not fit into any other classification. Samuelson puts Hayek in the category of "Chicago libertarianism," but Hayek is neither a follower of the Chicago school, nor is he a philosophical descendant of Walras and Marshall, as Samuelson suggests in the family tree. The Austrian school is really in a class by itself, a position necessary for it to qualify as the next economics, with founders Carl Menger, Eugen von Böhm-Bawerk, and Ludwig von Mises, all of whom came from Vienna.

WHY HAS THE AUSTRIAN SCHOOL BEEN SO UNPOPULAR?

Like the amazing story of Japan and the four tigers outlined in Chapter 16, the story of the Austrian school of economics deserves much more than a few passing references in the top 10 textbooks. Unfortunately, the Austrian school has been greatly censored over the years by the economics profession. It has undoubtedly been one of the most unpopular groups among economists in terms of securing a position on a major campus or getting published in one of the major journals. Austrian economics has taken hold in a few universities, such as George Mason University, Auburn University, New York University, and the University of Nevada at Las Vegas. The number of such universities appears to be growing, but it is still pitifully small.

There are a number of reasons for this unfortunate neglect. First, the modern Austrians are advocates of extreme laissez-faire policies in both macroeconomics and microeconomics. They accept the Jeffersonian principle that government which governs least governs best. The only legitimate function of government is to defend liberty; all other forms of government intervention are counterproductive. According to the Austrians, state involvement in the economy is not the solution to a recession or depression, but the original cause. Beginning with the Great Depression and continuing under the influence of Keynes, most economists have regarded such views as antediluvian to say the least. Only in the past few decades, when many governments around the world have suffered (or caused) serious problems, has the Austrian position begun to be taken somewhat seriously. Nevertheless, the staunch anti-state attitude of the Austrians has hurt them more than it has hurt the Chicago school, which also promotes the free market but endorses a government fiat money standard, albeit limited. (The Austrian school is one of the few schools of economics to endorse a genuine gold standard.)

Second, the Austrians—apart from the Chicago school—are highly skeptical of the use of mathematical and econometric models in economics. In the most extreme case, Mises refused to include any graphs or charts in his works because he did not believe in them. Most of Mises' students have not been so purist, however, and frequently use supply and demand curves and other graphic techniques to demonstrate certain concepts. They favor the logical exposition of economic concepts, however, rather than mathematical formulas. Austrian methodology is highly individualistic; economic analysis is based on deductive reasoning rather than empirical studies. Austrians emphasize that economics is the study of human action—in which there are no constants—which is radically distinct from the mechanistic approach of the physical sciences. The economics profession's penchant for borrowing phrases from physics and biology—such as elasticity, velocity, friction, and circulation—is criticized by the Austrians. In a time when most professional journal articles are highly mathematical and empirical, it is no wonder that the Austrian school has had trouble being accepted.

Third, the battle over economic philosophy has often been acrimonious and has in the past evolved into bitter ad hominem attacks. The interventionist atmosphere on campuses following World War II was so biased that Mises was never offered a paid, full-time position at a major university. He ended up as a visiting professor at New York University, financed by outside sources and "visiting" for 20 years. Even Hayek had difficulty securing a position at the University of Chicago. Meanwhile, former students of Mises who were converted to Keynesianism had no difficulty obtaining positions at Harvard, Princeton, and other prestigious schools. Mises was often accused by his critics as being uncompromising, polemical, and intolerant; he would often dismiss those who disagreed with him in a terse sentence or two, calling them "anti-economists" or "pseudo progressives." But the disdain and intransigence were mutual. Mises and other free-market economists were labeled "reactionaries" and "narrow-minded fanatics." It was a dark chapter in the history of American academia.

CARL MENGER AND THE EARLY AUSTRIANS

Such divisiveness and censorship were not always the case. Before World War II and the Keynesian revolution, the Austrian school enjoyed a highly favorable reputation.

Carl Menger (1840–1921) founded the Austrian school of economics when he published his innovative work, *Principles of Economics,* in 1871. Soon thereafter he became a professor at the University of Vienna. Menger's *Principles* was a remarkable achievement that revolutionized the way economists viewed the world. His book greatly influenced economists in both Europe (e.g., William Stanley Jevons in England) and America (e.g., Frank Fetter and Frank Taussig). In microeconomics, Menger broke away from the classical economics of Adam Smith and David Ricardo, who claimed that value was determined by costs of production (the labor theory of value). Instead, he proved that values are determined solely by the subjective demands of consumers. The classical economists tried to resolve the famous "diamond–water paradox"—why are diamonds so expensive compared to water when water is far more essential to life? They attempted to resolve the paradox by distinguishing between "use" value and "exchange" value. But Menger unraveled the paradox of value that had eluded the classical economists by showing that the value of goods is determined by their marginal rather than their total utility. In other words, diamonds are worth more than water because normally an *extra* diamond has greater utility than an *extra* cup of water. The greater the quantity, the lesser the marginal value or price.

Menger also developed a new basis for analyzing the economy as a whole. According to Menger, all goods go through a time-consuming process of production, from higher-order raw materials to lower-order consumer goods. This stages-of-production approach forms the basis of the capitalist system. The time-structure approach has also proven useful in making investment decisions.

Menger was a strong advocate of free-market capitalism because, he felt, it maximizes the quantity, quality, and variety of goods and services. Because of his achievements, Carl Menger must be regarded as one of the greatest economists who ever lived. His book *The Principles of Economics* is a well-written, compelling work that should be required reading for all students in economics. It is an unhappy commentary that Menger is mentioned only briefly by 3 of the top 10 textbooks, and then only in connection with his discovery of the principle of marginal utility (along with Jevons and Walras). None of the textbooks that highlight outstanding economists includes Menger.[2]

BÖHM-BAWERK AND THE THEORY OF CAPITAL

Eugen von Böhm-Bawerk (1851–1914), continuing the Menger vision, was one of the most influential economists of his generation. He was the Austrian minister of finance around the turn of the century and helped return Austria to the gold standard. But his most important impact came from his writing about the theory of capital and interest, as well as his devastating critique of Marx. His most significant theoretical work is *The Positive Theory of Capital*, which forms the basis of the modern theory of economic growth. Böhm-Bawerk argued that individuals and businesses adopt more roundabout processes of production in order to achieve economic growth and a higher standard of living. By *roundabout*, Böhm-Bawerk means the sacrificing of current consumption to produce more capital goods and longer processes of production, which in turn leads to greater future consumption. Most economists, including Samuelson, acknowledge Böhm-Bawerk's theory that more roundabout processes (however risky) are necessary to achieve economic growth. Referring to Böhm-Bawerk's theory, Bronfenbrenner admits, "The record of the so-called 'industrial revolution' of the past two hundred years shows that roundabout production works."

Böhm-Bawerk was also one of the first economists to dispute the anti-savings doctrines of pre-Keynesians. He demonstrated that savings and investment were critical to economic growth and should be encouraged.

THE MISES LEGACY

Ludwig von Mises (1881–1973) followed in Böhm-Bawerk's footsteps to become the foremost leader of the free-market Austrian school in the 20th century. In the 1920s and early 1930s, Mises conducted his famous private seminar at the University of Vienna, which included such students as Friedrich Hayek, Gottfried Haberler, Fritz Machlup, and Lionel Robbins. Mises left for Switzerland in 1934 in the wake of Nazism and emigrated to the United States in 1940. He lived and taught in New York City for more than 30 years.

Mises was the first Austrian to develop a comprehensive theory of subjective economics. The earlier Austrians dealt primarily with individual prices and firms, but Mises integrated microeconomic analysis into the macroeconomic sphere of money and banking. In his first work, *The Theory of Money and Credit,* published in 1912, Mises applied Menger's theory of marginal utility, Wicksell's natural interest rate hypothesis, and Böhm-Bawerk's capital theory in a full-scale analysis of money and the business cycle. He demonstrated the nonneutral impact of money on relative prices, income, and business activity.

Mises was the first to raise the problem of inefficient allocation of resources without a price mechanism in socialist economies. In 1920, Mises wrote a short article entitled "Economic Calculation in a Socialist Commonwealth," demonstrating that socialism could not efficiently calculate prices and output in a complex economy without relying on the market mechanisms of profit and loss. Two years later he wrote a full-scale critique of central planning, entitled simply *Socialism.*

His lifework culminated in his magnum opus, *Human Action,* originally published in 1949 by Yale University Press. The work is considered difficult reading for new students (e.g., Chapter II includes a section entitled "The Formal and Aprioristic Character of Praxeology"). Mises wrote numerous articles for the lay public, however, and the best compilation is *Planning for Freedom,* now in its fourth edition. It includes the extremely readable article "The Essential Von Mises," by Murray Rothbard.

Mises, like his predecessors, stressed the importance of savings and capital formation in the economy. As he stated, "The essence of Keynesianism is its complete failure to conceive the role that saving and capital accumulation play in the improvement of economic conditions. . . . It is one of the foremost tasks of good government to remove all obstacles that hinder the accumulation and investment of new capital."[3]

HAYEK AND THE KEYNESIAN REVOLUTION

Mises' most famous student was Friedrich A. Hayek. Hayek studied under Mises and was director of the Austrian Institute for Business Cycle Research during the late 1920s. He raised dire warnings about the state of the world economy prior to the Great Depression (see Chapter 9). At the invitation of Lionel Robbins, Hayek moved to London in 1931 to teach at the London School of Economics. During the early 1930s, he presented his theory of the business cycle as an explanation of the Great Depression. His thesis, published in a little book entitled *Prices and Production,* was initially well-received in England and was, according to Sir John Hicks and other contemporaries, the principal rival to Keynesianism during the 1930s.

Based on Menger's time-structure view of the economy, Hayek explained how monetary inflation misdirects economic resources and creates an artificial boom in the higher-order industries that eventually must end in an economic downturn. But although his explanation of the business cycle made sense, economists gradually became disenchanted with Hayek's laissez-faire cure for the stubborn depression and eventually turned to Keynes for the answer. The Keynesian revolution eclipsed the new theories of Hayek and the Austrians, which were not to be resurrected until decades later. Hayek moved on to political philosophy, writing the controversial tract *The Road to Serfdom* in 1944, which argued that authoritarian governments spell economic and political disaster for countries that adopt them.

JOSEPH SCHUMPETER AND THE FUTURE OF CAPITALISM

Joseph Schumpeter (1883–1950) was a student of Böhm-Bawerk and, like his teacher, was the Austrian minister of finance, though only briefly in 1919. He moved to the United States in 1932 and was professor of economics at Harvard University until 1950. He was president of the American Economic Association in 1949. In most of his writings, Schumpeter focused on the entrepreneur as the central character who plays a vital role in the economy, which, as we have seen, is a strong Austrian theme. Schumpeter's entrepreneur is the business-person who constantly searches for innovative ideas and seeks improvements in a process Schumpeter called "creative destruction." To Schumpeter, entrepreneurship is at first a move away from equilibrium, whereas the other Austrians view the entrepreneur as one who moves the economy toward equilibrium. Schumpeter opposed the stagnation theory as popularized by Alvin Hansen in the 1940s (the mistaken notion that the Great Depression and lack of innovative opportunities were permanent fixtures in the world economy). He rejected the perfect competition model, although he criticized big business for becoming too bureaucratic and managerial rather than entrepreneurial. In a book written during World War II, *Capitalism, Socialism, and Democracy,* he predicted that this lack of creativity would gradually doom capitalism.

In other ways, Schumpeter was an *enfante terrible* and renegade from the Austrian school as it developed under Mises and Hayek. He rejected the Mises–Hayek theory of the business cycle and opted instead for a trade cycle based on innovation as well as the Kondratieff long waves, a belief that history repeats itself in 50 to 60-year cycles. He also rejected the gold standard as the basis of an ideal monetary system and, despite his emphasis on disequilibrium in economic activity, considered the French economist Leon Walras to be the greatest of all economists.[4] The theory of time preference, which the Austrians regard as a universal phenomenon and the basis for a positive rate of interest, was also dismissed by Schumpeter, who mistakenly believed that interest rates would fall to zero in long-term general equilibrium.

MILTON FRIEDMAN AND THE CHICAGO SCHOOL

The renaissance of the free-market counterattack began in earnest in the 1960s and 1970s as the Keynesian edifice began to crumble under the wear and tear of inflation and monetary crises. The first challenge to the Keynesian revolution came from the Chicago school, which was under the brilliant leadership of Milton Friedman. His monumental study, *A Monetary History of the United States, 1867–1960,* coauthored with Anna J. Schwartz, demolished the fiction held by many early Keynesians that money does not matter and the belief that an expansionary monetary policy during a recession was like pushing on a string. According to Friedman, Keynes and his followers misinterpreted the cause of the Great Depression. The deficiency in aggregate demand was not a failure of capitalism, but of the government's central bank, which permitted the money supply to decline by one third. At the same time, Friedman wrote a popular bestseller, *Capitalism and Freedom,* questioning the benefits of Keynesian fiscal policy and other forms of government intervention. It has gone through many printings and remains one of the best expositions on free-market capitalism ever written.

As a young college student in the 1960s, I found that Friedman and the monetarists solved many of the riddles in Keynesian economics. Unfortunately, they were silent on the Keynesian paradox of thrift, which many students found baffling, and failed to provide a full understanding of the mysteries of banking and the origin of money. The monetarists also favored a fiat money system rather than a genuine gold standard, which raised the ethical question of legal counterfeiting by government. The monetarist model was implying a something-for-nothing idea by advocating the slow expansion of the money supply without any gold backing. In a sense, monetarists believed that they could create real value by printing fiat money without paying full value for it. Under a pure commodity standard, on the other hand, the money supply could only be increased by investing resources and extracting gold out of the ground.

MURRAY ROTHBARD AND THE NEW AUSTRIAN SCHOOL

The only other free-market school to offer an alternative philosophy was that of the Austrians, led by Ludwig von Mises. But Mises did not provide the detailed answers I was looking for. His responses to Keynesianism in *Planning for Freedom* were too simplistic, and his philosophical approach in *Human Action* was too formidable. His running battle against the interventionists often shed more heat than light. Some say his German background was a barrier. He reminds me of a brilliant math teacher who always comes up with the correct answers to difficult problems but is so bright that he skips many steps along the way, leaving his students unsure how he got there.

Then along came Murray Rothbard, an American economist who could translate Misesian economics for the intelligent layperson. He has the unique ability to present scholarly material in an understandable and readable fashion. In fact, Rothbard's books and pamphlets have probably been far more popular and influential than those of Mises. Accordingly, Rothbard is often acknowledged as the dean of the new Austrian school. Not all neo-Austrians give their allegiance to Rothbard, however, because, like Mises, he has had run-ins with opponents that are sometimes rancorous and divisive. Nevertheless, most economists agree that his theoretical works have had a profound influence.

I was first introduced to Rothbard through an article in an anthology entitled *Views on Capitalism,* edited by Richard Romano and Melvin Leiman. Rothbard's article criticizing President Johnson's "Great Society," although only nine pages, was brilliant, pithy, and electrifying. After reading this short essay, I realized that an exciting new school of thought had been denied me throughout my undergraduate years.

Rothbard's first work, *Man, Economy, and State,* published in 1962, is an enormous treatise that appeals primarily to economics majors. I read it as a graduate student and found it more persuasive than any other theoretical work I had read. (My wife will attest to its influence over me, as I read it on our honeymoon.) It offers a full-scale critique of Keynesian doctrines as well as an in-depth discussion of the theories of production, interest, supply and demand, savings and economic growth, and government policy. His principal thesis is that government intervention in money and spending is counterproductive and antigrowth. Rothbard's magnum opus went beyond Friedman in answering my questions. After reading Rothbard, I felt as Paul Samuelson had when he read Keynes's *General Theory*—to quote Wordsworth, "Bliss was it in that dawn to be alive, but to be young was very heaven!"

In terms of popularity, Rothbard's next two books had a far greater impact on general audiences. *America's Great Depression,* published in 1963, is a revisionist history of the 1930's depression. It explains in clear terms how the government's inflationary policies, not the free market, are responsible for the boom–bust cycle, and he applied his thesis to the depression. In addition, the 1972 edition of *America's Great Depression* offered the first Austrian-style explanation of inflationary recession (see Chapter 8).

Rothbard's next work, *What Has Government Done to Our Money?,* written in 1964, is a 60-page pamphlet that has probably had a greater influence on students of the free market than any other work ever published. Although not strictly a political tract, it has a punch and religious fervor akin to Marx's *Communist Manifesto.* To thousands of hard-money investors and true believers, it was both shocking and exciting in its revelation of the origin and nature of money. National currencies such as the dollar, the pound, and the franc were not inventions of the state but were valued by citizens because they were originally defined as gold or silver, commodities that had value in the first place. His defense of a 100 percent genuine gold standard and his indictment of government inflationary policies made sense for the first time. He showed why central banking is an unnecessary invention of the state. The history of money came to light like a bolt of lightning. (Rothbard has since written a textbook called *The Mystery of Banking.*) In 1970, Rothbard followed his economic treatise with a scholarly work entitled *Power and Market,* on the theory of taxation and government policy. His analysis of taxation is particularly provocative.

Of course, Rothbard is a prolific writer on many subjects besides economics, including politics, philosophy, and history. Nevertheless, there is a great deal of prejudice against him in the economics profession, similar to that exhibited toward Mises. Although he has a Ph.D. in economics from Columbia University and has written numerous scholarly works, Rothbard is to a large degree a persona non grata among professional economists. Despite his numerous achievements, he is simply not quoted in the textbooks and seldom referenced in the economics journals. In Mark Blaug's otherwise exhaustive *Who's Who in Economics,* Rothbard is not even listed. Blaug's explanation is that Rothbard was not sufficiently cited in the academic journals to be included in the list of 1,000 famous economists. Radical economists have a difficult time fitting traditional standards of recognition.

For decades, Rothbard was consigned to an economics professorship in a little-known technical school in New York City. But Rothbard is finally gaining some of the recognition he deserves. He was recently appointed professor of economics at the University of Nevada at Las Vegas. And Dolan, in one of the top 10 textbooks, actually quoted him. But I doubt if Rothbard will ever be awarded a Nobel Prize.[5]

THE EXPANDING AUSTRIAN UNIVERSE

Other scholars in the Austrian tradition include Israel Kirzner and Ludwig M. Lachmann at New York University, Leland Yeager and Roger Garrison at Auburn University, George P. O'Driscoll, Jr., at the Dallas Federal Reserve, D. T. Armentano at the University of Hartford, Don Lavoie at George Mason University, Steve Hanke at Johns Hopkins University, Walter Block at the Fraser Institute in British Columbia, Richard Ebeling at Hillsdale College, Joseph Salerno at Pace University, and Hans Sennholz at Grove City College.

James Buchanan, who won the Nobel Prize in economics in 1986 for his public choice theory of government, is also at Gerald Mason University and considers himself a fellow traveler with the Austrian school. Half of the top 10 textbooks have recently added new chapters or discussions on public choice theory, including Buchanan's version. Buchanan is highly critical of government spending programs and the federal bureaucracy, which has expanded far beyond its useful functions and is inherently bloated because of the vested interests of the bureaucrats. Adopting an Austrian perspective, Buchanan views the government as a group of individual decision makers who seek to protect their own self-interests and whose acts are determined according to the risk and reward to their careers.

Some of the most original thinking on macroeconomics has come recently from Auburn University's Roger Garrison. His theme is that Austrian economics is not as extreme as some economists make it out to be, but rather it serves as a middle ground. In a recent journal article, Garrison contends that Keynesianism and monetarism are two extreme poles in the monetary relationship between the supply of and the demand for goods. According to Garrison, the Keynesians view money as a "broken joint" in the monetary system, whereas the monetarists view money as a "tight joint" in the monetary system. The Austrians, on the other hand, represent the middle ground by suggesting that money is a "loose joint" in the economy.[6]

Several scholarly journals in the Austrian tradition are now available: *The Cato Journal,* published quarterly by the Cato Institute in Washington, D.C.; *The Review of Austrian Economics,* published annually by the Ludwig von Mises Institute at Auburn University; and *The Market Process,* published by the Center for the Study of Market Processes at George Mason University.

Finally, there is a wide variety of think tanks and research organizations devoted to the free market in general. The oldest group is the Foundation for Economic Education (FEE) in New York, founded by Leonard Read in the late 1940s. Others include the Reason Foundation, publisher of *Reason* magazine; the Heritage Foundation; the Pacific Institute; and the Manhattan Institute. In Britain, organizations include the Institute for Economic Affairs and the Adam Smith Institute. In Latin America, they include the Instituto Libertad y Democracia.

SUMMARY

The inability of the mainstream economists to explain the crises of the past 20 years has led to a search for new theories and even a return to old ideas that were wrongly ignored a generation ago. The latter include the economic studies of Mises and Hayek, which are based on the importance of microeconomics, time, entrepreneurship, and capital. We are witnessing the renaissance of the Austrian school of economics. It may be too much to expect government leaders to accept the noninterventionist approach of the Austrians, but academics, businesspeople and investors may be surprised at the insights the Austrian school can provide about the world in which we live.

NOTES

1. Peter F. Drucker, *Toward the Next Economics, and Other Essays* (New York: Harper & Row, 1981), p. 13.
2. Schumpeter lists Menger, as well as his compatriot Böhm-Bawerk, in his classic work, *Ten Great Economists* (Oxford University Press, 1951). But that was a generation ago. Today's writers have largely forgotten the founders of the Austrian school.
3. Ludwig von Mises, *Planning for Freedom*, 4th ed. (Spring Mills, Penn.: Libertarian Press, 1980), pp. 207, 214.
4. Joseph Schumpeter, *History of Economic Analysis* (New York: Oxford University Press, 1954), p. 827.
5. But first read the delightful article by Gary North, "Why Murray Rothbard Will Never Win the Nobel Prize!," in *Man, Economy, and Liberty: Essays in Honor of Murray N. Rothbard* (Auburn, Ala.: Ludwig von Mises Institute, 1988), pp. 89–109.
6. Roger Garrison, "Time and Money: The Universals of Macroeconomic Theorizing," *Journal of Macroeconomics* (Spring 1984). This article must be regarded as the most penetrating contribution ever written about the debate over macroeconomics.

RECOMMENDED READING

For general readers:
Butler, Eamonn. *Ludwig von Mises: Fountainhead of the Modern Microeconomics Revolution*. Hants, England: Gower Publishing, 1988.

von Mises, Ludwig. *Planning for Freedom.* 4th ed. Spring Mills, Penn.: Libertarian Press, 1980.

Rothbard, Murray N. *America's Great Depression.* 4th ed. New York: Richardson and Snyder, 1983.

Rothbard, Murray N. *What Has the Government Done to Our Money?* 2nd ed. Novato, Calif.: Libertarian Publishers, 1981.

Skousen, Mark. *What Every Investor Should Know About Austrian Economics and the Hard Money Movement.* Auburn, Ala: Mises Institute, 1988.

For economists and economics majors:

Hayek, F. A. *Prices and Production.* 2nd ed. New York: Augustus M. Kelley, 1967.

Menger, Carl. *Principles of Economics.* New York: New York University Press, 1976.

Mises, Ludwig von. *Human Action.* 3rd ed. Chicago: Regnery, 1966.

O'Driscoll, Gerald P., Jr. and Mario J. Rizzo, *The Economics of Time and Ignorance.* New York: Basil Blackwell, 1985.

Rothbard, Murray N. *Man, Economy, and State.* Los Angeles: Nash Publishing, 1970.

Skousen, Mark. *The Structure of Production.* New York: New York University Press, 1990.

CHAPTER 21

THE FUTURE OF ECONOMICS

If the theory were not logical, or if the theory failed to be confirmed by real-world facts, it would be readily discarded by economists.

—Roy J. Ruffin and Paul R. Gregory
Principles of Economics (1988)

I wish I could be as generous as Ruffin and Gregory are with regard to the alleged open-mindedness and adaptability of the economics profession. Unfortunately, my experience is that economists in general are more likely to modify their already established models than to scrap them entirely and adopt a whole new conceptualization. In introducing his new theory of the economy, Keynes himself warned his fellow economists of the "struggle of escape from habitual modes of thought and expression."[1] In the early 1930s, Keynes compared his new theory of aggregate demand to economists' stepping into a new pair of trousers, and castigated them for trying to keep an embroidered version of the old pair of classical pants. It's a longstanding problem.

The same commentary can be made regarding today's orthodox economists and their determination to hold onto the tattered pair of neoclassical trousers. They just don't seem to fit. (Perhaps they never did fit. Such economists are more like the shopper who bought a coat on sale that didn't fit but couldn't bear to throw it out because it was such a bargain.) The crises of the 1970s and 1980s necessitate a new theory. In the previous chapters on both macroeconomics and microeconomics, I have argued for getting a new pair of theoretical pants rather than patching up the old ones.

NEW ECONOMIC REALITIES OF THE 1990s

What principles should guide our thinking as we approach the beginning of a new century and a new millennium? I list seven basic ideas:

1. Production is more important than consumption. Despite the implications of GNP and other misleading national statistics, the world's economies are not consumer-driven. Industry plays a central role in society's well being.

2. Deficit spending and an excessive national debt are a drag on society, not a benefit. The Treasury debt market is the largest financial market in the world and, as such, reduces the liquidity and size of other more essential markets, thus substantially penalizing economic growth. Government spending and the national debt can be reduced considerably through privatizing social goods and services.

3. A policy of encouraging consumption at the expense of savings, of promoting debt at the expense of equity, is detrimental to economic growth and the standard of living. The consumption–savings ratio is in imbalance in many countries. We need to shift policies toward encouraging savings and investment by reducing taxes on interest, dividends, capital gains, and business activities.

4. Central planning and socialist totalitarianism do not work. Command economies and welfare states need to encourage competition by deregulating their industries, eliminating monopolies, privatizing government businesses, and decentralizing decision processes.

5. A new monetary system is necessary to establish a stable financial and economic framework, one which minimizes boom–bust cycles, inflation, and uncertainty. A pure commodity standard (based on gold) is a possible solution.

6. The best long-term policy of peace and prosperity is that of global freedom in the movement of capital,

money, and people. Countries should adopt liberal immigration policies.

7. As nations increase their productivity and standard of living, individuals, businesses, and governments should develop efficient ways to reduce pollution and other negative environmental externalities as much as possible.

If countries around the world, both rich and poor, do not pursue these seven principles, then they will continue to suffer from artificial booms and busts, massive inflations and sudden deflations, credit crunches and monetary crises, unbalanced budgets and bureaucratic nightmares, stagnation and environmental pollution, and wars and rumors of wars. To the extent that individual nations adopt sound economic policies, they will prosper and expand, their currencies will strengthen, their interest rates will fall, their stock markets will show remarkable strength, and they will be the envy of their neighbors. Truly the fortunes of each nation lie in the destiny of their leaders.

WHAT'S NEEDED IN THEORY AND PRACTICE

Economists in academia, business, and government play an influential role in determining the destiny of their fellow citizens. To incorporate the sound principles outlined above, a challenging new approach is necessary in economic theory. In macroeconomics, we need a theory that reestablishes the virtues of savings, capital formation, and productivity—one that does not contradict the principles of economic growth. We need a framework that describes the microeconomic inner workings of the economy far beyond the excessive aggregation of models currently in vogue. The aggregate supply and demand models are still too macro-oriented and therefore are unable to portray accurately and completely the economic events of the past two decades.

The time-structure model that I have highlighted in Chapter 3 offers just such an alternative and ought to be incorporated into today's economic thinking and tomorrow's textbooks.

As I have demonstrated, the stages-of-production approach not only focuses on the real dynamic process, but offers a comprehensive look at all economic activity, not just final goods and services. Unlike GNP, it includes the full range of intermediate products on their way toward final consumer use. It also stresses the importance of time in the marketplace and the production process, and reenthrones the importance of capital theory, which has been largely absent from macroeconomic thinking since the 1930s. The time-structure method also offers a more complete description of inflationary recession, runaway inflation, depression, and other economic crises and business cycles. Finally, it shows the impact of various government fiscal and monetary policies on the economy.

In microeconomics, the neoclassical competition and monopoly models are largely static and thus fail to include the entrepreneur, the central figure in the market process. In Chapter 18, I presented an alternative model that does not make artificial distinctions between monopolistic and perfect competition in the marketplace. I have also suggested that long-term costs are just as subjective as consumer prices in determining what goods and services are produced.

It is my conviction that these two positive contributions to economic theory would solve most of the problems inherent in today's economics and would replace the incomplete and inaccurate macro–micro models and their corollaries (the multiplier, the accelerator, the circular flow diagram, the paradox of thrift, perfect and imperfect competition, etc.). I frankly admit that the adoption of these new views would mean a wholesale, dramatic alteration of today's way of economic thinking, and I have no illusions that such changes will be made anytime soon. My main hope is that these concepts will at least be included among competing theories.

There are grave omissions from introductory textbooks, including an accurate analysis of the gold standard and the origin of money, economic success stories around the world, creative alternatives to government-provided services and programs, and the value of applying economic principles to the business world and personal investment strategies. Last but not least, I would like to see the economics profession acknowledge and utilize more the wide range of contributions made by the Austrian school of economics. Much of my analysis, both positive and critical, has come from this insightful and versatile school of thought. Dolan, Gwartney and Stroup, and Byrns and Stone, have already started to use Austrian concepts in their books, a positive signal.

WHAT'S RIGHT WITH ECONOMICS

My tour of the top 10 economics textbooks has been fascinating and fruitful. It has been both rewarding and challenging, depending on the topic. Economics has changed in many ways since I studied it as an undergraduate 20 years ago, but much in economics has also remained the same. A great deal ought to be altered, as noted above, although some concepts are sound and a consensus about them has been formed in the economics profession. Almost all of today's economics writers, like those of the past, defend free trade and oppose protectionist measures. Various forms of government controls (on wages, prices, and rents) are systematically attacked. Most economists wisely reject the doomsday scenario of a worsening energy crisis and the population explosion. On this count, the academic world deserves applause.

In addition, much has changed over the past 20 years. In many ways, the changes have been beneficial, reflecting a willingness of economists to be more open-minded than they were during the monolithic years of the Keynesian era. Today's textbooks, from McConnell's to Dolan's, include a wide variety of new concepts. During this period, almost all of the writers have added discussions about monetarism, supply side economics, rational expectations, and Marxism, and I would hope that they would add considerably more on the Austrian school. In addition, today's economists use a great many more real-world examples of how economies operate. Of the top 10 textbooks, I found Dolan's and Gwartney and Stroup's to be the most progressive in integrating new material.

Paul Heyne's unorthodox text, *The Economic Way of Thinking,* is a challenging alternative that is being used more and more in the college classroom. Now in its fifth edition, Heyne's book takes a very practical down-to-earth approach to economics, using numerous examples that students can understand. Using Heyne's textbook, one gets the impression that the teacher is not lecturing but conducting a discussion about economic decision making. His questions for discussion at the end of each chapter are extensive and make students think deeply about real economic issues.

In the microeconomics section, he does not even refer to the perfect-competition model because he does not believe in it. He talks about price takers and price searchers without making value judgments.

In the macroeconomics section, there are no production-possibility curves or circular flow diagrams. Heyne does use aggregate supply and demand curves to discuss macroeconomic issues, however. His section on money does not include a discussion of the origin of money and makes only a short reference to gold. He contrasts Keynes ("Demand creates its own supply") with supply-siders ("Supply creates its own demand"). Ultimately, says Heyne, macroeconomic instability is a coordination problem, which could be viewed as an Austrian perspective. But he does not refer to Austrian economists by name.

The growing use of nontraditional texts and the introduction of totally new concepts in the traditional textbooks are favorable signs.

THE CASE FOR ECONOMIC FREEDOM

This book is not an apology for historical capitalism, nor does it say that the free market will solve all our problems. A free market, however productive, may produce many morally repugnant things. I do not claim that the market is perfect or always good, but neither is it bankrupt. What this book is saying is that the free market and private enterprise encourage the widest variety of economic activity and the most productive use of resources. If indeed the purpose of economics is to seek the best way to transform unusable resources into usable products, then the free market provides the best way to do it. Virtually all forms of government intervention—controls, subsidies, taxes, inflation, nationalization, and bureaucracy—limit the universal possibilities of mankind. Government leaders must provide a vision of leadership, political stability, individual rights, and the defense of liberty itself. It must provide an even playing field for all economic actors. On a macroeconomic level, this means a stable monetary system, low taxes, and a balanced budget. On a microeconomic level, this means equal justice under the law, individual rights, no special privileges, and noninterventionism. When individuals seek to pass a law, they should always consider two critical issues: (1) what the long-term, not just the short-term, effects of this new law are, and (2) how it will affect all groups or areas of the economy, not just one group. Henry Hazlitt has wisely called this test the one lesson everyone should learn in economics.[2]

The defenders of liberty have always, throughout history, called for an international open community where the government administers the law but does not interfere with the individual's freedom of movement. The state should guarantee individual rights and assure the freedom of movement in three areas—goods, people, and money. The issue is whether individuals will control their own destiny or the government elite will control their lives. Our goal can be summed up in one simple phrase: freedom in our time for all people.

THE SEARCH FOR TRUTH

In the past few hundred pages, we have examined a wide variety of issues in an effort to separate good from bad economics. In a broader sense, it has been a search for truth and common sense in the field of economics. Undoubtedly, my consistent defense of the free market as the best solution to the wide variety of economic problems may not be popular with many of my fellow economists. But as Josh Billings would say, "As scarce as truth is, the supply has always been in excess of the demand."

NOTES

1. J. M. Keynes, *The General Theory of Employment, Interest and Money* (London: Macmillan, 1936), p. *xxiii.*
2. Henry Hazlitt, *Economics in One Lesson,* 2nd ed. (New York: Arlington House, 1979), p. 17.

RECOMMENDED READING

Heyne, Paul. *The Economic Way of Thinking,* 5th ed. Chicago: Science Research Associates, 1987.

Naisbitt, John, and Patricia Aburdene, *Megatrends 2000: Ten New Directions for the 1990's.* New York: William Morrow & Co., 1990. A virtual libertarian document, the authors predict prosperity for countries that adopt free trade, privatization, and individualism.

APPENDIX

WHERE TO GET THE BEST INFORMATION ON ECONOMICS

Intelligent citizens can no longer afford to be innocent of economics textbooks.
—William J. Baumol and Alan S. Blinder
Economics: Principles and Policy (1988)

Throughout this study of economics, I have referred to many books and articles that you may be interested in reading. Although many of these works can be found in university libraries, the following sources should also be useful in locating these recommended materials.

Books, Cassette Tapes, and Videos

Laissez Faire Books
942 Howard St.
San Francisco, California 94103
800–326–0996

Laissez Faire Books has a large selection of books and cassette tapes on economics as well as other subjects. Ask for their free catalog.

JOURNALS AND ORGANIZATIONS

Reason Magazine
The Reason Foundation
2716 Ocean Park Blvd. Suite 1062
Santa Monica, California 90405

The Freeman
The Foundation for Economic Education (FEE)
Irvington-on-Hudson, New York 10533
(Published monthly, free)

The Cato Journal
The Cato Institute
224 Second St., SE
Washington, D.C. 20003

The Review of Austrian Economics
The Ludwig von Mises Institute
Auburn University
Auburn Alabama 36849

Pacific Research Institute for Public Policy
177 Post St.
San Francisco, California 94108

The Heritage Foundation
214 Massachusetts Ave., N.E.
Washington, D.C. 20002

American Enterprise Institute
1150 17th St., NW
Washington, D.C. 20036

Institute of Economic Affairs
2 Lord North St.
Westminster SW1P 3LB, England

Adam Smith Institute
23 Great Smith Street
London SW1P 3BL, England

NEWSLETTER ON ECONOMICS AND FINANCE

Mark Skousen's Forecasts & Strategies
Phillips Publishing Inc.
7811 Montrose Rd.
Potomac, Maryland 20854 ($99 a year, 12 issues)
800–722–9000 or 301–340–2100 for free sample

REFERENCES

Specific page references to the top 10 textbooks mentioned in *Economics on Trial: Lies, Myths, and Realities* are listed below. This book's page number appears first, followed by the source authors and page reference. Excerpts and longer quotations are referenced at the end of each chapter.

Chapter 1
14 Bronfenbrenner, Sichel, and Gardner, p. 15

Chapter 2
20 McConnell and Brue, p. 25

Chapter 3
28 Ruffin and Gregory, p. viii
31 McConnell and Brue, p. 46
31 Baumol and Blinder, p. 140
31 Bronfenbrenner, Sichel, and Gardner, pp. 130–38
31 Lipsey, Steiner, and Purvis, pp. 52–53

Chapter 4
38 Miller, p. 205
41 Dolan and Lindsey, p. 156

Chapter 5
47 Baumol and Blinder, p. 192
48 Lipsey, Steiner, and Purvis, p. 572
48 Samuelson and Nordhaus, p. 8
49 Samuelson and Nordhaus, p. 183
52 McConnell and Brue, p. 242

Chapter 6
63 Baumol and Blinder, p. 185
68 McConnell and Brue, p. 257
69 Miller, p. 302
69 Samuelson and Nordhaus, p. 182
69 Dolan and Lindsey, p. 260
72 Samuelson and Nordhaus, p. 216
72 Lipsey, Steiner, and Purvis, pp. 558–59

Chapter 7
74 Gwartney and Stroup, p. v

Chapter 8
88 Byrns and Stone, p. 306

Chapter 9
102 Gwartney and Stroup, p. 328
107 Baumol and Blinder, p. 85
107 Lipsey, Steiner, and Purvis, p. 719
111 Lipsey, Steiner, and Purvis, p. 573

Chapter 10
119 Miller, p. 162
119 McConnell and Brue, p. 93

126 Samuelson and Nordhaus, p. 769

Chapter 11
128 Samuelson and Nordhaus, p. 700
130 Samuelson and Nordhaus, p. 942
131 Bronfenbrenner, Sichel, and Gardner, pp. 341–44
140 Ruffin and Gregory, p. 316
141 Lipsey, Steiner, and Purvis, p. 843
141 McConnell and Brue, p. 343
143 Samuelson and Nordhaus, p. 949

Chapter 12
145 Lipsey and Steiner, p. 406
147 Gwartney and Stroup, p. 717
153 Samuelson and Nordhaus, p. 45
153 McConnell and Brue, p. 92

Chapter 13
158 Samuelson and Nordhaus, p. 795
158 Samuelson and Nordhaus, p. 794
168 Byrns and Stone, p. 673
170 Baumol and Blinder, p. 716

Chapter 14
177 McConnell and Brue, p. 296
179 Byrns and Stone, p. 296
181 McConnell and Brue, p. 402
182 Miller, p. 319
182 Baumol and Blinder, p. 331
183 Byrns and Stone, p. 295
183 Dolan and Lindsey, p. 280
184 Samuelson and Nordhaus, pp. 400–404
185 McConnell and Brue, p. 411

Chapter 15
187 Samuelson and Nordhaus, pp. 652–53
187 Samuelson and Nordhaus, p. 652
187 Baumol and Blinder, p. 825
194 Samuelson and Nordhaus, p. 641
194 Miller, p. 729

Chapter 16
198 Lipsey, Steiner, and Purvis, p. 735
198 Miller, p. 428
198 Samuelson and Nordhaus, p. xi
199 Samuelson and Nordhaus, p. 832
199 Bronfenbrenner, Sichel, and Gardner, pp. 796–98
200 Gwartney and Stroup, p. 804

Chapter 17
208 Samuelson and Nordhaus, p. 837
208 Samuelson and Nordhaus, p. 836
213 Lipsey, Steiner, and Purvis, p. 888
213 Ruffin and Gregory, p. 914
214 Lipsey, Steiner, and Purvis, pp. 885–86
217 Ruffin and Gregory, p. 908
217 Miller, p. 888
222 Samuelson and Nordhaus, p. 39
223 Baumol and Blinder, pp. 893–94
224 Lipsey, Steiner, and Purvis, pp. 870–80

Chapter 18
238 Ruffin and Gregory, p. 913
243 Miller, p. 565
246 Dolan and Lindsey, p. 603
248 Dolan and Lindsey, p. 681
252 Miller, p. 540

Chapter 19
255 Ruffin and Gregory, p. 2
257 Samuelson and Nordhaus, p. 251
258 Baumol and Blinder, p. 671
265 Baumol and Blinder, pp. 669–70

Chapter 20
274 Dolan and Lindsey, p. 678
280 Bronfenbrenner, Sichel, and Gardner, p. 631
287 Dolan and Lindsey, p. 679

Chapter 21
291 Ruffin and Gregory, p. viii

Appendix
299 Baumol and Blinder, p. iii

INDEX

Ability-to-pay principle, 165–67
Aburdene, Patricia, 298
Accelerator principle, 71–73
Adam Smith Institute, 288, 300
Affluent Society (Galbraith), 156, 194, 197 n
Aggregate demand curve, 74–84
Aggregate final demand, 38–39
Aggregate production structure (APS), 34–35
  and depression structure, 110–12
  to explain inflationary recession, 84–85
Aggregate supply and demand model, 74–84
  versus aggregate production structure, 84–87
Aggregate supply curve, 74–84
Agriculture, imperfect competition, 224–45
Air pollution, 148–50
Alchian, Armen, A., 249, 254 n
Allen, William R., 249, 254 n
Allende, Salvador, 221
American Economic Association, 10
American Economic Review, 115
American Enterprise Institute, 300
American Institute for Economic Research, 105
America's Great Depression (Rothbard), 101 n, 118, 286, 290
Anderson, Benjamin, 105
Annalist, 106
Antisavings mentality, 47–49; *see also* Savings
Antitrust Policy (Armentano), 254
APS; *see* Aggregate production structure
Arbitrage, 247
Argentina, 80, 218
  bankruptcy, 183
Armentano, D. T., 246, 253 n, 254 n, 287
Arrow, Kenneth J., 86–87
Auburn University, 277, 288
Australia, gold discoveries, 135
Austrian Institute for Business Cycle Research, 282
Austrian Institute for Economic Research, 104
Austrian school of economists, 295
  Böhm-Bawerk's influence, 280
  on econometric models, 277–78
  Hayek, 282
  leaders and characteristics, 274–75

Austrian school of economics—*Cont.*
  Menger, 278–79
  Mises' legacy, 280–81
  neglect by economists, 275–76
  reasons for neglect, 276–78
  recent scholars, 287–88
  on role of government, 277
  Rothbard, 284–87
  Schumpeter, 282–83

Babson, Roger, 103
Balanced budget
  amendment, 185
  laws, 174
  and multiplier, 69–70
  opposition to, 179
Band, Richard, E., 260, 272 n
Bank of England, 140
Bank of France, 140
Bankruptcy
  Argentina, 183
  federal government, 182–83
  United States potential, 182–83
Banks
  cash reserves, 59–60
  failures in 1930s, 108
  failures in 1980s, 114–15
  gold reserve system, 130
  gold standard reserves, 132–33
Bauer, P. T., 206
Baumol, William J., 13, 47, 73 n, 117 n, 196 n, 235 n, 236 n, 255
  central planning, 228–29
  circular flow model, 31
  competition, 240–41
  current economics, 1
  debt default, 182
  economics text, 10
  efficient market theory, 257
  externalities, 146
  Great Depression, 107
  income distribution, 187, 188 n, 190
  Marx, 208–9
  multiplier, 63–64
  random walk method, 258
  savings, 47
  Soviet Union, 214

Baumol, William J.—*Cont.*
 speculators, 265
 Sweden, 223
 taxation, 162, 170, 171 n
Bawley, Dan, 175–76
Benefit principle
 national basis, 168–69
 of taxation, 167
Bernhard, Arnold, 259, 272 n
Bethell, Tom, 236 n
Beyond Our Means (Malabre), 185, 186
Billings, Josh, 297
Birdzell, L. E., Jr., 270
Black, Fischer, 259, 271 n
Black market, 220
Blaug, Mark, 116 n, 247–48, 254 n, 287
Blinder, Alan S., 47, 73 n, 101 n, 117 n,
  196 n, 235 n, 236 n, 255
 central planning, 228–29
 circular flow diagram, 31
 competition, 240–41
 debt default, 182
 economics text, 10
 externalities, 146
 Great Depression, 107
 income distribution, 187, 188 n, 190
 investing, 257
 Marx, 208–9
 multiplier, 63–64
 Phillips curve, 97–98
 random walk method, 258
 savings, 47
 Soviet Union, 214
 speculators, 265
 Sweden, 223
 taxation, 162, 170, 171 n
Block, Walter, 287
Blodgett, Ralph H., 18, 19 n
Blum, Walter, J., 176 n
Böhm-Bawerk, Eugen von, 276, 280, 282,
  289 n
Bond market, federal, 184–85
Bordo, Michael David, 91, 100 n, 136, 137 n
Boskin, Michael, 12, 176
Boulding, Kenneth E., 12, 36
Bourne, Randolph, 112
Brand name preferences, 244
Brazil, 80
British pound sterling, 131
Bronfenbrenner, Martin, 131
 circular flow diagram, 31
 economics text, 11
 Japan, 199
 learning economics, 14
 roundabout production, 280
Brown, C. Cary, 109
Brown, Lawrence, 272 n
Browne, Harry, 186, 273
Brue, Standley L., 53 n
 costs and benefits, 20
 economic text, 10
Brzezinski, Zbigniew, 216–17, 218, 235 n,
  236 n, 237
Buchanan, James, 126, 156, 176, 287–88
Buffett, Warren, 259
Bureaucracy, 125–26
Business, gross outlays for production, 41–42

Business cycles; *see also* Depression; Great
  Depression; *and* Recession
 Hayek on, 282
 inflation-induced, 88–100
 Schumpeter's view, 283
Butler, Eammon, 289
Buy-and-hold strategy, 258
Byrns, Ralph T., 77 n, 118 n, 295
 economics text, 11
 federal budget, 179, 183
 Great Depression, 103
 inflation/unemployment, 88
 value-added tax, 168

California, gold discoveries, 135, 138
Canada
 capital gains tax, 179
 low savings rate, 52
Capital (Marx), 221
Capital formation, 89
Capital gains tax, national comparison,
  170–71
Capital goods industries
 and credit expansion, 92
 and recession, 179
Capitalism, Socialism, and Democracy
  (Schumpeter), 283
Capitalism and Freedom (Friedman), 73, 284
Cartels
 compared to perfect competition model,
  244–45
 weakness of, 243–44
Case for Gold, The (Paul and Lehrman), 144
Cash hoarding, 59–60
Cato Institute, 288, 300
Cato Journal, 288, 300
Center for the Study of Market Processes,
  288
Central banks; *see also* Federal Reserve
  Board
 and gold standard, 139–40
 money creation, 91–92
 role in recession and inflation, 90–92
Central planning; *see also* Socialism
 economists' defense, 232
 faults, 217–22
 failure, 292
 reasons for failure, 225–29
 in Sweden, 223–24
Chamberlain, John, 232
Chamberlin, Edward, 239, 245
Chase, Stuart, 113, 118 n
Chesapeake, Bay, 149
Chiang Kai-shek, 203
Chicago school, 276, 277
 Freidman and, 283–84
Chile, 221–22
China
 bankruptcy, 183
 full employment, 121
Circular flow diagram
 analysis and criticism, 28–34
 limitations, 31
 purchasing power fallacy, 30–31
Circulating capital, 19
Clark, John Bates, 29

Clason, George, 273
Classical range of inflation, 20
Clean Air Act of 1977, 150
Coase, Ronald H., 153, 156 n
Collectivism; *see* Central planning *and*
   Socialism
Commodities, price fall, 83–84
Communism, 208–18; *see also* Central plan-
   ning; Marx, Karl; *and* Socialism
Communist Manifesto (Marx and Engels),
   209–10
Competition, critique of classical model, 245–
   46; *see also* Imperfect competition model
   and Perfect competition model
Competition and Enterpreneurship (Kirzner),
   245, 254
Constitution, balanced budget proposal, 185
Consumer demand, 50–51
Consumer spending
   exaggeration of 42–43
   in GNP data, 39–43
Consumption
   during the depression, 60–61
   present and future, 54–56
   versus production, 45–46
Contrary investing theory, 266–67
Corporate capitalism, 255
   flaws, 233–34
Corrections Corporation of America, 254
Cost and price, 22–53
Cowen, Tyler, 156
Crandall, Robert, 150
Creative destruction, 283
Credit Anstalt, 104
Credit expansion, 92
Crowding-out effect of deficits, 184–85
Cuba, 218
Currencies
   on gold standard, 130
   origin of, 131
Cutting Back on City Hall (Poole), 151
Cyclical unemployment, 122–23
Czechoslovakia, 218

Debt market, 186
Decision-making processes, 24–26
Deficit; *see* Federal deficit *and* Government
   spending
Deflation
   cause of unemployment, 123
   and economic growth, 78
   fear of, 90–94
   and gold standard, 132–33
Demand; *see also* Supply and demand
   costs determined by, 252
   and future consumption, 54–56
Demand-pull inflation, 80
Demand-side economics, 74–75
Demsetz, Harold, 156
Depression; *see also* Great Depression *and*
   Recession
   denial of recurrence, 102, 113–16
   and gold standard, 138–39
   increase of savings, 48–51, 59–62
Depression-proof economy, 113–16
De Soto, Hernando, 220–21, 236 n, 237

Diamond-water, paradox, 279
Disequilibrium, 79–80
Dolan, Edwin, G., 12, 42, 174, 175 n, 254 n,
   287, 295
   and Austrian school, 274, 275
   competition, 248
   economics text, 11
   entrepreneurs, 246
   federal deficit, 183
   gross national product, 40–41, 43
   tax cuts, 69
Dollar, origins of, 131
Dominguez, Kathryn, M., 118 n
Dow Jones Industrials, 200, 257
Dreman, David, 260, 272 n, 273
Drucker, Peter, F., 75, 127 n, 289 n
   criticism of Keynesian economics, 274
   on federal bureaucracy, 126

Ebeling, Richard, 245, 287
Econometric models, 277–78
Economic activity
   dynamism, 19
   everyday, 16–17
   transformation process, 17–18
Economic booms
   artificial, 98
   sustained versus artificial, 92–95
Economic calculation
   Mises on, 281
   under socialism, 228–29
"Economic Calculation in a Socialist
   Commonwealth" (Mises), 281
Economic census, 44–45
Economic freedom, 296–97
Economic goals, 128–29
Economic growth
   Böhm-Bawerk on, 280
   and capital gains tax, 170–71
   definition, 19
   and deflation, 78
   and gold standard, 141
   Keynesian prescription, 206 n
   savings and, 51–62
   simplistic notions, 202
Economics; *see also* Keynesian economics
   aggregate reduction structure, 34–35
   battles over, 278
   chief textbooks, 10–11
   circular flow diagram, 28–34
   commonsense decision making, 24–26
   current definition, 14
   errors of, 1–3
   factors of production, 18–19
   full employment concept, 52–54
   gross national outlays, 43–46
   gross national product data, 38–43
   information sources, 229–300
   marginal value theory, 15
   need for new theory, 293–95
   new definition, 18–19
   new realities, 292–93
   objectivity in, 12–13
   opportunity cost, 21
   paradox of thrift, 47–62
   power of habitual thinking, 291

Economics—*Cont.*
  production chain, 16–19
  production-possibility curve, 20–27
  purchasing power fallacy, 30–31
  qualitative science, 265–66
  scarcity theory, 14–16
  schools of thought, 276
  stages of production, 32–36
  supply and demand connection, 16–17
  theoretical versus practical, 3–5
  theory of subjective, 281
  time element, 28–30
  transformation process, 17–18
  usefulness, 267–68
  valid concepts, 295–96
  value-added approach, 40–41
Economics (Bronfenbrenner, Sichel, and
    Gardner), 11
Economics (Byrns and Stone), 11
Economics (Dolan and Lindsey), 11
Economics (Lipsey, Steiner, and Purvis), 10
Economics (McConnell and Brue), 10
Economics (Samuelson and Nordhaus), 10,
    47, 62
*Economics: An Introduction to Traditional
    and Radical Views* (Hunt and Sherman),
    12
Economics: Principles and Policy (Baumol
    and Blinder), 10
Economics: Private and Public Choice
    (Gwartney and Stroup), 11
Economics of a Pure Gold Standard (Skou-
    sen), 144
Economics of Time and Ignorance (O'Driscoll
    and Rizzo), 290
Economics Today (Miller), 11
Economics Time Bomb (Browne), 186
Economic Way of Thinking (Heyne), 12, 249,
    295–96, 298
Economists
  influence of, 2–3
  investment advisers, 255–71
  practical experience, 6–9
  reaction to depression, 106–13
  rejection of gold standard, 128
Economy; *see also* Free markets
  resource market and product market, 28
  structure of, 34–35
Efficient market theory, 257
  objections to, 259–60
Eisenstadt, Gale, 156 n
Eisner, Robert, 180–81
Employee benefits, 124
Employment
  taxes, 124
  during World War II, 112
Employment Act of 1946, 119
Engles, Friedrich, 209–10, 212, 235 n
Entrepreneurs
  creative destruction, 283
  definition, 246–47
  role in markets, 246–48
  speculators, 264–65
Entrepreneurs, The (Sobel and Sicilia), 232,
    254
*Equality, the Third World, and Economic
    Delusion* (Bauer), 206

Equilibrium
  without full employment, 78–80
  long-term, 250–51
  Schumpter's view, 283
Erhard, Ludwig, 222–23, 236 n
*Essays on Some Unsettled Questions of Politi-
    cal Economy* (Mill), 46
"Essential Von Mises" (Rothbard), 281
Exogenous monetary inflation, 72–73
Expected value, 33–34
Expenditures; *see* Government spending
Externalities, 145–46
  air and water pollution, 148–50
  in public education, 147

Factors of production, 18–19, 33
Fair, Ray C., 118 n
Fallacy of composition, 48–49
Farmers, 245
Federal deficit
  consequences, 180–83, 184
  and government bankruptcy, 182–83
  huge increases, 180–82
  as income redistribution, 181–82
  interest costs, 182
  monetarist view, 179–80
  need to reduce, 292
  and private debt, 185–86
  public credit fallacy, 181–82
  during a recession, 179
  relative to GNP, 177–78
  Samuelson's view, 184–85
  solutions to, 185
  taxation and, 173–74
  threat of, 177
  Treasury bills, 184
Federal Reserve Board, 90, 104–5, 108, 116,
    140
Fetter, Frank, 279
Fiat money, 70–71; *see also* Money creation
  versus gold standard, 139
  results of, 92–93
Final aggregate demand theory, 38–39
Financial markets, 114, 255–71; *see also* In-
    vestment markets
Fire protection, 151–52
Fiscal policy; *see* Federal deficit; Government
    spending; *and* Taxation
Fisher, Irving, 104, 115–16
  and depression, 102–3
Fisher, Irving Norton, 116 n
Fitzgerald, Randall, 154, 157
Five-dollar day, 231
Fixed capital, 19
Ford, Henry, 231
Foundation for Economic Education, 288,
    299–300
Fractional reserve banking, 130
Franklin, Benjamin, 3, 62
Free banking arrangement, 143 n–44 n
Freeman, 299
Free markets
  absence of system, 224–25
  alleged failings, 145
  case for, 296–97
  Chile, 221–22

Free markets—*Cont.*
    criticism of, 229–30
    environmental issues, 149–50
    externalities, 145–46
    failure versus government failure, 155
    fire protection, 151–52
    flaws of corporate capitalism, 233–34
    income distribution, 187–96
    as job destroyer, 121–22
    lighthouses, 153
    long-term equilibrium, 249–50
    price-cost relationship, 252–53
    production of goods, 232
    profit seeking, 249–51
    provision of public goods, 154
    and public education, 147–48
    responsibility for depression, 107–9
    road services, 152
    role of entrepreneurs, 246–48
    versus socialism, 224–25
    strengths and weaknesses, 233
    unemployment, 120–22
Free rider problem, 151–53
Free to Choose (Friedman), 37
Friedman, Milton, 2, 37, 73, 117 n, 118 n,
        144 n, 257
    bank failures, 108
    Chicago school, 283–84
    deficit spending, 179–80
    depression-proof economy, 113–14
    depressions, 102
    Federal Reserve Board, 116
    gold standard, 141
    monetarist policy, 75
Fringe benefits, 154
Full employment
    analysis of, 52–54
    disadvantages, 121–22
    government policy, 119
    inflation during, 80–82
    and savings, 48–59
Full Employment and Balanced Growth Act
        of 1987, 199

Galbraith, John Kenneth, 156, 194, 197 n,
        233, 274
Gardner, Wayland
    economics text, 11
    learning economics, 14
Garrison, Roger, 140, 144 n, 274, 287, 288,
        289 n
Gemmill, Paul F., 18, 19 n
General Accounting Office, 121
General Motors, 63–67
*General Theory of Employment, Interest, and
    Money* (Keynes), 2, 65, 106, 262
George Mason University, 277, 288
Germany
    bankruptcy, 183
    economic turnaround, 219–20
    postwar recovery, 222–23
    savings and growth, 52
Gilder, George, 254
Glasnost, 217
GNP; *see* Gross national product (GNP)

Gold
    cost of, 140
    major producers, 141–42
    supply and economic growth, 141
    world production, 134, 135
    world stocks, 133
Gold exchange standard, 142–43
Goldman, Marshall, 214, 235 n, 237
Gold standard
    advantages, 132–40
    case against, 140–42
    and deflation, 132–33
    and depressions, 138–39
    false, 142
    and inflation, 89–90, 133–38
    monetarist view, 144 n
    nature of, 129–30
    need for, 292
    and need for central banks, 139–40
    obstacles to, 142–43
    rejection by economists, 128
Gosplan, 217
Government; *see also* Federal deficit
    Austrian school view, 277
    bankruptcy potential, 182–83
    bias toward inflation, 90–95
    cause of unemployment, 123–25
    failure versus market failure, 155
    flawed financial theory, 165
    full employment policy, 119
    impact on investment markets, 268–69
    income distribution, 196
    increase in bureaucracy, 125–26
    money creation and inflation, 80–82
    pollution policies, 149–50
    responsibility for depression, 107–9
    role in free economy, 297
    role in Japan's economy, 201
    role in Pacific Basin nations, 200
    role in Singapore, 204–5
    subsidizing education, 147–48
Government spending; *see also* Federal deficit
        and Money creation
    cure for depression, 109–11
    civilian versus military, 20–24
    in gross national product, 45
    multiplier and, 67–69
    and taxes, 173
Graham, Benjamin, 267
Grand Failure (Brzezinski), 216, 237
Great Britain
    capital gains tax, 171
    colony of Hong Kong, 203
    income distribution, 190–91
    low savings rate, 52
    privatization, 155
Great Contraction, The (Friedman and
        Schwartz), 118
Great Depression, 59–62
    argument over causes and cures, 89–90,
        106–13
    blame for, 107–9
    failure to predict, 102–4
    Friedman on, 284
    and government spending, 109–11
    Hayek's warning, 282
    importance of thrift, 270–71

Great Depression—*Cont.*
  lessons of, 107–9
  likelihood of recurrence, 113–16
  Rothbard's analysis, 101, 286
  and World War II, 111–13
Great Society, 285
Gregory, Paul R., 28
  competition, 238
  definition of economics, 14
  on economics, 255
  economics text, 11
  economic theory, 291
  federal deficit, 180
  gold standard, 140
  government spending, 109–10
  Soviet Union, 213, 217
  use of economics, 28
Gross national product (GNP)
  analysis and criticism, 38–43
  consumer spending data, 42–43
  data flaws, 41–43
  equation, 39
  excluded data, 39–41
  and federal deficit, 177–78
  and multiplier, 63–64
  as net value-added approach, 40
  potential, 99–100
  Soviet Union, 213–14
  during stagflation, 82–83
Gross national outlays, 43–45
Gwartney, James D., 108, 148, 216, 295
  economics text, 11
  Great Depression, 102
  macroeconomics, 74
  public education, 147–48
  socialism, 218

Haberler, Gottfried, 280
Hanke, Steve, 287
Hansen, Alvin, 283
Harcourt Brace Jovanovich, 10
Harper and Row, 10
Harrington, Michael, 233
Harris, Nigel, 204, 206 n
Harvard Economic Society, 103, 115–16
Harwood, E. C., 105, 117 n
Hawaii, 149
Hawtrey, Ralph, 62
Hayek, Friedrich A., 36, 88–89, 117 n, 217, 228, 229, 233, 236 n, 275–76, 280, 282, 283, 288, 290
  prediction of depression, 104–5
  view of money, 263
Hazlitt, Henry, 66, 73 n, 297
Heilbroner, Robert L., 212, 229, 235 n, 236 n
Heritage Foundation, 288, 300
Hession, Charles, H., 117 n
Heyne, Paul, 12, 249, 254 n, 295–96, 298
Hicks, John R., 36, 282
Holt, Rinehart and Winston, 10
Homogeneous products, 244
Hong Kong
  economic success, 202–3
  standard of living, 219
Hong Kong: A Study in Economic Freedom (Rabushka), 207

Hoover, Herbert, 108
How the West Grew Rich (Rosenberg and Birdzell), 270
Hughes, Johathan, 232
Human Action (Mises), 281, 285, 290
Hungary, 218
Hunt, E. K., 12, 236 n
  on socialism and free markets, 229–34

Immigration policies, 292–93
Imperfect competition model, 239–42
  in agriculture, 244–45
Imperfect knowledge investors, 263–64
Incentives
  and income inequality, 190–93
  under socialism, 228
Income distribution
  absolute wage levels, 195–96
  artificial methods, 192–93
  egalitarian goal, 187
  and increased outputs, 193–96
  inflation's impact, 196
  Latin America, 191
  Lorenz curve, 187–94, 196
  Marx's slogan, 234
  need for inequality, 189–93
  results of equality, 189
  Sweden and Great Britain, 190–91
  theory, 196
Income tax; *see also* Taxation
  ability-to-pay principle, 166–67
  alternatives to, 168–69
  loopholes and brackets, 161–63
  progressive, 158–59
  federal deficit, 181–82
Index of Leading Indicators, 43
India, 219
Inflation
  bias toward, 90–95
  cause of unemployment, 123
  classical range of inflation, 80
  exogenous monetary, 72–73
  factors influencing, 97
  from federal deficit, 180, 183
  and full employment, 80–82
  and gold standard, 89–90, 133–38
  gold versus flat money, 139
  government-induced, 71
  impact on investments, 269
  and income distribution, 196
  Japan, 201–2
  and multiplier, 70–71
  role of central banks, 90–94
  runaway, 80–82
  and taxes, 174
Inflationary recession, 74–76, 82–84
  aggregate production structure, 84–85
  causes, 88–100
  energy crisis, 95–96
  inevitability of, 100
Informals (black markets), 220
Insider trading, 260
Institute for Economic Affairs, 288, 300
Instituto Libertad y Democracia, 288
Interest
  impact of rates, 182

Interest—*Cont.*
  natural rate, 89–90
Intermediate stages of production, 40–42
Internal Revenue Service
  and national sales tax, 169
  and underground economy, 175–76
Investment
  benefits of, 56–59
  during depressions, 60–61
  and savings, 50–52
  taxation, 48
Investment advice, 7–8
Investment markets
  contrary investing theory, 266–67
  cycles, 263–64
  economics text neglect, 255–56
  efficient market theory, 257
  government policy impact, 268–69
  inflation's impact, 269
  January effect, 260
  Keynesian economics view, 262
  keys to understanding, 261–64
  principles of success, 269–71
  random walk theory, 258–59
  speculators, 264–65
  usefulness, 255–56
  usefulness of economics in, 267–68
Invitational Conference of the Principles of
    Economics Textbooks, 12
Israel, 23, 80
Italy, 52
Izvestia, 215

Jackson, Andrew, 140
January effect, 260
Japan
  economic success, 198–202
  savings and growth, 52
  taxation, 169–73
Jevons, William Stanley, 35, 279
Joachimsthaler, 131
Job destruction and creation, 121–22
Johnson, Lyndon B., 285
Johnson, Paul, 211, 215 n, 271 n
Joint Council on Economic Education, 12
Jones, Charles, P., 271 n

Kalven, Harry, Jr., 176 n
Keynes, John Maynard, 2, 39, 46, 59, 62, 75,
    117 n, 140, 197 n, 230, 277, 286, 296,
    298 n
  causes and cures of depression, 106–13
  on economic theory, 291
  failure to predict depression, 103–4
  income distribution, 190
  on investment, 262
  personal investments, 272 n
  on Say's law, 109
Keynesian economics
  accelerator principle, 71–73
  aggregate supply and demand model, 78–84
  antisavings assumptions, 47–62, 270
  basic tenets, 49–51
  Chicago school reaction, 283–84

Keynesian economics—*Cont.*
  Drucker's criticism, 274
  on economic growth, 206 n
  final aggregate demand theory, 38–39
  flaws in, 54–56
  full employment issue, 52–54
  fundamental error, 48
  Garrison's view, 288
  GNP theory, 38–43
  and government growth, 155, 172–73
  impact on Austrian school, 282
  impact on stages of production model, 36
  investment theory, 262
  lack of microeconomic foundation, 86–87
  Mises' criticism, 281
  the multiplier, 63–63
  Phillips curve, 97–99
  principles, 106–7
  rejected by Pacific Basin nations, 19
  results, 3
  solution to recession, 179
  support for tax increases, 174
  worker productivity, 125–26
Kirzner, Israel, 176, 244, 247, 253 n, 274, 287
Knowledge, investment, 261–64
Kondratieff waves, 283
Kuznets, Simon, 38, 39

Labor force flexibility, 120
Labor theory of value, 210
  Austrian school view, 279
Lachman, Ludwig, M., 287
Laffer curve, 24, 162–64, 173
Laissez Faire Books, 299
Lange, Oskar, 228, 233, 236 n
Latin America, 80–81
  economic situation, 220–22
  income distribution, 191
Lavoie, Don, 236 n, 287
Leakages, 31
  savings as, 49–50
Lee, Dwight R., 176
Lehrman, Lewis, 144
Leiman, Melvin, 285
Lerner, A. P., 228
Lighthouses, 153
Lindsey, David E., 41 n, 175 n, 248, 254 n
  Austrian school, 274
  economics text, 11
Lipsey, Richard G., 10, 48, 117 n, 118 n
  accelerator principle, 72
  circular flow diagram, 31
  economics text, 10
  ending of depression, 111–12
  federal deficit, 177–78
  free markets, 224–25
  gold standard, 141
  Great Depression, 107
  inflation, 80–81
  Japan, 198
  Soviet Union, 214
  state intervention, 145
Liquidity preference, 59, 109
London School of Economics, 282
Long-term equilibrium, 249–50
Lorenz curve, 187–94, 196

Los Angeles freeways, 152
Losing Ground (Murray), 193, 197 n
Ludwig von Mises (Butler), 289
Ludwig von Mises Institute, 288, 300
Lynch, Peter, 259

Machlup, Fritz, 280
Macroeconomics
  aggregate production structure, 85–87
  aggregate supply and demand model, 74–84
  antisavings mentality, 47–49
  government control, 114
Magellan Fund, 259
Malabre, Albert, 185, 186
Malinvestment, 65
  definition, 94
Malkiel, Burton G., 257, 258, 271 n, 273
Man, Economy, and State (Rothbard), 285
Manhattan Institute, 288
Marginal tax rate
  Japan, 171–72
  and productivity, 159
Marginal value theory, 15
Market concentration, 243–44
Marketing, 36
Market Process, 288
Market rate of interest, 89
Mark Skousen's Forecasts and Strategies, 300
Marshall, Alfred, 252, 276
Marx, Jenny, 212, 256–57
Marx, Karl, 2, 229–30, 234, 235 n, 257
  family life, 212–13
  results of theories, 213
  theories, 208–11
Marxism-Leninism, 3
McConnell, Campbell R., 12, 28, 51–52, 53 n, 295
  federal deficit, 181
  full employment, 119
  circular flow model, 28–29, 31
  costs and benefits, 20
  economics text, 10
  lighthouse ownership, 153
  multiplier, 67–69
  paradox of thrift, 51–52
  role of debt, 185–86
  Soviet Union, 214
  taxation, 162, 170–71
McGraw-Hill, 10
McKenzie, Richard B., 121, 127 n
McKinley, William, 130, 132
Megatrends 2000 (Naisbitt and Auburdene), 298
Mehra, Jagdish, 117 n
Menger, Carl, 35, 132, 144 n, 210, 276, 287–79, 281, 289 n, 290
Microeconomics
  alternative model, 294
  neglect by Keynes, 86–87
  perfect competition model, 238–45
  teaching, 238
Mill, John Stuart, 45–46
Miller, Roger Leroy, 98 n, 99 n, 163 n, 239, 240 n
  aggregate supply and demand curve, 83

Miller, Roger Leroy—*Cont.*
  balanced budget multiplier, 69
  cost-price relationship, 252
  economics text, 11
  federal deficit, 182
  GNP, 38
  income distribution, 194
  Japan, 198
  on Marx, 234
  Soviet Union, 217
  unemployment, 119
Minimum wage legislation, 124–25
Ministry of Finance (Japan), 201
Ministry of International Trade and Industry (Japan), 201
Minsky, Hyman, 206 n, 271 n
Mises, Ludwig von, 88–89, 91–92, 94, 140, 217, 218, 228, 229, 233, 275–76, 277, 280–81, 283, 284–85, 288, 289 n, 290
  money, 281
  prediction of depression, 104–5
Mises, Margit von, 271 n
Mitchell, Wesley C., 103, 117 n
Modigliani, Franco, 51, 62
Moggridge, Donald E., 272 n
Monetarists
  economy, 74–75
  and gold standard, 144 n
  view of federal deficit, 179–80
Monetary History of the United States (Friedman and Schwartz), 108, 284
Monetary policy, and unemployment, 123
Money
  gold standard, 129–30
  Mises view of, 281
  origin, 130-32
  paper versus gold, 139
  Rothbard on, 286
Money creation
  by central banks, 91–92
  demand-pull inflation, 80–82
  economic imbalance, 104
  increases since 1960s, 115
  and interest rates, 89–90
  and multiplier, 70–71
  results, 92–95
Money in Crisis (Siegel), 144
Money-market instruments, 26
Money supply; *see* Money creation
Monopoly
  market concentration, 243–44
  state-granted, 243
Morgensen, Gretchen, 156 n
Morishima, Michio, 36, 207
Multiplier theory, 49, 63–73
  accelerator principle, 71–72
  government spending impact, 67–69
  and inflation, 70–71
  negative impact, 66–67
  operation of, 63–64
  savings and, 64–66
  taxation and, 69–70
Murray, Charles, 193, 197 n
Mystery of Banking (Rothbard), 286
Myths of Antitrust (Armentano), 246

Naisbitt, John, 298
National Bureau of Economic Research, 38, 103
National Conservancy (Hawaii), 149
National debt, 180–82; *see also* Federal deficit
National income theory, 168–69
National sales tax, 38–43
Natural rate of interest, 89–90
Net national product, 67–69
Net value-added approach, 40–41
New Classical School, 78
New Contrarian Investment Strategy (Dreman), 273
New Era economists, 102
Newly industrialized countries, 199–200
Newton, Isaac, 263
New York Times, 106, 125
New York University, 277, 278
Nikkei index, 200
No-knowledge investors, 261–62
Nordhaus, William D., 21 n, 73 n
  economics text, 10
  income distribution, 187
  socialism, 208
  taxation, 158, 170 n
North, Gary, 235 n, 289 n

O'Driscoll, George P., 287, 290
Oil glut, 253
Oil industry, 252–53
Oil prices, 95–96; *see also* Organization of Petroleum Exporting Countries (OPEC)
Opportunity cost, 21
  in decision making, 24–26
Organization of Petroleum Exporting Countries (OPEC), 95, 97, 244, 252–53
Other Path, The (De Soto), 237
Output; *see* Production

Pacific Basin nations, 1
  capital gains tax, 172
  economic success, 198–206
Pacific Research Institute for Public Policy, 288, 300
Padover, Saul K., 212, 235 n
Paradox of thrift theory
  analysis and criticism, 47–62
  definition, 4
  Friedman silence on, 284
Pattern of Failure: Socialist Economics in Crisis (Rydenfeldt), 237
Paula, Ron, 144
Payne, Robert, 212–13, 235 n
Pencil manufacture, 34
Perestroika, 217
Perfect competition model
  in agriculture, 245
  as cartel, 244–45
  characteristics, 238–39
  compared to imperfect competition, 239–42
  cost-price relationship, 252–53
  criticism of, 245–46
  economists' response to criticism, 248–49
  and entrepreneurs, 246–48
  flaws, 242–44

Perfect-knowledge investors, 261–62
Personal Finance, 260
Phillips, A. W., 97
Phillips curve, 74, 82
  flaws, 97–99
Phillips Publishing, Inc., 7, 300
Planning for Freedom (Mises), 281, 285, 290
Pollution
  controls, 150
  reduction, 293
Poole, Robert W., Jr., 151–52, 156
Positive Theory of Capital (Böhm-Bawerk), 280
Potential gross national product, 99–100
Poverty increase, 193
Power and Market (Rothbard), 286
Price
  and cost, 252–53
  gold standard, 133–38
  information coordinator, 228
  stocks, 266–67
Price discrimination, 166–67
Price-earnings ratio, 266
Prices and Production (Hayek), 282, 290
Price searchers, 249
Price stabilization theory, 103, 104
Price takers, 249
Principles of Economics (Menger), 278–79, 290
Principles of Economics (Ruffin and Gregory), 11
Principles of Economics (Taussig), 36
Private debt, 184–86
Privatization
  fire protection, 151–52
  government services, 154–55
  Great Britain, 15
  jails, 154
  lighthouses, 153
  and reduction of government, 155
  roads and highways, 152
Proctor, William, 272 n
Product differentiation, 244
Production; *see also* Stages-of-production model
  chain, 16–19
  versus consumption, 45–46
  decline during inflation, 80–82
  free market, 232
  gross national outlays model, 43–46
  homogeneous, 244
  importance, 292
  intermediate stages, 40–42
  roundabout, 280
  time factor, 28–30
  transformation process, 17–18
Production-possibility curve, 163–64
  analysis and criticism, 20–27
Productivity, and tax rates, 159
Product market, 28
Profit seeking, 249–51
Progressive income tax, 158–59
  loopholes, 161–63
Property taxes, 167
Prosperity, 45–46
Public credit fallacy, 181–82

Public education, 147–48
  benefit principle, 167
  externalities, 147
Public goods
  fire protection, 151–52
  free rider problem, 151
  lighthouses, 153
  road services, 152
  role of business, 154
Publishing business, 11
Purchasing power fallacy, 30–31
Purvis, Douglas D., 117 n, 118 n
  economics text, 10
  Japan, 198

Quantity theory of money, 80–81

Rabushka, Alvin, 207
Radical economics, 229–34
Random Walk Down Wall Street (Malkiel),
  258, 273
Random walk investing, 258–59
  objections to, 259–60
Read, Leonard E., 37, 288
Reagan administration, 162, 173, 180
Reason Foundation, 288, 299
Reason magazine, 151, 288, 299
Recession
  disequilibrium, 79–80
  factors influencing, 97
  increase of savings, 48–49
  inevitability, 100
  and inflation, 74–76
  inflationary, 82–84
  Keynesian solution, 179
Reed, Lawrence, W., 216, 235 n, 236 n
Regressive taxes, 169
Reserve requirements, 114–15
  gold standard, 130
Resource market, 28
Resources
  production-possibility curve, 20–27
  in production process, 16–19
  scarcity theory, 14–16
Review of Austrian Economics, 288, 300
Ricardo, David, 2, 140, 210, 279
Richest Man in Babylon (Clason), 273
Rizzo, Mario J., 290
Road services, 152
Road to Serfdom (Hayek), 282
Robbins, Lionel, 14, 19, 117 n, 280, 282
  definition of economics, 14
Roberts, Paul Craig, 176
Robinson, Joan, 239, 245
Rockwell, Llewellyn H., Jr., 144 n
Rollins College, 5
Romano, Richard, 285
Roosevelt, Franklin D., 109
Roots of Capitalism (Chamberlain), 232
Rosenberg, Nathan, 270
Rothbard, Murray N., 36, 118, 144, 254 n,
  274, 281, 284–87, 290
  Great Depression, 101 n
Roundabout production, 280

Rozeff, Michael, 272 n
Rueff, Jacques, 222–23
Ruffin, Roy J., 28
  competition, 238
  definition of economics, 14
  economics, 28, 235
  economics text, 11
  economic theory, 291
  federal deficit, 180
  gold standard, 140
  government spending, 109–10
  Soviet Union, 213, 217
Rural/Metro Fire Department, Inc.,
  (Arizona), 152
Rydenfeldt, Sven, 219, 236 n, 237

St. Joachim valley, Bohemia, 131
Salerno, Joseph, 287
Samuelson, Paul A., 11, 20–21, 47–49, 52, 53,
  73 n, 130, 156, 197 n
  accelerator principle, 71–72
  balanced budget multiplier, 69
  depressions, 102
  economic growth, 280
  economics text, 10
  "Family Tree of Economics," 276
  federal deficit, 184–85
  gold standard, 128, 140, 143
  government spending, 126
  growth of government, 173
  income distribution, 187, 190, 193, 194
  investing, 257
  Japan, 199
  on Keynes, 286
  lighthouse ownership, 153
  paradox of thrift, 47–49, 52, 53, 62
  random walk method, 258
  socialism, 208
  Soviet Union, 214
  taxation, 158–59, 162, 169–70
Savings
  benefits, 56–59
  Böhm-Bawerk on, 280
  and debt creation, 185–86
  and economic growth, 51–62
  future-oriented, 55, 57–59
  impact during recession/depression, 48–51,
    59–62
  increase during World War II, 113
  and interest rates, 89
  and investment, 50–52
  in Japan, 172, 201
  Keynesian view, 49–51
  Mises' view, 281
  in multiplier, 64–66
  need to encourage, 292
  reasons for, 55
  role in economy, 47–62
  taxation, 48, 174
Say, J. B., 4, 13, 247
Say's law, 46, 59, 77
  Keynes' criticism, 109
Scarcity theory, 14–16
Schecter, Kate, 216, 236 n
Schumpeter, Joseph, 246, 254 n, 275, 282–83,
  289 n

Schwartz, Anna J., 108, 116, 117 n, 118, 144 n, 284
Selgin, George, 14 n
Sennholz, Hans, 287
Shackle, G. L. S., 36
Shapiro, Matthew, 118 n
Sherman, A. J., 117 n
Sherman, Howard J., 12, 36, 236 n
  socialism versus free markets, 229–34
Sichel, Werner
  on economics, 13
  economics text, 11
Sicilia, David B., 254 n
Siegel, Barry N., 100 n, 136 n, 137 n, 144
Singapore, 204–5
Skousen, Mark, 46 n, 87, 144, 290
  definition of economics, 32
Smith, Adam, 2, 140, 210, 279
Sobel, Robert, 232, 247, 254 n
Socialism
  adverse to investment, 268–69
  central planning, 217–22
  economic apologists, 229–34
  economic calculation, 228–29
  failure of central planning, 225–29
  versus free market, 224–25
  Ghana, 219–20
  Latin America, 220–22
  main characteristics, 224
  Marx's theories, 208–11
  reasons for failure, 208–35
  revolutionary program, 209–10
  Soviet failure, 213–15
Socialism (Mises), 281
Somary, Felix, 103, 104, 105, 117 n
South Africa, 141–42
South Korea, 205
Soviet Union, 23, 141–42
  economic growth failure, 213–15
  standard of living, 214–17
Sowell, Thomas, 236 n
Speculators, 247, 264–65
Spirit of Enterprise (Gilder), 254
Stages-of-production model, 32–36
  aggregate production structure, 84–87
  in central planning, 227
  gross national outlays analysis, 43–46
  Menger's view, 279
  value of, 294
Stagflation, 74
  aggregate production structure, 84–87
  causes, 88–100
  and energy crisis, 95–96
  of 1970s, 82–84
Standard of living
  Lorenz curve, 192–93
  Soviet Union, 214–17
  during World War II, 112
Statute for Encouragement of Investment (Taiwan), 204
Steiner, Peter O., 48, 117 n, 118 n
  accelerator principle, 72
  circular flow diagram, 31
  economics text, 10
  ending of depression, 111–12
  federal deficit, 177–78
  free markets, 224–25

Steiner, Peter O.—*Cont.*
  gold supply, 141
  Great Depression, 107
  inflation, 80–81
  Japan, 198
  Soviet Union, 214
  state intervention, 145
Stiglitz, Joseph E., 12
Stockholm, 223
Stock market
  crash of 1987, 114, 260
  investment theories, 257–60
  Japan, 200
Stock price predictability, 266–67
Stone, Gerald W., 77 n, 118 n, 295
  economics text, 11
  federal deficit, 179, 183
  Great Depression, 103
  inflation/unemployment, 88
  value added tax, 168
Stoneman, William E., 116 n
Stroup, Richard L., 108, 149, 216, 295
  depression, 102
  economics text, 11
  macroeconomics, 74
  public education, 147–48
Structure of Production (Skousen), 36–37, 87, 290
Student vouchers, 167
Subjective economics, 281
Suicide Corporation, The (Weaver), 233
Sulfur emissions, 150
Supply and demand; *see also* Aggregate supply and demand model
  connection between, 16–17
  controversy, 45–46
  disequilibrium, 79–80
  micro and macro, 76–77
Supply shocks, 82–83
  and recession, 97–98
Supply-side economics, 173–74
Surtax, 174
Sweden
  central planning, 223–24
  income distribution, 190–91

Taiwan, 203–4
Taussig, Frank W., 36, 49, 270, 279
Taxation
  ability-to-pay principle, 165–67
  benefit principle, 167
  benefits and users, 165
  capital gains, 170–71
  economic efficiency, 22–23
  flaws, 176
  Hong Kong, 203
  impact on multiplier, 69–70
  impact on productivity, 159
  income brackets, 161
  income tax alternatives, 168–69
  Japan, 171–72, 200–201
  Laffer curve, 162–64, 173
  local versus national, 165
  loopholes, 161–63
  market efficiency, 162–64
  national comparisons, 169–71

Taxation—*Cont.*
national sales tax, 168–69
production possibility curve, 163–64
progressive income tax, 158–59
reactions to high rates, 159–61
regressive, 169
revenues and rates, 172–74
savings and, 174
on savings and investment, 48
underground economy, 174–76
user fees, 167
value added tax, 168
Vietnam War surtax, 174
Taxation and the Deficit Economy (Lee, ed.),
176
Tax shelters, 162
Taylor, Fred M., 228, 236 n
Templeton, John, 219, 236 n, 259, 268,
270–71
Tennessee Valley Authority, 155
Thaler, 131
Thatcher, Margaret, 155
Theory of Market Failure (Cowen, ed.), 156
Theory of Money and Credit (Mises), 281
Third World, 8
Time element in production, 28–30, 32–33;
see also Stages-of-production model
"Toward the Next Economics" (Drucker), 274
Trade-offs, 20–26
Transformation process, 17–18
Treasury bills, 182
to market debt, 184
Trinity House, 153
Tucker, Refus S., 134 n
Turning Point? (Somary), 105

Underground economy, 174–76
Unemployment; *see also* Full employment
cyclical, 122–23
employment taxes, 124
and equilibrium, 78–80
fear of, 119
in free market, 120–22
and inflation, 74–76
Keynesian view, 125–26
minimum wage legislation, 124–25
from monetary policy, 123
United Mine Workers, 150
United States
bankruptcy potential, 182–83
low savings rate, 52
tax rates, 169–71
United States Census Bureau, 44
United States Congress
environmental issues, 150
spending habits, 174
United States Department of Commerce, 43,
83, 112
United States Department of the Treasury, 70

University Economics (Alchian and Allen),
249
University of Chicago, 277
University of Nevada at Las Vegas, 277, 287
University of Vienna, 278, 280
User fees, 167
USSR in Crisis (Goldman), 237

Value, paradox of, 279
Value-added model, 40–41
Value-added tax, 168
Value Line Investment Survey, 259
Veblen, Thorstein, 230, 233
Victoria, Queen, 130, 132
Vietnam War, 174
Views on Capitalism (Romano and Leiman,
eds.), 285
Vital Few (Hughes), 232
Vouchers, 167

Wage income, and wage rates, 61
Wage levels, and income distribution, 195–96
Wages
Marx on, 210–11
purchasing power fallacy, 30–31
The Wall Street Journal, 174
Walras, Leon, 29, 76–77, 276, 279, 283
Walras' law, 77
War on Poverty, 193
Water pollution, 148–50
Weaver, Paul H., 223–34, 237 n
*What Every Investor Should Know about
Austrian Economics and the Hard
Money Movement* (Skousen), 290
*What Has the Government Done to Our
Money?* (Rothbard), 144, 286, 290
When Government Goes Private (Fitzgerald),
154, 157
Wholesale price indexes, 136, 137
Who's Who in Economics (Blaug), 287
Why Has Japan Succeeded? (Morishima), 207
*Why the Best-Laid Investment Plans Usually
Go Wrong* (Browne), 273
Wicksell, Knut, 88, 91–92
natural rate of interest, 89–90
Wimmer, Larry, 8
Women in labor force, 123
Worldly Philosophers (Heilbroner), 229
World War II, 111–13
Wordsworth, William, 286

Yeager, Leland, 287
Yugoslavia, 218

Zaychenko, Aleksandr S., 214–15